DEFINING MOMENTS

DEFINING MOMENTS

Reflections on Citizenship, Violence and the 2007 General Elections in Kenya

Edited by
Kimani Njogu

TWAWEZA
COMMUNICATIONS
"Working Towards a Better World"

© Copyright Twaweza Communications, 2011

Published in 2011 by:
Twaweza Communications Ltd.
P.O. Box 66872 - 00800 Westlands
Twaweza House, Parklands Road
Mpesi Lane, Nairobi Kenya
website: www.twawezacommunications.org
Tel: +(254) 020 269 4409

Design and Layout by Catherine Bosire
Cover design: Centrepress Media Ltd., info@centrepressmedia.com

With the support of The Ford Foundation, Office of Eastern Africa

ISBN: 978-9966-028-31-0

Dedication

To Kenyans who relentlessly work towards justice, peace and
fairness for all citizens.

Contents

Acknowledgements

This publication is part of ongoing work at Twaweza Communications to engage in national dialogue on citizenship as well as archive knowledge and emotions related to the violence before and after the highly contested 2007 general elections. The first publication titled *Healing the Wound: Personal Narratives about the 2007 Post-Election Violence in Kenya* sought to capture narratives of pain, narratives of mercy and narratives of aggression. *Healing the Wound* gave an opportunity to ordinary citizens to voice their experiences during that tragic period. Election related violence and the challenge of building a strong nation-state within a context of political manipulation of ethnicity is rigorously explored in *(Re)membering Kenya: Identity, Culture and Freedom* (Edited by Mbugua wa-Mungai and George Gona). *Defining Moments* provides other reflections about transformative moments after the 2007 elections. It is important that those moments be discussed openly so that yet another perspective to the violence can be provided and lessons learnt shared. Our commitment is not to capture a singular interpretation but rather to provide fora for a multiplicity of perspectives to be voiced. This perspective is underpinned by our dialogic reading of the world.

In this journey of archiving experiences and memory we are immensely grateful to the Ford Foundation, Office of Eastern Africa for supporting our initiative and more specifically Dr. Joyce Nyairo, Program Officer in charge of Media and Civil Society, for her continued engagement with us on this important subject. Through the support of the Ford Foundation, these reflections can now be shared with the world and provide a platform for major institutional reforms as we seek to build the Kenyan nation. We are also grateful to the contributors for generously sharing their thoughts with us and taking the time to write them down. This publication would not have been possible without the support of the Twaweza Communications team. Through their diligence and support we have been able to assemble yet again a body of key resources and I am grateful to them. I am also grateful to Catherine Bosire for designing this publication. May the spirit of sharing knowledge thrive in our midst.

Kimani Njogu
Nairobi.

Introduction

Fix Governance, End Impunity

The violence that followed the 27th December 2007 elections in Kenya shook every corner of the country and the region. About one thousand two hundred (1,200) lives were lost, thousands injured, over four hundred thousand (400,000) people internally displaced and a large number sought refuge in Uganda and Tanzania. Between January and February 2008, houses were burnt down and property destroyed across the country rendering many families destitute. Youth gangs were mobilized by power hungry politicians to harm innocent citizens and the police in many cases used excessive force in quelling demonstrations. Thousands of innocent people lost their lives over a period of fifty days or so and many others died later from shock and injuries incurred during the violence. There was overwhelming evidence of rape, sexual mutilation and painful deaths in the conflict areas. Furthermore, years after the mayhem, the lives of women and children are in jeopardy within the internally displaced persons (IDP) camps due to disease outbreak and hunger.

Ethnic identification is key to the control of the state and the allocation of resources in Kenya, as in most African states. Unsurprisingly therefore, in Nyanza, the Rift Valley, Coast, Central, Nairobi and Western provinces, the violence took an ethnic dimension and specific communities were targeted for elimination and displacement; they had voted for candidates other than those preferred by the perpetrators of violence. Also, groups used the opportunity to lay claim to land occupied by their opponents and take possession of abandoned property. Thugs were on the rampage and in some instances violence was meted with military precision. There were, moreover, incidents of retaliatory evictions and violence on innocent citizens especially in Naivasha and Nakuru as ethnic intolerance became rampant. New media (internet and mobile phones) and local language media were vital channels for perpetration of ethnic hate, including among "intellectuals." Urban Kenyan youth, who had not paid attention to ethnic identity, were confused and inter-ethnic marriages were put to unprecedented test.

Disturbingly, national political leaders did not do enough to calm their followers in order to create a space for national dialogue and peace. They neither openly denounced the rampant violence nor did they purposefully address honestly and systematically the issues that ignited the violence in the first place. They did not make efforts to visit violent areas to calm their supporters and urge them to respect life and property even as the country explored ways of dealing with electoral and other social injustices. On its part, the government initially took a hard-line position and rejected mediation efforts insisting that the legal and constitutional process be followed in coming up with a solution to the *impasse*. Also it temporarily banned live broadcasts and demonstrations organized by Orange Democratic Movement (ODM). Efforts by regional leaders and the Panel of Eminent African Personalities under the Chairmanship of Kofi Annan eventually led to the formation of a Coalition Government and the introduction of a Prime Minister's post currently occupied by Raila Odinga, the leader of ODM. Political power was shared in order to create room for key legislative and judicial reforms.

Immediately after the post-election violence broke out Twaweza Communications called a meeting of key civil society actors on 2nd January 2008. Dr. Joyce Nyairo represented the Ford Foundation at this brainstorming forum. Recommendations from this early meeting on the violence were mainstreamed into the "Independent Sector Initiative on Post-election Violence." The meeting, even without reaching total consensus on how to deal with the volatile situation, emphasized that a communication initiative for peace and reconciliation would add much needed value to the work being undertaken by peace and human rights organizations. Given the post election violence and disruption of identities that were in the formative stages especially among the youth, it was felt that the media can play a key role in ensuring healing, peace and reconciliation. Twaweza Communications undertook to engage the media in a number of important areas including lobbying media houses to focus on peace messages and linking centers hosting IDPs with media outlets through provision of cell phone airtime. For example, we worked closely with Urgent Action Fund in the provision of airtime to needy centers especially in the Rift Valley and Nyanza Province, and with the Legal Resources Foundation and the media to draw attention to the violence in Kipkelion, Londiani and Kuresoi areas.

Impunity is the second name of the Kenyan political elite; and this is best manifested during elections. Just like in the 1992 and 1997 elections, the 2007 voting pattern demonstrated once more the primacy of individuals and ethnicity over policy, ideology and class in Kenyan politics. The primary objective of most political leaders continues to be personal gain and individual preservation as well as financial advantage. Few have shown political principle in addressing fundamental national issues. Instead, poverty and deprivation, political expediency and support from ethnic communities have been used to perpetuate politico-ethnic violence. Virtually all elections in the multiparty era in Kenya have been manipulated and characterized by violence. The 1992 elections were a culmination of a tense and occasionally violent process in the pursuit of democracy and multi-party political participation that ended two decades of single party rule. With the erasure of Section 2 (A) of the Constitution that had transformed Kenya into a one party state, the path to democratization was opened. Many political parties were registered, although hugely populated by remnants of the former single party – Kenya African National Union (KANU). Elections held on December 29th 1992 were expected to lead to a change of president and government. Unfortunately, they were characterized by allegations of fraud and irregularities, including the stuffing of ballot papers, the destruction of opposition votes and other forms of count rigging. Africa Confidential reported in 1993 that *"Neither the foreign nor the local observer team had the capacity or resources to investigate comprehensively rigging allegations. Consequently, they reported only the most blatant and easily verifiable irregularities."*

According to Throup and Hornsby (1998), KANU won the 1992 elections due to three factors. First, the opposition was unable to present a united front and a single candidate to face Daniel Arap Moi at the polls. Second, the elections took an ethnic and regional dimension and, third, the state's bias and electoral malpractice to the advantage of the incumbent. But elections were also characterized by killing, intimidation, and displacement of individuals and communities perceived as opposition supporters. Unlike the 2007/08 violence, the 1992 election related violence took place prior to the polling day and sought to deny citizens the right to cast their vote.

The 1997 elections were also violent, especially at the Coast where upcountry people especially the Luhya, Luo, Kikuyu and Kamba were intimidated and their property destroyed. It would seem that the 1997 election violence at the Coast had three aims. First, KANU wanted to break the dominance of the unregistered Islamic Party of Kenya (IPK) which had denied it important votes in 1992. Secondly, it wanted to break the Swahili-Arab and Mijikenda elite and thirdly it sought to dis-enfranchise upcountry people in Mombasa and Kwale. The 2002 elections were also violent, although to a lesser degree. The use of vigilantes and ethnic 'warriors' was minimal. The relative peace that characterized the 2002 elections may be attributed to a number of things. First, Daniel Arap Moi had been barred by the Constitution from running for another term, relinquishing power to Mwai Kibaki who had won the election under the National Rainbow Coalition (NARC), a loose coalition of 14 opposition political parties. The common front ensured that the Coalition had support across the country and provided a formidable force to KANU. Second, different forums including the Electoral Commission of Kenya, Community Based Organization, and Non-Governmental Organizations had undertaken massive civic education against electoral violence. Nonetheless, the Central Depository Unit monitors did report that 116 lives were lost in election related violence, while the media reported 209 deaths. Thus despite the relative peace, life was lost in the 2002 elections.

But it is the 2007/08 post-election violence that shook the nation because of its spread, speed and ruthlessness. The closely contested presidential election was characterized by unrealistic promises, fragmentation, balkanization, media hype and strong expressions of ethnic nationalism. Inspired and buoyed by the rejection of the 2005 Referendum on a government sponsored proposed constitution and under the leadership of a charismatic team referred to as "The Pentagon", the main opposition party ODM went full throttle to wrest power from the incumbent in the General Elections. Further, the possibility of a 'majimbo' political system promised by ODM created anxiety in certain parts of the country notably in the Mt. Kenya region because of its association with balkanization, ethnic cleansing, 'insiders' and 'outsiders', 'us' and 'them'.

The highly emotive exclusionist majimboism was viewed as an affront to citizenship at the local level among the Mt. Kenya communities; the main supporters of Mwai Kibaki. But the concept also became a point of convergence among communities that have in the past supported it viewing it as an opportunity to curtail the power of majority communities, localize resources, and reap the benefits of citizenship. Consequently, the country became immensely polarized along zones seen to support the Party of National Unity (PNU) under Mwai Kibaki, on the one hand, and ODM under Raila Odinga, on the other. Although the casting of votes on 27th December 2007 was generally peaceful, delays in releasing results by the Electoral Commission of Kenya (ECK) and the subsequent declaration and swift swearing in of Mwai Kibaki as president, amid accusations of rigging by the main protagonists, led to unprecedented violence, looting, rape and destruction of property across the country. Opinion polls that preceded the elections had predicted a closely contested race to State House but not the level of violence experienced in the country.

The violence that engulfed Kenya after the 2007 elections was essentially about citizenship. What does it mean to be a citizen of Kenya? What are our rights and responsibilities? What does one need to do in order to 'belong' and enjoy rights in any part of Kenya? The violence was not just about who won or lost in the elections. Access to land, water, pastures and other resources coupled with political manipulation of ethnic difference have continued to heighten tensions among communities over the years. Furthermore, the 'winner- take-all' system and the real and imagined benefits associated with a powerful presidency put immense pressure and anxiety on political leaders and their supporters during election periods. Politicians ignite mistrust and encourage violence to reach their goals and maintain or acquire power. In certain cases, this means physically removing people from specific constituencies such as happened in Kuresoi and Mt. Elgon prior to the polling day in the 2007 election. Significantly, when the goals of politicians to acquire or maintain power merge with those of ordinary people in their quest for land and employment, a recipe for violence becomes potent. This potency can be aggravated by the existence of small arms, an inefficient and biased police force and poor infrastructure. This was precisely the situation in Kenya, and remains so to this day.

Although a Coalition government is in place, thousands of internally displaced persons are in camps, especially in the Rift Valley. Many would like to go back to their homes but are afraid of the harm that might befall them. There is evidence to show that individuals who attempt to go back to their homes are subjected to violence. In any case, the perpetrators of the violence were neighbours who sought to benefit from the evictions and are still free and roaming the fields with impunity. Further, without the IDPs, large chunks of land are available for tilling and pasture to neighbours who have taken possession. Clearly, the process of healing and reconciliation will be long and tedious but immensely beneficial if the country is to get back on its toes and recapture its esteem in the region.

These essays written by journalists, lawyers and cultural scholars, mainly in 2009 but with minimal revision thereafter in view of never-ending developments, capture the definitive moments during the violence. The first part revisits the various tensions and ruptures in Nairobi, Rift Valley and Nyanza giving us a glimpse of the forces at work. The second part discusses what was done, and is being done to ensure Kenya does not find itself on its knees again. The enactment of a constitution was a major step in the rebirth of the nation. Well implemented, it will unlock the nation and democratize leadership. The entry of the International Criminal Court (ICC) into Kenya has been transformative; it has completely reshaped social and political alignments. The implication of the indictments will be felt for decades to come. The "Waki list" presented by the Commission Investigating the Post-Election Violence (CIPEV) to Kofi Annan, Chair of the Kenya National Dialogue and Reconciliation process sent shock waves across the country.

A major consequence of the post election violence thus is the involvement of the International Criminal Court (ICC) which is governed by the Rome Statute. The ICC is the first permanent, treaty based, international criminal court established to help end impunity for the perpetrators of the most serious crimes of concern to the international community. The ICC sits at the Hague, Netherlands, and is an independent international organization. It is not part of the United Nations system. In the 1990s after the end of the Cold War, tribunals like the International Criminal Tribunal for the former Yugoslavia and for Rwanda were the result of consensus that impunity is unacceptable. However, because they were established to try crimes committed only within a specific time-frame and during a specific conflict, there was general agreement globally that an independent, permanent criminal court was needed. Thus on 17 July 1998, the international community reached a major and historic milestone when 120 States adopted the Rome Statute, the legal basis for establishing the permanent International Criminal Court. The Rome Statute entered into force on 1 July 2002 after ratification by 60 countries. Kenya is a signatory to the Statute.

Important Dates Related to ICC

December 25, 2007
There was violence as mobs in Nyanza beat up and killed at least 3 policemen accused of taking part in a plan to rig the December 27 elections in favor of the incumbent President Mwai Kibaki.

December 27, 2007
Kenya held parliamentary and presidential general elections. The highly contested elections were generally peaceful but tense.

December 30, 2007
Mwai Kibaki was declared the winner of the closest presidential election in Kenya's history, a contest marked by allegations of rigging and violence. Kibaki

beat Raila Odinga by 231,728 votes. Samuel Kivuitu, the Electoral Commission of Kenya chairman, acknowledged there were problems with the elections and said he was 'not sure that Kibaki had won fairly'. The opposition refused to go to court and called for mass action.

Many international and local observers agreed there were malpractices. The country was on fire in many hotspots.

January 1, 2008
The Kenya Assemblies of God Church in Kiambaa, Eldoret, was put on fire and many members of the Kikuyu community who had sought refuge there died, including children and a woman on a wheel chair. The country was shocked because there was no place to hide from the marauding gangs. Many churches were set ablaze especially in Kibera and the Rift valley.

January 9, 2008
President John Kufuor then Chairman of the African Union met Kenyan leaders to try to break the political stalemate. Hundreds of people had been killed, property destroyed and thousands of people displaced. Mwai Kibaki named half cabinet, signaling a willingness to accommodate the opposition in government but affirming that he was President.

January 10, 2008
An African Union statement said former UN Secretary-General Kofi Annan would take over mediation in Kenya's disputed presidential election. Kenya's feuding political leaders agreed to an immediate cessation of violence and any acts that may harm efforts to end the country's post-election crisis.

January 24, 2008
Mwai Kibaki and Raila Odinga talked for the first time since the elections, but the President angered the opposition by insisting after the hour-long meeting, mediated by Kofi Annan, that his position as Head of State was not negotiable.

January 29, 2008
Kofi Annan launched the Kenya National and Reconciliation process to end the post election crisis.

February 5, 2008
The International Criminal Court Prosecutor said his office has begun a preliminary examination of the post-election violence in Kenya.

February 26, 2008

Kofi Annan suspended the mediation talks after weeks of negotiations brought little progress. He committed to engaging Kibaki and Raila directly.

February 28, 2008

The Panel of Eminent African Personalities, under the chairmanship of Kofi Annan, oversaw the signing of a power-sharing agreement called the National Accord and Reconciliation Act, which established a coalition government with Mwai Kibaki as President and Raila Odinga as Prime Minister. It also set up the Commission of Inquiry on Post-Election Violence (CIPEV), which later became known as the "Waki Commission" after its chairman, Judge Philip Waki.

April 13, 2008

President Mwai Kibaki named Raila Odinga as Prime Minister, implementing a power-sharing deal after protracted negotiations over the Agreement they signed.

October 15, 2008

The Waki Commission submitted its Report and Recommendations to the Government of Kenya. The recommendations included the establishment of a Special Tribunal of national and international judges to investigate and prosecute perpetrators of the post-election violence.

The Report also stated that if the Tribunal was not set up within six months, information collected by the Waki Commission would be passed on to the ICC, including a sealed envelope of names of those suspected to be most responsible for the violence.

February 12, 2009

The Kenyan parliament voted against the establishment of the proposed Tribunal made up of Kenyan and international judges to address the post-election violence.

July 3, 2009

Three Kenyan Cabinet Ministers signed an agreement with the ICC committing Kenya to establish a credible and independent Tribunal to try perpetrators of post-election violence by August 2009.

July 9, 2009
Kofi Annan handed the International Criminal Court the names of key suspects in Kenya's post-poll violence. He said in a statement dated July 9 to Prime Minister Raila Odinga: "*I wish to inform you that the Panel of Eminent African Personalities has handed over to the Prosecutor of the International Criminal Court, the sealed envelope and supporting materials entrusted to me by the Waki Commission on 17th October 2008.*" The Chief Mediator further said: "*I have written in similar terms to President Kibaki.*"

July 16, 2009
Six boxes containing documents and supporting materials compiled by the Waki Commission during its investigations were sent to the Chief Prosecutor at the ICC.

November 9, 2009
Parliament begun debate on another Constitutional Amendment to form a Local Tribunal. The debate was not concluded.

November 26, 2009
ICC Prosecutor Luis Moreno-Ocampo filed a request seeking authorization from Pre-Trial Chamber II to open an investigation in relation to the crimes allegedly committed during the 2007-2008 post-election violence in Kenya.

March 31, 2010
Pre-Trial Chamber II issued its majority decision (2-1) that there was a reasonable basis to proceed with an investigation into the situation in Kenya in relation to crimes against humanity within the jurisdiction of the Court committed between June 1, 2005 and November 26, 2009.

April 1, 2010
The International Criminal Court announced that it will investigate members of Kenya's two ruling parties on charges that they instigated violence that killed more than 1,000 people after the disputed 2007 presidential election.

September 3, 2010
Kenya allowed the International Criminal Court to open an office in the country, a development that came after Kenya's commitment to the Court came into question when the nation hosted Sudan's indicted leader (President Omar al-Bashir) to the promulgation of a new Constitution.

September 21, 2010
ICC said it would launch cases against as many as six suspected instigators of postelection violence in Kenya that left more than 1,000 people dead in 2007/08.

December 15, 2010
The ICC Prosecutor requested the issuance of 'summonses to appear' for six people in the court's Kenya investigation: William Samoei Ruto, Henry Kiprono Kosgey, Joshua Arap Sang (case one) and Francis Kirimi Muthaura, Uhuru Muigai Kenyatta, and Mohamed Hussein Ali (case two) – for their alleged responsibility in the commission of crimes against humanity.

March 8, 2011
Pre-Trial Chamber II issued the summonses to appear for the aforementioned six individuals, as it found reasonable grounds to believe that they committed the crimes alleged by the Prosecutor. The charges in the case of Ruto, Kosgey and Sang relate to murder (article 7(l)(a)); forcible transfer of population (article 7(l)(d)); and persecution (article 7(l)(h)). The charges in the case of Uhuru, Ali, and Muthaura relate to murder (article 7(l)(a)); forcible transfer (article 7(l)(d)); rape (article 7(l)(g)); persecution (article 7(l)(h)); and other inhumane acts (article 7(l)(k)).

March 31, 2011
The Kenya Government filed an application challenging the ICC's jurisdiction over the cases.

April 4, 2011
The Judges of Pre-Trial Chamber II received the Application on behalf of the Government of the Republic of Kenya pursuant to Article 19 of the ICC Statute and begun the process of reviewing the application.

April 7, 2011
The first three defendants (Ruto, Kosgey, and Sang) made their initial appearance before the Court in The Hague.

April 8, 2011
The second three defendants (Muthaura, Kenyatta, and Ali) made their initial appearance before the Court in The Hague.

September 1, 2011
Confirmation of charges hearing is scheduled to begin for the first three defendants (Ruto, Kosgey, and Sang).

September 21, 2011
Confirmation of charges hearing is scheduled to begin for the second three defendants (Muthaura, Kenyatta, and Ali).

These individuals, although indicted at the Hague, are presumed innocent until proven guilty. For the avoidance of doubt, the effort to archive alternative voices and to record our history is informed by the tendency to "revise" the memory of national events for purposes of convenience and expediency. Kenyans deserve to hear other voices other than that of the state and its organs. Our aim is not to have a singular voice on the violence but rather to allow for multiplicity of interpretations of that dark period in Kenyan history. The essays do not seek to be conclusive statements of what happened in Kenya; rather they are attempts at understanding those transformative moments in the mayhem and to provide possible solutions to our political and social situation. They show how close Kenya was to total self destruction because of political power. These reflections are also a statement on the failure of institutions of governance, greed for power and ways in which unaccountable leaders can manipulate ethnicity to acquire or maintain power. The mediation process and the importance of crafting and implementing a people centred constitution as well as punishing crime are discussed. Impunity should never be elevated into a national culture. These essays suggest that violent conflict can be avoided; but for this to happen we must fix governance and make all citizens feel at home in their country. Further, we must strengthen our institutions including the judiciary and ensure constitutionalism and the rule of law.

We are grateful to the Ford Foundation, Office of Eastern Africa for encouraging us to venture into studies of public space, memory and healing. We hope that this journey to our recent past will present important learnings for the future.

Kimani Njogu
Nairobi.

Part One

Definitive Moments

Chapter 1

Reflections about the Events at Kenyatta International Conference Centre (KICC) on 27th-31st December 2007

Koki Muli

"Those who cast votes decide nothing. Those who count votes decide everything." - Stalin

Introduction

The events which occurred at Kenyatta International Conference Centre (KICC) between the 27th and 31st December 2007 fundamentally changed the democratic and electoral history of Kenya. These events and their implications are the subject of this chapter. This chapter will also examine what factors may have led to the events at KICC. This will involve examining events and factors before, during and after the elections and announcement of presidential results on 30th December 2007.

These events are captured in three parts;

Part One: relates to the period before the elections highlighting Kenya's history of elections and the emergence of ethnic and electoral tensions.

Part Two: Highlights specific events and factors that may have contributed to the electoral environment in which we found ourselves in 2007. This section also looks at the following issues:

- The ethnic tensions that have existed since 2005 Referendum on the proposed Kenya Constitution;

- Inadequate or inappropriate legal framework governing elections and a rich history of electoral malpractices;

- The administrative Framework of Elections and the composition of the ECK commissioners; and

- An unfair electoral system;

Part Three: Deals with the conduct of the media and the events that occurred at KICC from the 27th to the 31st December 2007. This part comprises the following:

- The conduct of the media
- The Events that Occurred at KICC between 27th and 31st December 2007

Part Four: Looks at the aftermath – the first few days of January, 2008, in relation only to the conduct of the disbanded ECK – statements attributed to its members and the responses they elicited from Kenyans and especially from key stakeholders in elections.

Part One: The Period before the 2007 Elections

Historical background and context of Elections in Kenya

To better understand the electoral violence that followed the 2007 general elections, it is important to understand the history of elections[1] in Kenya and put them in context. With the exception of the first independent elections; elections have always been tense and associated with intimidation and ethnic tensions. However, elections were not accompanied by ethnic violence until October 1991.

The independence Elections in 1963

There were three main contenders, Kenya African National Union (KANU), led by Jomo Kenyatta and Oginga Odinga, and Kenya African Democratic Union (KADU), led by Ronald Ngala, Masinde Muliro and Daniel arap Moi. There was also the African People's Party (APP) led by Paul Ngei. KANU was seen as an alliance of the two largest ethnic groups, the Kikuyu and the Luo, while KADU was an alliance of other groups such as the Mijikenda, the Kalenjin, Maasai and Luhya who wanted to resist domination by the big two. KANU favoured a unitary government but at the Lancaster House talks in London had given in to KADU demands for federal government known as *"majimboism."* The independence Constitution provided for independent candidates.

The 1963 elections were held in three phases. The first election on May 19, for the seven regional assemblies; May 22 for the 38 Senate seats (Upper

House) and on May 25-26 for the 112 House of Representatives seats. KANU won the majority and formed the Government, with Jomo Kenyatta as Prime Minister and Ronald Ngala as the leader of the Opposition.

The 1966 mini General Elections

In 1964 Kenya became a republic; Kenyatta became its President, and Oginga Odinga its Vice President. KADU and APP dissolved themselves and all their MPs "crossed the floor" to the government side in the House of Representatives making Kenya a *de facto* one party (KANU) State. However, in 1966 the left-leaning Odinga displeased with the ruling party KANU and its ideology, quit as Vice President and formed his own party, Kenya Peoples Union (KPU). 28 MPs and 10 Senators also resigned their seats. Kenyatta then caused a constitutional amendment requiring each legislator who left his sponsoring party to seek a fresh mandate in a by-election, at the same time abolishing the provision for independent candidates. This amendment also postponed[2] the next General Election to 1969, when KPU won only 10 seats but effectively became the Opposition taking the place of KADU. These elections marked the beginning of ethnic tensions and balkanisation of ethnic political support.

The 1969 General Elections

In 1969 KPU was banned and its leaders detained without trial. Detention without trial, in which an application for *habeas corpus* was not allowed, became the preferred weapon against political dissent and for stifling leaders and their communities who did not tow the political line of the ruling elite. Some constitutional amendments were passed; the provision for Bi-cameral[3] Houses was removed; merging the 2 Houses together into a Parliament of Representatives from 158 Constituencies. Daniel Moi had been appointed Vice President after the short-term of Joseph Murumbi who had resigned just seven months after succeeding Odinga.

Since 1966, KANU elections always preceded the general elections and were part of the elections, during which candidates were nominated or selected unopposed. The KANU primaries began on December 6, 1969 and were followed by the general elections, held on January 3, 1970. All the candidates were sponsored by KANU. This excluded all other candidates who had left KANU to join KPU; criminalising political dissent and diversity; and creating a very disgruntled and disenfranchised group of politicians and their primary support, their ethnic communities. Kenyatta was declared elected unopposed as president.

1974 General Elections

The KANU Constitution was further changed to allow only its life members to vie as candidates. The provision further required that candidates had to have been life members of KANU, for at least three years, before they could be cleared for an election. This disqualified nearly all KPU members. Kenyatta was again declared elected unopposed as President.

On 22 August 1978, Kenyatta died in office. His Vice President, Moi, succeeded him as was stipulated in the Constitution allowing him to hold office for ninety (90) days. This was not without elaborate scheming and machinations to change the constitution to ensure Moi (who came from a minority community), did not automatically succeed Kenyatta in the event of the latter's death; but Moi amassed sufficient support to retain the constitutional provision that made him the heir apparent. Charles Njonjo was central to the affirmation of Moi's constitutional right to replace Kenyatta, and the silencing of his opponents.

1979 General Elections without Kenyatta

On October 14, 1978 Moi was elected unopposed and sworn in as President. He coined *"fuata nyayo"* (meaning follow the footsteps of Kenyatta and the previous government) - a clear message to political dissenters and their communities that there was not going to be fundamental political change. He chose Mwai Kibaki, from Kenyatta's community, as his Vice-President. Following in Kenyatta's foot-steps, he further had the KANU constitution amended with a requirement that, in addition to being a KANU life member for three (3) years, candidates had to get endorsement from their local KANU branches; and had to demonstrate their "loyalty" to the party. While many could manage an endorsement from their local KANU branches, many were unable to "demonstrate loyalty" to the party and therefore were locked out of the elections. Many former KPU leaders including Jaramogi Oginga Odinga, and other voices of dissent such as former Kitutu East MP and detainee George Anyona were locked out for not having shown a "change of heart."

These elections saw an increase in the number of disenfranchised and disgruntled politicians whose ethnic communities felt left out because they didn't have representatives of their choice. They were also sidelined on the management of national affairs and, therefore, unable to partake in the sharing of the national "cake" – national resources and development opportunities – further heightening ethnic tensions. The elections were held on November 8, and Moi was declared elected unopposed as President.

1983 General Elections

On August 1, 1982 there was an attempted *coup d'etat* to remove Moi and according to the organizers allow for political participation by all communities. The attempted coup led Moi to postpone the general elections to enable him to consolidate his grip on power. Soon thereafter, a constitutional amendment was passed to make Kenya a *de jure* one-party (KANU) State.

Raila Odinga (current Prime Minister and son of Oginga Odinga), was detained without trial for the first time, accused of involvement in the coup attempt. Many former members of KPU and others implicated in the attempted coup were locked out of the 1983 elections and detained without trial. Moi was again declared elected as President unopposed.

1988 General Elections

These elections were intended to assist Moi to consolidate his control over the elected representatives and their communities. The method of voting in the KANU primaries was changed to the infamous queue-voting known in Kiswahili as the *"mlolongo"* elections in which the top two or three candidates in the KANU primaries were elected through queuing to face-off at the general elections. Any candidate who won 70 percent of the vote at the queue-voting stage was declared elected unopposed. Where no one attained this amount, the candidates were required to compete at the general elections. The KANU primaries saw the most blatant elections rigging in Kenya's electoral history, in which the longest queues were declared losers and shortest queues winners.

Following the attempted coup, there had been a serious crackdown on political dissent or free expression of divergent officials. Scores of academics, politicians, human rights and political activists were detained or forced into exile. Torture and imprisonment on trumped-up charges was the order of the day in the crackdown against alleged *Mwakenya* and other dissident movements. Expulsion from KANU, the sole legal political party became routine. All-powerful KANU became *"Mama na Baba"* (Mother and Father). The Special

Branch; the Criminal Intelligence Department (CID) and other security organs were law unto themselves; they followed "dissidents" around and listened to their private conversations. They even seized reading materials, including personal diaries and arrested people for private entries in their diaries. Many people were arrested or labelled dissidents by association.

The number of Parliamentary seats was increased from 158 to 188. The first round of the elections by *mlolongo* was held on March 21, 1988. A total of 65 parliamentary candidates were either unopposed or declared unopposed on attaining the 70 percent benchmark. Moi was elected unopposed as President. Kibaki easily retained his Othaya seat by garnering over 80 percent at the primaries. However, he was dropped as Vice President and appointed the Minister for Health.[4] Josephat Karanja[5] was appointed as Vice-President but served for just one year before being unceremoniously removed to make way for George Saitoti.

1992: Return of multi-party

The excesses of the Moi regime sowed the seeds for the campaign that would ultimately result in return of the multi-party system. In the absence of a legal political opposition, the churches, academics, professional organizations and other groupings (there were hardly any civil society organizations due to refusal of registration) including the branded political "dissidents" constituted themselves into the unofficial opposition. Under great pressure President Moi eventually gave in and allowed the removal of Section 2A of the Constitution, legally ushering in multi-parties.

However, Moi predicted that the re-introduction of multi-party politics would result in ethnic clashes because Kenyans were not cohesive enough. His predictions were realized when in October 1991, the first ethnic clashes broke out in Tinderet in the Rift Valley Province between Moi's Kalenjin community on the one hand and the Luo, Kikuyu, Kisii and Kamba communities living in the Province on the other. An Africa Watch Report[6], documents how these clashes were state-sponsored as if to fulfill Moi's prediction.

This report records in great detail the patterns of the violence, the identity of the perpetrators and how the State armed and supported them; the helplessness of the victims and how the State, while claiming to support them, closed out the Rift Valley (Moi's home Province) to outsiders to ensure only residents of the province knew what was happening there. The report confirms that ethnic clashes associated with elections began in Kenya in 1991 (the year before elections) after the repeal of Section 2A which had made Kenya a *de jure* one-party State.

The violence continued during the campaigns and elections of 1992 and even after the elections. The aim of the ethnic/political violence was to disenfranchise other communities who did not support Moi and KANU by dispossessing them of their land and killing them. Another objective was to allow the Kalenjin to occupy the land of the victims that they had chased away from Rift Valley, either for free or by forcing the victims to sell their land cheaply as they had no alternative.

The Forum for Restoration of Democracy (FORD) was registered by leaders who had been banished from KANU. Kibaki registered his Democratic Party (DP).[7] Unfortunately, FORD could not contain all the political superstars, and it soon split into two; Ford-Kenya led by Oginga Odinga and Ford-Asili led by Kenneth Matiba. As time went by, Ford-Asili split further into Saba Saba Asili and Ford-People. More political parties were also registered, most representing ethnic and regional support.

The Electoral Commission of Kenya (ECK), dormant since independence, was re-activated and the late High Court Judge Zacchaeus Chesoni was appointed its chairperson. Other Commissioners were nominated by the leaders of the main political parties and appointed by Moi. A total of 711 candidates for Parliamentary elections were formally nominated by the party and the ECK to vie for seats in 188 constituencies.

KANU was the only party that managed to get a candidate in every constituency. Other major parties fielding parliamentary candidates were DP (153), Ford-Asili (141) and Ford Kenya (138); and their presidential candidates, Kibaki, Matiba and Odinga respectively. KANU's nominations were finally de-linked from General Elections nominations.

The elections were held on 29 December. Moi won the presidency even though he got the least votes cast; 36.8 percent; against a majority combined opposition votes; of Matiba (26.8 percent), Kibaki (19.3 percent) and Odinga (17.7 percent). KANU got the majority of Parliamentary seats – 94 (sparking controversy as there were numerous allegations of rigging); Ford-Asili 31; Ford-Kenya, 30; and DP, 23.

1997: Moi win improves but more violence

In 1994 Oginga Odinga died and his son Raila's attempt to dethrone Michael Wamalwa as party chairperson of his father's party, Ford-Kenya, failed. Raila Odinga quit Ford-Kenya and took over the National Development Party (NDP). As a result, a by-election was called, which he won, retaining his parliamentary seat in Langata, Nairobi.

The elections approached with Kibaki's DP as the most stable and organised opposition party, and its leader the strongest opposition candidate, but still he could not remove President Moi, who was re-elected for his final term with an improved 40.1 percent of the total votes cast. Kibaki was second with 31.1 percent followed by Odinga with 10.9 percent, Wamalwa 8.3 percent and Charity Ngilu of SDP with 7.7 percent. Another nine candidates in the large field of 14 shared the rest of the vote, with none of them even reaching the one percent mark. Most of the presidential candidates sought their primary support from their ethnic communities. This continued to entrench ethnic block-voting patterns in our elections.

Shortly after the 1997 General Elections, Raila Odinga and his NDP party began to cooperate with KANU and he and some of his NDP MPs were appointed to the Cabinet. Before the 2002 general elections, the NDP merged with KANU. The 1997 elections were also characterised by the same politically motivated and state-sponsored violence that was witnessed for the first time in 1991. After the General Elections of 1992, the ethnic/political violence had continued and had spread to other parts of the Rift Valley and Kenya.

In 1994 this violence took another form. Police Stations in the Coast Province were raided, suspects in police custody set free, and up-country residents in the Coast Province targeted for eviction. Talk of federalism intensified; communities from the Rift Valley and the indigenous people of the Coast provinces began demanding a federal government in which they could determine their own destiny without interference from Nairobi /up-country and central government.

Survivors and other victims in Rift Valley sold off their land or fled and did not return. Most of their documents including their voters' cards and or Identity Cards were burned or destroyed in the violence. They were therefore, not able to vote by reason of not having the required documents or because they were not in the polling stations where they were registered.

The worst violence was witnessed in the Coast Province. In August 1997, the Likoni and Kwale areas of the Coast Province erupted in violence targeted at Kenyans of upcountry origin. The violence was "widely regarded as state engineered in an attempt to "cleanse' the area of its upcountry population in order to weaken the opposition in the1997 General Elections. The fact that there was a disproportionately large number of registered Luo voters in the Likoni Constituency who were instrumental in the FORD-Kenya win during the 1992 General Elections, and the further fact that members of the Likoni Luo community seem to have been especially targeted by the raiders, lend credibility to the view that the violence was state engineered."[8]

There were also allegations that local KANU politicians were involved in perpetrating the violence peppered with calls for majimboism aimed at securing the Coast Province for the alleged "rightful owners," - the indigenous communities. This violence though allegedly planned as early as May 1997,[9] seemed to intensify after the dissolution of Parliament in readiness for the General Elections. The results were death, destruction, dispossession, displacement and despair. Most of the victims who survived could not vote as their documents were either destroyed or they had to run away from their polling areas. Although subsequently a Commission of Inquiry into the 1997 and the 1992 violence was established and prepared a report, the findings and the report were never made public or acted upon by the government. 1997 continued the pattern of elections violence.

2002: The transition General Elections

Since Moi had served his two 5-year presidential terms (1992 and 1997), he was ineligible to vie for president in 2002. He hand-picked his successor to the KANU chairmanship, Uhuru Kenyatta, and had KANU nominate him as its presidential candidate. In doing this, Moi had taken for granted that Odinga, Saitoti, Kalonzo Musyoka and Joseph Kamotho would support his choice. However, they left together with their supporters. This heralded the end of KANU rule.

Leaders of opposition political parties, Kibaki, Wamalwa and Ngilu, decided to unite and sponsor one presidential candidate to remove KANU and defeat Kenyatta. In a move strongly backed by youthful back-bench MPs and civil society groupings, the three opposition leaders united under first, the National Alliance for Change, which was later renamed the National Alliance

Party of Kenya (NAK). This was achieved through a change of name of Ngilu's National Party of Kenya (NPK). Odinga, Saitoti, Kalonzo, Kamotho and others who had left KANU joined NAK, and renamed it the National Rainbow Coalition (NARC). Odinga endorsed Kibaki as the sole candidate by declaring, "Kibaki tosha" (Kibaki is enough), to the surprise and chagrin of the others, who nevertheless decided to remain and support Kibaki.

This was the first time in many years an alliance that brought together a significant section of the Kikuyu, Luo, Luhya, Kamba and other communities came together. Surprisingly, ethnicity was not a problem in this instance. In fact Moi's choice of Kenyatta, and Kenyans desire to usher in change by removing KANU from power, seemed to unite all ethnic communities to vote against KANU.

Consequently, Kibaki was overwhelmingly elected president and Kenyatta conceded defeat. Moi peacefully handed over power to Kibaki in a ceremony that was very hostile to Moi and which was conducted by the military. These were the first elections since 1991 that happened without electoral violence or tribal clashes, breaking the cycle of electoral violence. Also, majority of Kenyans voted without inducements or bribery. It showed that elections can happen in Kenya without violence.

Unfortunately, upon election, Kibaki allegedly failed to honour a Memorandum of Understanding (MoU) with Odinga. In February 2003, murmurings of the private MoU began to appear in the public, with claims that Kibaki had failed to honour an agreement between Odinga and himself in which he had allegedly agreed to share appointment of cabinet ministers and other public appointments 50-50. This led to the eventual break-up of NARC, the creation of NARC-Kenya (of Kibaki) and the return of the Liberal Democratic Party led by Odinga.

Kibaki and his colleagues had promised a new constitution for Kenya within one hundred days after the elections. That, of course, did not happen. Nevertheless, the National Constitution Review Commission in April 2004, convened the National Constitutional Conference (NCC) in the Bomas of Kenya. The political elite did not reach consensus on the constitution. The 2005 Referendum on the proposed Draft Constitution and the process leading to it is discussed later as one of the factors and events contributing directly to the heightened tensions and the post-elections violence in 2007/8.

2007 Rejected presidential elections results and the electoral violence

Although there were nine (9) presidential candidates in these elections, only the three main candidates attracted the greatest attention. These were the incumbent President Kibaki, his main challenger Raila Odinga and leader of ODM-Kenya Kalonzo Musyoka, now the Vice President. Kibaki's support mainly came from his community (and the diaspora in Kenya) - Central Province and the Mount Kenya area[10]; Odinga's support came from Nyanza, Western, Rift Valley, Coast and Nairobi Provinces while Musyoka's support came mainly from the Ukambani areas of the Eastern Province. Odinga and his supporters expected to win the elections using the same math and tabulations they had used during the 2005 Referendum.[11] It is worth noting, however, that Raila Odinga and Uhuru Kenyatta were in the same camp during the Referendum.

The real battle was, therefore, fought between Kibaki and Odinga. Odinga's belief in his popularity was also buoyed by opinion polls before the elections which showed him as the leading presidential contender ahead of Kibaki. These opinion polls also showed people's disaffection with Kibaki's government's handling of corruption scandals such as the Anglo Leasing, military and Immigration Department's procurements which had been questioned by Parliamentary Committees and the Office of the Auditor General. Opinion polls also told of Kenyans' desire for genuine reforms, especially the enactment of a new constitution.

Part Two – The Electoral Environment

Factors and events that shaped the 2007 electoral environment

This section highlights some of the key factors and events that shaped the 2007 electoral environment. Many of these factors and events although directly contributing to the events that occurred in 2007, were not necessarily directly cultivated to achieve these results. With benefit of hind-sight we can identify specific actions that could have been undertaken to evade or avoid the post-elections violence.

There were clear signs that the 2007 elections results were likely to be very closely contested, especially the presidential election and that the voter turnout would be a key determinant. As early as around April 2007, the disbanded Electoral Commission of Kenya (ECK) chairperson, Samuel Kivuitu, warned that presidential elections were going to be closely contested and that there was some risk of rejection of results and subsequent tensions and violence. He, however, informed Kenyans that the ECK was pre-empting such eventualities by ensuring that the ECK was independent, credible, and transparent, and would endeavour to oversee free and fair elections.

Other factors significantly contributed to the heightening of tensions and the subsequent post elections violence. These factors, some of which happened long before the elections, include:

1. The ethnic tensions that existed since 2005 Referendum on the proposed Kenya Constitution;

2. Inadequate or inappropriate legal framework governing elections and a rich history of electoral malpractices;

3. The administrative framework of elections and the composition of the ECK commissioners; and

4. An unfair electoral system.

2005 Referendum on the proposed Constitution

In April 2004, the National Constitutional Conference (NCC) opened with a divided and querulous ruling NARC party. There was the group that gravitated around Raila Odinga – mostly of politicians who were unhappy with President Kibaki. Odinga's group was mainly drawn from Nairobi, the expansive Rift Valley, Luo-Nyanza, Coast, Eastern and Western Provinces – a large group at this time comprising majority of the ethnic communities in Kenya.

Kibaki's support was drawn mainly from his ethnic community of Central Province and their close cousins from the Mount Kenya area. They were later (after the Referendum) joined by the Leader of Official Opposition and Chairman of KANU, Uhuru Kenyatta and his political party supporters. Other supporters who joined Kibaki especially after the Referendum were drawn from parts of Kisii-Nyanza, the North Eastern Province, central and upper Eastern Province.

The NCC discussions and support on constitutional issues played out along these ethnic and political lines. In their campaigns, Odinga's supporters reiterated the issues in the proposed constitution that the religious and civil society organisations were unhappy with.

The ECK assigned the "Orange" symbol to the "No-vote" and the "Banana-symbol" to the "Yes-vote" for the Referendum. The campaigns for and against the proposed constitution and the Referendum greatly heightened ethnic tensions, with the group for the "Yes-vote/banana" led by President Kibaki drawing a lot of support from the populous Mount Kenya area while the group for the "No-vote/orange" led by Odinga drawing support from the rest of Kenya, because of the politicians[12] who were then aligned to the "NO campaign." The No-side went on and won the Referendum. Buoyed by the win against President Kibaki, Odinga's No-vote team went ahead and converted the "Orange" symbol to the Orange Democratic Movement (which later split into two – ODM and ODM-Kenya). Kibaki fired Odinga and his colleagues from the Cabinet and sealed the ethnic divide that became the fault-lines along which the 2007 General Elections were conducted. Many see this as a result of Kibaki's failure to reconcile Kenyan communities after the Referendum defeat and embrace dissent from within his then coalition partners. A large group of disgruntled and scorned politicians and their supporters then began to prepare to "teach Kibaki a lesson in the 2007 elections." They anticipated marshalling support against Kibaki, defeating him during the 2007 General Elections and thereby denying him a second term as president of Kenya. This strategy was, however, complicated by Uhuru Kenyatta decamping to join Kibaki and Kalonzo Musyoka going it alone in ODM-Kenya.

The Referendum campaigns were also marred by violence where 8 people were reported to have been killed in Western and Coast Provinces – mainly 'No-Vote' strong-holds. There was also a lot of tension, especially between the Luo and the Kikuyu communities, and between the Kikuyu and the Kalenjin in the Nyanza, Coast and Nairobi Provinces in the former case and in Rift Valley Province in the latter case. In the Rift Valley, the tensions were turning into intimidation .

The legal framework governing 2007 elections and management of electoral malpractices

This section deals briefly with the laws that govern elections in Kenya and the institution that has been managing and administering elections in Kenya. It will also look at the management of electoral malpractices.

The 2007 elections were held within the umbrella of the previous constitution of Kenya replaced in 2010 Referendum. Generally, every stage and step in the electoral cycle and process is governed by the law in a very detailed manner. The law also prescribes all the essential and non-essential materials used during the electoral process. Therefore, the law plays a vital and critical role in the electoral process. The elections management body, in our case, the Electoral Commission of Kenya (ECK) managed the electoral cycle/process and oversaw the electoral system in accordance with the law. Other agencies of the government also played a significant role in the electoral process. For example, the security personnel including the Police provided security and investigated election offences. The Office of Police Commissioner was therefore engaged throughout the electoral process and, together with the Office of the Attorney-General, investigated and prosecuted election offences and other electoral malpractices. The ECK also required support and cooperation from other government agencies to ensure efficient and effective management and administration of the electoral cycle. For example, the Registrars of Births and Deaths and of Persons are critical in the registration of voters and maintenance of an updated and current Register of Voters. The Kenya Bureau of Statistics and Ministry of Education are also critical as the former provides population data (both for registration of voters and for the design of voter education and other programmes) while the latter provides almost all of the polling stations in Kenya.

However, there was a clear lack of cooperation and coordination of activities between these government agencies to facilitate the smooth operations of the ECK even though coordination initiatives were made by ECK.

Although the ECK was disbanded in 2008 and replaced with the Interim Independent Electoral Commission (IIEC), this section will focus on the ECK because it conducted the 2007 General Elections and the other elections previously since 1992.

As per the previous constitution, there is no one consolidated law but nine (9) pieces of legislation governing the electoral process in Kenya. The three (3) elections: Presidential; Parliamentary and Civic are governed by 4 separate laws. The Constitution of Kenya, The National Assembly and Presidential Elections Act (Cap 7) governed presidential and parliamentary elections, while the Local Government Act (Cap 246) governed civic elections. Elections Offences Act prohibited offences related to the 3 elections. Other electoral administrative and management matters were governed by other laws, including:

1. The Constitution of Kenya
2. The National Assembly and Presidential Elections Act (Cap 7),

3. The Local Government Act (Cap 246)
4. Election Offences Act (Cap 66),
5. Police Act (Cap 14),
6. The Kenya Broadcasting Corporation Act (cap 221)
7. Public Order and The Preservation of Public Security Act (Cap 56),
8. The Political Parties Act,
9. Penal Code (cap 63).

This multiplicity of laws made it difficult for the ECK and the Police to implement and enforce electoral laws. The ECK lacked enforcement capacity. Although the ECK constituted Committees to implement the Electoral Code of Conduct (CoC) and even attempted to fine and impose other sanctions on those who breached it, they had no powers to enforce these sanctions and most of those who got fined for breaching the Electoral CoC got away without paying the fines.

Multiplicity of electoral laws also makes it difficult for key stakeholders to adhere to all of them, as many people will focus on the key laws that govern the actual process of elections, and will have only copies of these with them. For example, many people, including candidates, political parties, their agents, the media and voters often focus on Cap 7 and Cap 246 which govern the elections of President, Members of Parliament and Councillors and pay no heed to Cap 66 and others that criminalise election offences and other electoral malpractices.

The police and other security personnel were seconded to the ECK during elections, during which time they were at the disposal of the ECK. In my experience of elections observation in Kenya,[13] the security personnel seconded to ECK interpreted their role as that of ensuring security for ECK and stakeholders during elections. In the past, the Police and the ECK generally ignored the Election Offences Act.[14] There is also some confusion regarding whom the Police owe accountability to - is it to the Commissioner of Police and the chain of command or is it to the ECK? The training that the police and other security personnel received from ECK relates mainly to their role during elections – securing the polling stations and the elections process, voting, counting and announcement of results, law and order during elections, escorting elections officials and general security duties. I have witnessed electoral bribery and intimidation taking place in many polling stations under the watch of security officers.[15] This, coupled with a very rich history of electoral malpractices with impunity, has over time given candidates, political parties, their agents and voters a free hand to engage in corruption, vote-buying and bribery, intimidation and electoral violence.

In the by-election of Kisauni, following the death of the former MP Karisa Maitha, the ECK and the Police created a joint mobile unit to drive around the Constituency smoking out political parties, their candidates and agents and voters involved in vote-selling and buying, intimidation, and other forms of electoral malpractices. This was noticeably successful and was conducted by a unit comprising ECK Commissioners and Senior Police Officers.[16] It was a pilot project and was abandoned after this by-election.

Election malpractices and offences have been routinely committed with incredible impunity during elections. This has been the tradition since independence. Some of these include: electoral corruption – vote-buying, intimidation, electoral violence, misuse of public resources (funds, vehicles/planes, public offices); creation of new districts and administrative divisions, issuance of title deeds by the incumbent president; contribution to harambees during campaigns to build public schools, dispensaries or the installation of rural electricity/power or building of roads. Other forms of electoral corruption relate to increments of salaries and allowances for teachers and civil servants during the election campaign period by the incumbent government. Also, incumbent presidents tend to issue title deeds to government or forest land as a way of inducing voters to support them. These are aimed at winning favour and support for the ruling party and the incumbents.

The impunity associated with electoral malpractices emboldened political parties, their candidates and supporters to incite people to electoral violence which has so far generally gone unpunished. Even though the ECK fined some candidates suspected of electoral violence, some of them issued statements informing ECK that they would not pay the fines. Indeed, they didn't pay and ECK did nothing about it. This breeds a culture of impunity. People believe that one can participate in electoral violence and get away with it. This impunity greatly contributed to the electoral violence that followed the rejection of Kenya's 2007 presidential results.

There is also the perceived manipulation of the Judiciary by politicians and its failure to uphold the rule of law. The Judiciary has been accused of being corrupt and totally unable to independently and exhaustively address corruption, impunity and promote respect for human rights. Many aggrieved parties have no confidence that they can find justice in our courts and tend to seek it elsewhere, mainly from the streets – demonstrations, protests, violence and civil disobedience. Others prefer "direct and immediate" actions such as mob-justice and other forms of revenge violence. This is one of the factors that led the Odinga team who rejected the results of the presidential election to completely refuse to file a petition in the High Court – they had no confidence in the Judiciary.

The near breakdown of law and order and lack of respect for the rule of law by the political elite creates a degree of helplessness amongst citizens. Key institutions of accountability and public governance have also collapsed or been ineffective. There are no sustainable checks and balances and citizens are incapable of holding their elected leaders to account, other than removing them through the ballot every five years. So when voters feel cheated out of an election, redress can only be expected in five years. This situation contributed to the protests by many voters against what they perceived as a lack of institutional framework to resolve election disputes. This problem was aggravated by lack of a specific elections court.

The administrative framework of elections and the composition of the ECK Commissioners

The third part of this section focuses on the Electoral Commission of Kenya and how it has organised and managed elections in Kenya. This section looks at how the ECK was established, how it was constituted, and how it was perceived and related issues. It also looks at the factors that may have influenced its conduct and management of the 2007 general elections and what could have been done if at all to prevent or minimise the electoral violence that followed the announcement of the disputed 2007 presidential elections results.

The ECK was a Constitutional Commission but did not have a facilitative Electoral Commission Law. Its operations were classified under the Ministry of Justice, National Cohesion and Constitutional Affairs since 2003. Yet, the ECK was accountable through Speaker of Parliament and had a separate Finance Vote, receiving funding like other Constitutional Commissions directly from the Treasury but not from the Consolidation Fund as they would have preferred.

The ECK was established in 1963 under Section 48 of the Constitution (Chap 3). The Speaker of Senate was Chairperson. Other members were the Speaker of House of Representatives, who was the Vice-Chairperson, a member appointed by the Governor-General with advice from Prime Minister and 8 Members from each of the 8 Regions appointed by the Governor-General with advice of the President of the respective Regional Assembly.

In 1966 when Regional Assemblies were abolished by a Constitutional amendment, a new structure of the ECK was therein created with the following members: The Speaker of the National Assembly was Chairperson, 2 members appointed by the President and a member representing each of the 8 provinces also appointed by the President. In 1969 another Constitutional amendment provided as follows: That the appointment of the Chairperson will henceforth be done by the President plus that of not less than 4 other Commissioners. From 1969 to 1991, ECK played a very minimal role and did not exist independently. Elections were conducted by civil servants, directed by the Director of Elections who was based at the Attorney-General's Chambers. In the Constituencies, elections officials were mostly drawn from Provincial Administrations – District Commissioners mainly served as Returning Officers supported by District Officers and other Civil Servants.

In 1990 and 1997 through Constitutional amendments No. 17 and No. 7 respectively, Section 41 was amended to establish the ECK, consisting of a Chairperson appointed by President and not less than 4 and not more than 21 Commissioners also appointed by the President. The Chair and Vice-Chair of the ECK had to be qualified to hold office as either High Court Judge or a Judge of Appeal. The Vice-Chairperson was elected by Commissioners from among themselves. The ECK Commissioners served for a term of 5 years and were eligible for re-appointment at the pleasure of the President. By the 2002 General Elections there were 22 ECK commissioners who served on a permanent and pensionable basis making them executive staff. These provisions relating to the composition and establishment of ECK remained until 2008 when the ECK was disbanded and replaced through a Constitutional amendment that created the Interim Independent Electoral Commission (IIEC).

By the 2002 General Elections the ECK had established a fully functioning Secretariat headed by a Secretary with two deputy secretaries in charge of elections and human resources respectively. There were also Heads of Departments and other senior staff charged with direct management of different aspects of the electoral cycle. The ECK was managed on the basis of Committee which were constituted and chaired by Commissioners with senior staff serving as secretaries and members. The roles of commissioners vis-a-vis those of senior staff were almost always not clearly demarcated resulting in a lot of tension between them. Senior staff often felt micro-managed by the Commissioners while the commissioners felt the senior staff were sometimes overstepping their boundaries.

Many members of staff didn't have clear job descriptions and had to await instructions on a daily basis. This resulted in wasted time and skills. It also resulted in low morale amongst the staff. There were also ethnic politics and issues of nepotism, favouritism and allegations of discrimination, where some members of staff complained of being unable to function because their immediate bosses were not supportive or never approved any proposed projects or activities. The above situation may have contributed to the undermining or sabotaging of the operations of the ECK by some of its members to spite each other, a situation the Kriegler Commission generally described as "incompetence".

The ECK collaborated with many Civil Society Organisations and Development Partners. It had capacity to conduct and manage many of its responsibilities. However, the ECK relied heavily on its Commissioners for guidance, direction and leadership. Senior staff members were unable or unauthorised to take actions or make decisions without reference and deference to the Commissioners. This sometimes slowed down activities and other times led to delay in implementation of programmes. Collaborative initiatives also suffered as the bureaucracy created by this mode of operations was slowing down activities.

Since 1992, the government and public servants have in one way or the other participated in elections to the benefit of the incumbent. Since 1992 to date, public resources such as cars, planes, public servants, public broadcaster (Kenya Broadcasting Corporation- KBC) and development opportunities (water, roads, electricity, schools, health centres, bursaries), and gerrymandering have been used to benefit the incumbent. Negative ethnicity is also a factor. Since the 2005 Referendum, voters voted for or against the proposed Constitution on the basis of ethnicity. Politicians managed successfully to balkanise Kenyans along ethnic lines to vote, not on the basis of the issues in question or content of the Constitution, but on the basis of ethnic affiliation. These electoral malpractices/offences have unfortunately gone unpunished, resulting in impunity. It is virtually impossible to expect the incumbent president to lose an election, however unpopular he may be. This is a culture that seems to defy even the best of voter/civic education, as even the educated and informed voters seem incapable of rising above these sectarian interests.

Appointment of ECK Commissioners

In 1992, former president Moi extensively involved the late Jaramogi Oginga Odinga in the selection and appointment of the ECK commissioners. In fact, many of the 1992 ECK commissioners were Oginga's own selection. Other political parties and candidates who participated in the 1992 General Elections were also consulted and involved. There were no disputes relating to the composition of the ECK at that time.

In 1997, in order to level the political playing field, Moi gave in to pressure from professionals and Civil Society Organisations, and the then opposition political parties, to form an Inter-Parliamentary Parties Group (IPPG), led by Kibaki (the then Leader of Official Opposition), which recommended a variety of constitutional amendments among them an agreement to share appointments of Commissioners to the ECK. The joint opposition political parties were given 10 slots for Commissioners while the ruling party then, KANU, retained 11 slots, excluding the chairperson (a total of 22 Commissioners). The IPPG further aimed at making the ECK more independent by providing that it shall not be directed in its functions or interfered with. The amendments also clearly spelt out its functions. Disturbingly this IPPG arrangement was not enacted into the Constitution and operated as a gentlemen's agreement. However, in 2002, all the ECK Commissioners were re-appointed in readiness for the 2002 General Elections without any serious concerns, since the re-appointment did not upset the IPPG status quo.

During the first tenure of President Kibaki (2003-2007), he appointed and re-appointed commissioners without consulting parliamentary political parties. Most of the appointments were to fill vacancies left by commissioners who had passed away. Others were appointed to replace those whose terms were not renewed. However, no political party complained that Kibaki didn't consult the parliamentary parties as was required under the IPPG agreement. Since the numeric positions and composition of parliamentary political parties had changed, it had been expected that Kibaki, having led the IPPG in 1997, would honour the spirit and the principle of IPPG to secure democracy and fairness.

On 11th January 2007 (an election year), Kibaki single-handedly appointed nine (9) new ECK Commissioners causing outrage and indignation from the public, professionals, media, civil society, international community and political parties. In November 2007, Kibaki, again, without reference to opposition parliamentary political parties, appointed seven (7) Commissioners to the ECK, five (5) new and two (2) re-appointments, only a month to the General Elections. This action triggered national outrage. Kibaki's action was seen as aimed at crowding the ECK with his supporters in order to influence the outcome of the 2007 presidential elections. This unilateral action had the effect of undermining the credibility of ECK as an independent body.

The General Elections of 2007 were conducted by 18 Commissioners who had never overseen General Elections before (only one of the 18 had been there during the Referendum of 2005 for the proposed constitution). This meant that only five (5) Commissioners including the chairman had practical experience in the management of elections. The foregoing may have contributed to break-down of chain of command during the 2007 General Elections and to the "gross negligence and incompetence" in the management of the 2007 General Elections that the Kriegler Commission reported on.

In addition, it also emerged that new Returning Officers (RO) without any experience in elections were also engaged to conduct the elections. Some of these ROs were later to confess- to the alarm of Kenyans- that they had messed and mixed up results as they were collating them and announced losers as winners. A case in point was the RO of Kirinyaga Constituency who confessed that he had announced the loser as the winner of the election. It is quite possible that many sitting members of parliament were not legally elected.

Credibility, confidence in and legitimacy of the ECK

The appointments of new commissioners, especially in an election year and without involvement of political parties participating in the 2007 General Elections, greatly undermined the credibility of ECK and cast doubts on its independence, thereby eroding the confidence of the people in the electoral body. On 14th October 2007, the term of Gabriel Mukele expired. He was not reappointed. Instead, another new commissioner was appointed. This was a great blow to the ECK. Mukele had been in ECK since 1997 and had also been Kivuitu's right-hand man. He had in April 2007 led a delegation to Nigeria to support and observe the Local Government elections in Nigeria. He had also been managing the ECK in Kivuitu's absence and was important link within the ECK.

On 11ᵗʰ November 2007, Kibaki, to the relief of both national and international community, (re)appointed Kivuitu chairman of the ECK. Kivuitu became the Chairman of ECK in 1997 and oversaw the 1997, 2002 and 2007 General Elections. He also oversaw the 2005 Referendum on the proposed Constitution. Kivuitu was first appointed to the ECK in 1992. His appointment came as opposition politicians, religious leaders, media, international community, donors, civil society and professional organizations mounted pressure on Kibaki to reappoint him.

Kivuitu had tremendous experience in elections and – at the time – a reputation to match in Kenya, Africa and abroad. Therefore, his re-appointment greatly enhanced the credibility of ECK and increased people's confidence that the ECK would conduct free and fair elections. His reappointment was also welcomed by the then three main political parties– Party of National Unity (PNU), Orange Democratic Movement (ODM) and Orange Democratic Movement-Kenya (ODM-Kenya). Other political parties participating in the 2007 General Elections also welcomed the reappointment of Kivuitu as ECK chairman, stating that they had confidence in his ability to oversee the elections. This heightened the expectations that the General Elections were going to be conducted in a professional and credible manner, even though the majority of ECK Commissioners were relatively new.

Upon his reappointment, the rating of ECK by people in Kenya, based on opinion polls, drastically increased. More than half of the 14.5 million voters were confident the ECK would oversee free and fair elections in 2007. According to a Steadman poll, "confidence in the ECK has increased from 38 per cent in early November 2007 to 59 per cent by mid this month [December 2007]."[17]

The International Commission of Jurists (Kenya Section) also named Kivuitu, "the Jurist of the Year" on 10ᵗʰ December 2007 because of his contribution to democratic governance and the rule of law. Kivuitu, while receiving the Jurist of the Year Award, promised that he would oversee the General Elections without fear or favour, and that the process would be both professional and transparent. In addition, the public in Kenya had a lot of trust and confidence in the 5 commissioners' ability to deliver credible, free, fair and peaceful elections that would be professionally managed. This heightened the expectations that all was going to be well.

The electoral system

An electoral system generally means the means by which votes cast in an election are translated into seats. Kenya inherited from the British an electoral system based on electoral districts known as constituencies for Members of Parliament and wards for councillors: The First-Past-The-Post electoral system (FPTP). This electoral system belongs to the larger category of Majoritarian systems. It is likened to a horse race where the first horse that crosses the post becomes the winner of the race. This in elections means, the candidate with the highest number or majority of the total votes cast wins the election and all other votes don't count. Although this system is simple and easy to use, it wastes all the votes that are not cast for the winner and it does not promote the principle of equality of votes. This is the electoral system Kenya has practised since independence.

According to the previous Constitution of Kenya, our system allowed for nomination of 12 additional Members of Parliament and many councillors whose number was determined by the size of their councils. These nominated MPs and Councillors were supposed to ensure fair and equitable representation. "First-past-the-post" is an electoral system in which the winning candidate is the person who wins the most votes. This means electors cast one vote for the candidate of their choice in single-member constituencies, and the candidate with the largest number of votes is elected, regardless of the proportion of the vote obtained. For example, in a constituency of 75,000 votes where there are 15 candidates, if the candidate with the majority votes has only 15,000 out of a turn-out of 60,000, the candidate wins with only a quarter of the votes of those who cast their ballots. the rest of the 45,000 votes are wasted and count for nothing.

The concept of one-person-one-vote is completely diluted by our electoral system in which different regions have different value for their vote. There is no equity in electoral areas, population and other important considerations which ensure fair and equitable representation. As mentioned above, the candidate with the highest votes wins whether that candidate has the majority backing of his or her constituents or not.

The electoral boundaries are drawn every ten years in Kenya after national population census has been conducted. Periodic drawing of boundaries is aimed at ensuring equitable and fair representation of every voter in Kenya. Unfortunately, this electoral system is prone to abuse. Because of gerrymandering the constituencies in Kenya do not ensure equitable and fair representation, all factors considered. There are constituencies with over 200,000 registered voters while others have 25,000 registered voters and their Members of Parliament have equal weight in representation. There are also constituencies as large as a province while others are so small geographically an MP can walkthrough them within an hour or so. A fair and equitable electoral system requires reliance on the international principles of boundary delimitation. The following factors need to be considered in boundary determination:

- Density of population, and in particular the need to ensure adequate representation of urban and sparsely-populated rural areas;

- Population trends;

- Means of communication; and

- Community of interest, historical, economic and cultural ties.

The above factors should be balanced- none of them should be given more weight than the other. The practice in Kenya of Proportional Representation (one-person-one-vote) favours only densely populated areas. This means that densely populated areas will have the most number of constituencies irrespective of their geographical size. This is unfair to the sparsely populated areas with very large constituencies whose communication and other infrastructure is poor. Therefore, the argument for one-person-one-vote should be balanced with the argument for one-kilometre-one-vote. Under the Constitution of Kenya, promulgated in 2010, the electoral system and process is guided by a set of principles found in Chapter 7. The principles affirm the right to fair representation for all citizens. The Constitution also establishes the Independent Electoral and Boundaries Commission which will conduct or supervise referenda and elections of elective bodies and offices (Article 88).

The current Constitution addresses the problem of unequal representation of women and ethnic minorities and sets the stage for the reduction of electoral malpractices as witnessed in 2007. In a sense, the Constitution responds to the unfair electoral system, cited by some as a possible reason for the 2007/8 violence.

Part Three: During the Elections

This part deals with role and the conduct of the media before and during the general elections. It also deals with the events that ocurred at KICC between 27th And 31st December 2007

The role and conduct of the media

The media play a very key role in the electoral and democratic processes in Kenya. They are a medium for voter and civic education – mostly through paid up spaces and air-time and also as part of news, features and information released through press releases, media briefings and press conferences. The media also extensively cover campaigns, nominations[18] and political rallies of political parties and their candidates.

"On January 22, 2008, international reports began to appear, claiming that media, and particularly local language (commonly called vernacular) radio stations in Kenya, were responsible for fanning ethnic hatred and fuelling violence. The reports echoed previous such allegations, including around the 2005 referendum campaign in Kenya. While the mainstream media has been praised for trying to calm the situation, people within and outside the media argue that it has failed to live up to professional and ethical standards and has contributed to the crisis."[19] For instance, according to a BBC World Service Trust Policy Briefing report released in April 2008 in London, "some local language radio stations have incited fear and hatred particularly at the height of the violence. Local language radio stations are routinely partisan and flout codes of ethics. Talk shows have provided the greatest opportunities for hate speech and talk show hosts are not trained in conflict reporting or moderation." There have also been serious allegations that journalists demand bribes to file reports and that corruption tends to determine editorial content more and more. This is generally attributed to "poor remuneration, status and safety of journalists, hampering a free and plural media."[20]

The BBC Policy Report conclusion stated that, "there is no independent public service broadcaster in Kenya. If there had been, the scale of the violence and of the crisis may well have been much less severe." The Kenya Broadcasting Corporation (KBC) – Radio and Television services – is publicly owned and managed. It is supposed, in collaboration with the Electoral body, to ensure fair and balanced coverage for presidential candidates and their political parties under the KBC Act which also is the only law that defines the 21 days official campaign period. Unfortunately KBC lost its independence a long time ago. Indeed, during the time of KANU's single party rule, which is since the late 1960s, KBC (formerly Voice of Kenya – VoK) was the ruling party's mouth piece and propaganda machine. This did not change even after the re-introduction of multi-party politics in 1992.

Privately owned media, allowed to operate only in the 1990s, generally censor themselves or adopt self-interested editorial policies. Therefore, there is really no free and balanced media house in Kenya. "Recently the media has been accused of fanning the flames of ethnic hatred, of having become politically co-opted, of marginalizing voices of reason at a time of ethnically polarised politics and failing to uphold its function as a source of investigation of abuse of power. Many of these accusations have been made by those within the media itself."[21] This report further concluded that, "recent record of the media, according to many within it, is that media has undermined as well as invigorated democracy."

During the 2005 Referendum and 2007 General Elections, the media played a very critical role. While some media houses promoted civic and voter education, others clearly fanned ethnic tensions and propagated hate speech, while others, especially commercial media, restricted its content and access by the public, clearly taking political sides and excluding politicians and parties they did not associate with.[22] "A lot of co-option happened during the last elections," says David Makali of the Media Institute of Kenya. "Some of the journalists were affiliated to certain groups, some media houses have been alleged to have some leanings towards or against certain politicians. The editorial content or the drift of analysis would point which direction the media were. The media in totality were co-opted and corrupted in this election; there is no doubt about that."[23]

There were many mysterious happenings. All the main television stations (*Kenya Television Network, Nation Television*, and *Citizen Television*) claimed that their elections databases crashed. "At Nation Media Group we invested heavily in very expensive software that provided us with an Election Database," says Emmanuel Juma, Head of TV News at Nation TV. "We had people in all the tallying centres and were meant to know the results long before the Electoral Commission announced them. But to everybody's shock and horror, the database crashed and that happened to the Nation, to Citizen TV and even KTN... they all crashed which is very mysterious. We're trying to find out what really happened... but there's no way all the databases could have crashed accidentally at the same time."[24]

At the height of the tension the government banned live coverage of the elections results, heightening suspicions that rigging was going on or that results were allegedly "being cooked" in favour of the incumbent. According to the BBC Report, "a ban on live news reporting instigated by the government was designed to defuse public anger, but arguably did the opposite as rumour spread over SMS text messages and other networks took over from live journalistic reporting. When the media was prevented from doing its job, the public clearly missed it and the country almost certainly suffered as a result. The ban was largely considered ineffective because international broadcasters continued to broadcast coverage, including through national partners." The situation was worse at the KICC because those who were there began to "manufacture" and spread their own information to the outside world. Since they were at KICC, they were bound to be believed.

The ECK at KICC had been relying heavily on live media coverage to reach out to Kenyans all over the country in order to diffuse suspicions and to preach peace and calm as the results were being awaited. The ban on live broadcasts curtailed this process, further increasing the fear that, the delays in the transmission of results, especially from areas where Kibaki was strong, were deliberate so as to allow for "cooking of presidential elections results", as Kivuitu had intimated.

"The violence after the announcement of the polls was due to the polarity in the media, especially vernacular media which were turned into political tools,"[25] Samuel Poghisio, Minister for Information is quoted as saying. Stations recruited 'quacks' as news anchors and editors according to Poghisio, and he cited a case where a media house broadcast ethnic war songs targeting certain communities.

Some journalists, both local and international, played a calming critical role while at KICC. Some local journalists tried hard to get genuine information from ECK which they relayed to Kenyans through international journalists after the ban. Other journalists tried to allay rumours and misinformation that were going on at KICC by providing counter-information or corroborating genuine information. Some of them also diffused some really volatile situations. A good example was Linus Kaikai who spent days and nights at KICC trying to get genuine information and diffusing rumours that could have resulted in more tension.

The events that occurred at KICC between 27th and 31st December 2007

The ECK had set up a national tallying centre for the 2007 presidential elections results at the KICC at Nairobi. The centre was equipped with computers (with access to internet and wireless connections), communication devises, printers, scanners, fax machines, television screens and other information and communication gadgets, that were used to facilitate accurate, current and transparent tallying of the final presidential elections results from all Kenya's 210 constituencies. These results were transmitted from Constituency tallying centres to KICC by Returning Officers (ROs) first through telephone calls and or faxes and subsequently in person.[26]

According to the ECK all the results (of the elections) were to be received by ECK officers at KICC from Returning Officers in the field who were to verify the same after receiving a faxed copy of the statutory form on which the final results are recorded and signed by the officer and the candidates. The final results of the presidential election were announced by the ECK chairman, Samuel Kivuitu, in accordance with the law.

To ensure there was adequate security, the ECK made special arrangements with the police to ensure that KICC and the ECK headquarters at Anniversary Towers were secured against any political hooligans throughout the voting, counting, tallying and announcement of results.[27] This was also personally supported by the former Commissioner of Police, Hussein Ali, who issued several statements from the KICC and his Vigilance House offices. 27th December 2007 was the date for the General Elections. There were long queues of voters waiting to vote outside all polling stations long before they opened their doors. The voter turn-out was very high. Official figures given by the ECK were 70% voter turn-out. There were very many young first-time voters. The ECK had registered over 60% young voters under the age of 35 years.[28]

The voting and counting processes in most polling stations went smoothly except in some areas where voting and/or counting were disrupted, for example, in Kilgoris, Dagoretti and Starehe constituencies.[29] Observers concluded that the polling and counting processes at polling stations in most constituencies was credible and the election process relatively free and fair.

However, there were doubts cast on the tallying of General Elections results at the constituency tallying centres and the transmission of results from constituency tallying centres to KICC in Nairobi and the tallying of presidential results at KICC. Many observers and the Kriegler Commission concluded that the problem occurred from the constituency tallying centres stage to KICC.

On 28th December 2007, a day after the general elections, Samuel Kivuitu, the ECK chairman, spoke of difficulties in accessing ECK's Returning Officers (ROs), who, he said, could not be reached through telephones. He said that, like all other Kenyans, he was anxious about the delays over dispatch of presidential results from the constitutiencies' level. He even commented that such delays could be misinterpreted by some to mean that those who are delaying the results may be involved in "cooking them." This statement planted seeds of suspicion and doubts as to the integrity of those delayed presidential elections results.

On 29th December 2007, there were further delays. Government suspended live media broadcasts of presidential results. ODM and Raila Odinga claimed the rigging of results was taking place democracy was being sabotaged. At this stage, the ECK was also tense and seemed "nervous", casting doubts on and inviting serious questions about the integrity and credibility of the presidential results it was announcing.

As a result, the chairman of ECK agreed that the only way to ensure the integrity and credibility of the presidential results was to allow party agents from the ODM and the Party of National Unity, (PNU), and domestic observers to go inside the tallying room at KICC. A team of party agents of ODM, ODM-Kenya and PNU and observers were allowed inside the tallying centre at KICC to scrutinise and review all the available files from the Returning Officers (ROs) in order to compare the results from polling stations with those from the constituency tallying centres. The materials to be used were the files that had been physically delivered to KICC by Returning Officers: one containing results, forms and other materials for presidential, parliamentary and civic results for each of the 210 constituencies as captured in Forms 16A completed by Presiding Officers at the polling stations, as well as Forms 16 completed by ROs from constituency centres.

The "scrutinisers" were asked by Chairman Kivuitu to carefully examine the files containing presidential results. They were supposed to note any suspiciously high voter turn-out, inflated or deflated figures, alterations, missing statutory forms, any results forms which were in photocopies, and any forms that were inappropriately filed (some parliamentary results forms had been filed in presidential results files). The chairman said these anomalies, if noted, would be used to invalidate presidential results in the affected areas. "Announcement of presidential results would be delayed, in the cases of constituencies whose results were not filed in statutory forms, until the forms were physically at KICC," the chairman added.

The "scrutinisers" worked throughout the night of 29th December 2007. Before scrutiny work began, the party agents agreed on a number of files to begin with and work their way through as many files as they could find. Most of the ROs had already arrived with their files. The ECK staff at KICC were able to pull out the files and surrender them for scrutiny by parties' agents and observers. The political parties' agents sat around one large table while the observers were moving from one table to the other, observing what was going on. A number of original files could not be traced – only their photocopies were availed to the scrutinisers. In addition, there were some altered results that were made available.[30]

On 30th December 2007 morning[31] the "scrutinisers" were asked to leave the tallying centre although they had stated that they had not finalised their assignment. They however submitted through the Commissioners and the ECK legal officer their findings. I learnt later from the Chairman that the report submitted to the Commissioners and the Legal Officer, and later submitted to him showed absolutely no irregularities and indeed indicated consensus among the PNU and ODM agents and the observers. Therefore, there was no serious problem to warrant the delay in announcement of presidential results.

The purpose of the scrutiny, the chairman informed us, was to enable him and Commissioners to discuss and resolve the issues that may have arisen from the scrutiny process on the night of 29th December, 2007. However, the report that was prepared and presented to the Chairman did not raise any issues of concern that warranted further discussions. This report had been prepared by the senior staff and commissioners who were present at KICC during the scrutiny process.

On 30th December, several attempts to announce presidential results were interrupted by ODM supporters, although Kivuitu and his Commissioners generally ignored these interruptions. At the raised stage, security personnel physical shoved and elbowed ODM supporters to stop them from interrupting the announcement of results.

Both the ODM and PNU supporters issued statements from the KICC castigating each other and claiming and counter-claiming that the elections had been rigged in ODM strongholds in favour of ODM, and in PNU strongholds in favour of PNU. There was confusion at one stage when an ODM supporter seized one micro-phone to object to Kivuitu's announcement of what was claimed to be altered results. Kivuitu ignored this and continued to make the announcements.

Although the ODM on several occasions publicly objected to the results being read out at KICC by the ECK and demanded a recount, they did not put their demands in writing as is required by the law. Then, an officer who had been seconded to the ECK at KICC to oversee the collating of presidential election results spoke to the media at KICC claiming that he had witnessed alteration and incorrect tabulation of elections results at KICC and that he felt obliged to state the truth. He later fled the country for his own security.

In the mid-morning of 30th December, word went out that preparations for the swearing in of Kibaki as president were at high gear in State House. By this time, most ROs had not yet arrived at KICC to physically deliver the results of the elections. This triggered more angst amongst supporters of ODM and ODM-Kenya, who began to question why preparations for swearing were on-going yet the ECK had not announced the results. By about 5pm, armed General Service Unit and Police arrived at the Media Centre at KICC where the journalists, observers, invited guests, ECK staff, political parties' agents and supporters were waiting for results. They then asked everyone to vacate the room and escorted everybody out of the KICC parameter fences and closed all the gates.

As people tried to understand what had happened, car radios began to announce- through KBC radio- that Kibaki had won the elections. Immediately, there were more armed security re-enforcements who demanded that all the journalists, observers and party supporters vacate and go home. They also denied everyone re-entry to KICC. All those journalists who had left equipment at KICC were asked to come another day.

On the evening of 30th December 2007, Chairman Kivuitu and his colleagues announced the presidential election results in a secluded room amid complaints of rigging and heavy presence of security personnel. Soon thereafter, Kivuitu was escorted by armed security men to State House to deliver the certificate of results that he had announced. Soon afterwards, a swearing in ceremony of President Kibaki was conducted under night cover at State House.

Part Four: The Aftermath

The electoral violence witnessed after the announcement of the 2007 presidential results was fast and furious. The State security apparatus responded with maximum force, further aggravating the violence. Strangely, the number of people reported to have died and those reported to have been displaced was almost the same as was reported in the 1991-1993 ethnic violence – 1,500 dead and more than 300,000 displaced. This was an uncanny coincidence. But the ferocity of the 2007/8 violence could not be compared with that of 1991, as just in days, the violence was enacted as though the perpetrators had been ready for it. The violence was enacted around the same areas as was the case in 1991 – 1993 – Rift Valley, Nyanza and Western Provinces, although the Coast Province was not very much affected by the violence in 2007/8, which also saw some parts of Central Province being similarly affected.

From the 31st December 2007, it was clear the ECK believed something had terribly gone wrong in the manner in which they tallied and announced presidential results. Indeed, Samuel Kivuitu and four of his Commissioners colleagues cast doubts on the election results through the statements they made on 31st December, 2007 and 1st and 2nd January, 2008. They repeated their doubts in the subsequent weeks of January 2008. They indicated that there were irregularities and they had noted some which required serious scrutiny and investigations. They agreed that there was a need to establish an independent body to investigate these irregularities.

After the announcement of the results and the swearing in ceremony, Kivuitu received evidence of manipulation, which had been placed on his table at KICC, anonymously. He had not had the opportunity to open the envelope which contained some forms 16A and 16 which were clearly altered. He began to doubt the results he had announced. He also began to believe that there may have been serious evidence of irregularities far worse than he had thought. This may explain his conduct. He was extensively quoted as saying, "I do not know whether Kibaki *fairly* won the presidential elections". This statement added to the already serious doubts about the credibility of the presidential elections results.

On 31st December 2007, four Commissioners issued a press statement in which they further cast doubts about the credibility of the election results. They said: "it is noted that some of the information received from some of our

Returning Officers (ROs) now casts doubts on the veracity of the figures. The complaints raised following the audit[32] are weighty and in our view merit careful consideration."

On the evening of 1st January 2008 after Kivuitu and his colleagues cast doubts on the results, calm returned in some areas torn apart by the violence because people began to believe that the ECK had understood that something had gone wrong and that a solution was probably in the offing.

On claims that he was under undue pressure to declare results, Kivuitu said: "Some PNU (Party of National Unity) and ODM-Kenya leaders put me under pressure by calling me frequently, asking me to announce the results immediately". On Tuesday, 1st January 2008, Kivuitu said, "I had thought of resigning, but thought against it because I don't want people to say I'm a coward". He said he "announced the results because the Commission [ECK] had no legal mandate to investigate complaints raised by the opposition immediately."[33] That is why despite the scrutiny at the KICC on the night of 29th December 2008 by party agents and observers, no action was taken by ECK before the election results for the presidential elections were announced. This was regardless of the report prepared by the party agents and commissioners that it was necessary to re-examine and scrutinize results from over 44 constituencies they had agreed on.

In the end, the "scrutiny" of the files/returns for presidential results was an exercise in futility - perhaps meant to buy time. After all, the chairperson and the Commissioners did mention, after the fact, that they would do nothing, no matter what the agents and observers found from the scrutinised files, since "their hands were tied by the law." They instead said that whatever was found from the files would be used in an election petition. Kivuitu also said, "We are culprits as a Commission. We have to leave it to an independent group to investigate what actually went wrong."

The announcement of presidential results itself came as a surprise because many people in Kenya believed that Kivuitu would never announce results that were openly contested by key stakeholders; results he believed incorrect or inaccurate, or results whose authenticity he doubted. Yet, Samuel Kivuitu went ahead and announced the presidential results from a secluded room at KICC surrounded by tens of armed security men. Then he left KICC under heavy security guard to deliver the Results Certificate in person to the President in State House as stipulated by the law.

At State House, Kivuitu handed over the election certificate to Mwai Kibaki, informing him he was duly elected President of Kenya. Kivuitu even made a joke about the process, though the faces of the people at the ceremony were rigid and solemn. Thereafter, a brief swearing in ceremony followed, and Mwai Kibaki began his second term as the President of Kenya.

By mid-February 2008, the violence ended with the arrival of the mediation team led by His Excellency Kofi Annan. Soon thereafter, the ECK did an about-turn and denied ever casting doubt on the presidential elections results. These denials, explanations and counter-accusations against the ODM political party by the ECK Commissioners were made through daily newspaper advertisements.

Notes

[1] The reference materials for the information on the history of elections was mainly from Elections Data Book published by the Institute for Education in Democracy (IED) – and from its unpublished elections materials and resources, source - Jumuia Place, Lenana Road, Nairobi in September and October 2009.

[2] Kenya's general elections are conducted at an interval of five years.

[3] With its removal, the provision for federalism, also known as *majimboism,* was removed marking the end of devolved government and the tightening of central government.

[4] It was expected that Kibaki would reject his appointment by Moi to the Ministry of Health. After all, it was seen as a demotion from being Vice President. Furthermore, it had become clear that Kibaki had lost favour with Moi. But Kibaki chose to remain a Minister.

[5] Yet another Kikuyu Vice-President. Moi's vice-presidents were consistently from the same ethnic community, the Kikuyu; even George Muthengi Saitoti is said to be a Kikuyu, though with a Maasai surname. He was said to want to appease the Kikuyu community, the largest in Kenya and the community of Kenyatta and his close cronies who ensured that Moi became President even though he came from a small ethnic community. The short-lived appointment of Musalia Mudavadi in October 2002, two months before the general elections was aimed at rewarding him and his community for not snubbing Moi as did Raila Odinga and the others who walked out on Moi when he picked Uhuru Kenyatta as his preferred heir apparent.

[6] "DIVIDE AND RULE: State-Sponsored Ethnic Violence in Kenya, Human Rights Watch/Africa Watch, New York, November 1993.

[7] Interestingly when he was Vice President and a Minister in Moi's government, Kibaki had opposed the re-introduction of multi-parties stating that, "introducing multi-parties was impossible – it's "like cutting a *mugumo* tree with a razor-blade."

[8] "Kayas of Deprivation, Kayas of Blood: Violence, Ethnicity and the State in Coastal Kenya," Kenya Human Rights Commission (KHRC), Nairobi, 1997, p. 50.

[9] The KHRC 1997 Report, above note, p. 1.

[10] Although Kibaki also got support through his coalition partners of Party of National Unity (PNU), KANU led by Kenyatta had declared support for Kibaki and brought support from North Eastern and others. However, most of PNU supporters were mainly from Central and Mount Kenya areas – and supporters of these communities in other parts of Kenya (diaspora).

[11] Even though Musyoka had left the ODM party with a piece of the "Orange" in the name of ODM-Kenya, he didn't leave with a lot of supporters to clinch the presidency.

[12] The expansive Rift Valley province represented by William Ole Ntimama, William Ruto, Henry Kosgey and the late Kipkalya Kones; Nairobi Province led by Odinga; The Eastern Province was represented by Kalonzo Musyoka, current Vice-President, Charity Ngilu, the late Bonaya Godana, Yusuf Haji and others, while the Coast Province was represented by Najib Balala and others. The North-Eastern Province was also ably represented by Billow Kerrow, as was Western Province by the Deputy Prime-Minister Musalia Mudavadi with part of Central Province represented by the other Deputy Prime-Minister Uhuru Kenya who was then the Official Leader of Opposition.

[13] I have been observing general elections and by-elections in Kenya since 1992 and I have never missed any General Elections observation. Even in 1997, when I was based abroad, I travelled to Kenya purposely to vote and observe the general elections of that year.

[14] Many of them, even including key stakeholders – candidates, political parties, voters, have been unaware of the existence of the Election Offences Act, which has remained almost entirely unchanged since independence.

[15] This may be because the security officers seconded to the ECK also included General Service Unit, Kenya Youth Service and others, not just the Police. In addition, they often see themselves playing a different role other than arresting suspects during the elections. This is because arresting suspects will also require them to take and book them in Police Stations, thereby removing them from their duties at the polling stations. Furthermore, they are often spread too thin as there are usually more than 27,000 polling stations. Also, as mentioned earlier, most Police Officers know and understand the Penal Code with some knowing the Criminal Procedure Code, but only a few are aware of Economic Crimes Laws (on corruption, bribery) and Elections Offences Act.

[16] This was a roving unit completely separate from the Police Officers stationed at the polling stations. It was possible to create this unit because this was a by-election involving only Kisauni Constituency and it was possible to deploy additional officers to the field. This is usually not possible during General Elections, when almost all officers are deployed either to polling stations or to guard our politicians and diplomats.

[17] Nation Reporters, "**Most voters confident in Kivuitu team**," *www.nationmedia.com*, Tuesday, December 18, 2007.

[18] Political parties and ECK nominations. There were reports that some of the nominations of the political parties were generally a sham in which some candidates received automatic nominations while in some cases, alleged losers of party nominations eventually got the parties' certificates to vie for the general elections. ECK nominations were no better. ECK instituted

first-come-first-served policy where whichever candidate of any participating party arrived first was given the ECK nomination. This led to political parties issuing more nomination certificates than was required per constituency and candidates who had lost nominations becoming the official candidates. ECK and political parties ignored all complaints stating that their hands were tied because there was no law governing the party nomination process and how ECK was to liaise with political parties in relation to nominations.

[19] Policy Briefing, by the BBC World Service Trust, London, UK, April 2008.

[20] BBC Report, above note, p. 2.

[21] BBC April 2008 Report, p. 3.

[22] IED was a host of an observation initiative that monitored the referendum including the media, at the time, I was the Executive Director of IED.

[23] Quoted in the BBC Report above, p. 9

[24] Quoted in BBC Report above, p. 9

[25] Quoted also in the BBC Policy Briefing report, April 2008.

[26] The law requires that all certificates and Forms 16A must be transported to the national tallying centre in the original form before any presidential results can be announced. Presidential results can however be announced, if the remaining results are not so many as to substantially change the elections results.

[27] Odhiambo Orlale, The Daily Nation, *www.nationmedia.com* 23rd December 2007.

[28] Through a collaborative initiative between the ECK and the Institute for Education in Democracy (IED) known as *vijana tugutuke* Voter Education and Registration campaign and other ECK efforts, more first time voters most of them youth registered between 2006 and 2007. This was the first time in the history of elections that such a large number of young people (over 60% of the total 14.5million registered voters) participated in any elections process.

[29] Kilgoris and Starehe elections were repeated while the results of Dagoretti parliamentary elections were announced at a Police Station.

[30] Upon inquiry it was established that the alterations mostly occurred because the ROs had phoned in provisional results from the constituencies earlier because the staff at KICC had put a lot of pressure on them to do this. Therefore, when they later phoned in the final results, the earlier results forms had to be altered to make the necessary changes. Other forms were altered by ROs when they arrived at KICC to reflect some changes. Some alterations could not, however, be explained. Some ROs indicated that they had left their files in the District Election Coordinators offices or that some of their materials had got lost following scuffles or that they were too tired and didn't know where the forms and the files were. Some ROs refused to explain themselves, leaving the ECK staff and commissioners to explain the situation.

[31] A report of the proceedings of the night of 29th December was prepared listing areas of agreement with regard to the constituencies scrutinised and areas of disagreements. It was evident

that throughout the country, there were anomalies. Some constituencies recorded over 90% voter turn-out, while in others the presidential elections results appeared inflated compared to parliamentary and civic elections results, even in rural constituencies. This is mostly a pattern of results that comes from urban areas. In some files, it was clear that the arithmetic (additions) was inaccurate and other anomalies were detected.

[32] Sanctioned by the ECK on 29th December 2007 where PNU, ODM, ODM-Kenya and 5 domestic observers were allowed to scrutinise ROs files at the tallying centre at the KICC overnight.

[33] Those who object to results can do so at constituency level or at national level (to the chairperson) with regard to presidential elections. Their objection must be in writing and should be submitted 24 hours before the final results are announced. Any objection after the announcement and swearing in can only be brought to a petition court. James Orengo made a well-publicised objection to the results in good time to the chairman which was aired by both the international and local media. However, when I asked why he didn't take any action on the objection, Kivuitu later told me that the objection had not been made in writing as was required by law!

Chapter 2

Violence in Kibera: A Reflection of the Country's Ailments

Simiyu Barasa

When the 2007 presidential elections were being announced, I was busy previewing a wedding video of my girlfriend's (now my wife) brother. The newly weds constantly shifted their eyes from the wedding video on the computer to the TV screens, where both opposition and the incumbent ruling party members were having a shouting match over the delayed release of presidential results. We were in Ngumo estate, less than 500 metres from Kibera slums, whose area MP, Raila Odinga, was widely seen as the winner against the incumbent, Mwai Kibaki. Suddenly, on the TV screens, a contingent of the elite paramilitary General Service Unit (GSU) forced their way in as a besieged Samuel Kivuitu, the then chair of the Electoral Commission of Kenya, announced the results. Pandemonium broke out, and Kivuitu was quickly escorted out of the Kenyatta International Conference Centre where the Electoral commission had set up its headquarters. When Kibaki was announced the winner, the first loud yells and screams of disbelief erupted from Kibera slums, and we looked at each other. We did not need to voice it, we knew it. Kenya was definitely erupting into a civil war.

As if setting the agenda for the rest of the country, Kibera was up in flames in a few minutes. We got out of the house, and quickly climbed onto the rooftop. From across the stone-walled fence and relative security of the Ngumo upper middle class estate, I saw the first fires start, literally. Smoke billowed in the air, screams and gunshots were everywhere, as a crowd of young men appeared from deep within the slums marching militantly on the main road; obviously heading towards the city centre which was less than four kilometres away. With similar Houdini acts, the anti-riot GSU appeared too intent on blocking the youth from their mission. There were several people running for their lives as angry mobs chased them, and a few more rusty brown iron sheet-walled houses went up in flames. It was clear: Kikuyu and Luo youth were hunting each other down, and torching property belonging to the other community. What was happening in Kibera was a microcosm of what was happening in the rest of Kenya. And once more, Kibera was displaying, in its essence, the traits of dangerous, explosive issues that have besieged Kenya from colonial times. If anyone wanted answers as to why Kenya was burning, all they needed was to ask why Kibera was aflame. Then copy paste the answers against the larger Kenya question.

Though it is in Lang'ata constituency, the area Member of Parliament, the long-time firebrand opposition politician, Raila Odinga, enjoys fanatical support within the Kibera slums to the extent that most people just refer to his constituency as Kibera. From the days of his father, the doyen of Kenyan opposition politics, Jaramogi Oginga Odinga, any time people rioted against the dictatorial regime of Daniel Arap Moi, Kibera youth were noticeably at the forefront. When Raila took over from where his father had left off, Kibera became synonymous with him, and for every fight that he had against the government of the day, Kibera provided him not only with the votes, but with the people power vital during demonstrations. It had earned Raila both political strength and an Achilles heel. He had street muscle, since Kibera is densely populated, especially by members of his ethnic Luo community. Representing an urban constituency also gave him a national appeal, since he was the only Luo MP of a constituency outside his geographical ethnic home of Luo land. His Achilles heel is the fact that Kibera is the largest slum in Africa and has one of the most deplorable living conditions in the world, about which critics would argue he had done nothing, and was only being voted in due to the huge number of Luos who migrated to Nairobi City from the shores of Lake Victoria in western Kenya in search of jobs. This ethnic angling immediately reflects the problem in Kenya and hence offers an easy answer as to why Kenya was burning. However, several other factors at play in Kibera point to a complex web of issues that are at play in Kenya, making this country an explosive keg of gunpowder that went off in December 2007.

Located roughly 3 Kilometers from the city centre of Nairobi, the capital city of Kenya, Kibera is a huge mass of mud-walled shanties, whose roofs of rusty brown corrugated iron sheets spread over an estimated 780 hectares of land. Much of its southern area is bordered by Nairobi River and the artificial Nairobi Dam, which is supposed to provide water for the Nairobi City. The Kenya-Uganda Railway splits the Kibera slums into two halves. On its southern side, immediately after you cross the Nairobi River, is the upper middle class Lang'ata Estate, and to the north immediately you cross the tarmac road, is the upper middle class Ngumo Estate. Sandwiched between these two upper middle class estates, is this shanty town housing approximately 177,000 people according to the 2009 Kenya Population and Housing Census reports, 300,000-1 million people according to UN-Habitat estimates, or 2.6 million according to popular opinion. Its unplanned infrastructure, extreme poverty and its unknown number of residents have always posed a potential danger, yet successive Kenyan governments have largely ignored it.

A few months prior to the elections, I had accompanied a local publishing house to a school inside the slums for a storytelling competition. Driving into Kibera, we were struck by the numerous signposts crowding together along the tarmac. Each of these signposts proudly announced that the NGO displayed on it was here to alleviate the suffering of the Kibera people. I had never seen so many NGOs working in such a small geographical area, and we loudly mused, "if half these NGOs did half of what they were promising, Kibera would surely not be having housing, sanitation, crime, HIV and AIDS, cholera, TB, alcoholism and all the myriads of problems it chokes under."

In the school, adults and children were well prepared with short performance narratives. We were welcomed with smiling faces and cheerful handshakes, and assurances that we shouldn't fear Kibera because all those stories about Kibera being hostile were untrue. I was mesmerized by the narratives the children gave. All the children in the area we had gone to first had Dholuo names. In every short story, whether it was a traditional hare-and-hyena story or a modern 'I-went-to-the-city-one-day…' kind of story, Raila Omolo Odinga had to feature in them. So a child would begin: 'Once upon a time there lived a hare and hyena…' Midway through the story, would suddenly go… 'and as the hyena waited for the hare, my grandmother stopped telling me the story and told me to rush to the DC's office compound. When I got there I found a huge crowd and Raila was giving flour and sugar to the people, so I took the flour and rushed back home and told my grandmother to finish the story. She told me the Hare said to the hyena…' The onlookers would cheer at this narrative mastery of giving a Raila twist to the story.

It was clear even then that the country was deep into a fanatical hero-worshipping of leaders. When I went to another section of the slums, the children there were invariably Gikuyu, and they too would drag Raila's name or his Luo people into the story but with a negative connotation. For example, 'My mother told me to stop being lazy like the Luo and get up and work' or similar statements.

It was no wonder then, that by December 2007, as was the rest of the country, Kibera had been so polarized not only ethnically, but also in relation to personality cults. You either liked Kibaki or you were the enemy, you either liked Raila or you were the enemy. No middle ground. Political tolerance had no room in people's discourse, and when the closely contested elections were bungled emotions ran high, everyone who was Luo or Gikuyu became the enemy of the other side's cult-hero, and hence needed to be exterminated.

Marooned in the house for three days, we spent time climbing up on the roof top and watching as the people in the slums fought it out and burnt whatever structures they would come across. Smoke billowed skywards, as the shouts, which would escalate as police in riot gear shot at the rioters to repel them, rent the air. A momentary peace would return only to be shattered by another attempt to march out of Kibera and into the city centre.

By the third day, I could venture out a bit. In Laini Saba, the *matatu* stage, a gang of Mungiki youth (a predominantly Gikuyu militia gang), had taken control of the area. Obviously drugged to their eyelids and talking recklessly, they made it clear that only 'the circumcised' would gain access into the slums through that route. Laini Saba is one of the major entry points to Kibera for the residents. They had set up crude check points where they would scrutinize the identity cards of residents getting in and out of the slums, and if your name suggested that you were Luo (who don't circumcise as a form of initiation and in the olden days, initiated their young into adulthood by removing a set of teeth), you were in trouble. A few unlucky Luos were nabbed as they tried to get out of the area, and in broad daylight, forcibly circumcised, or rather had their genitalia mutilated.

Using the elections as an excuse, misguided ideas of masculinity were acted out. As a final humiliation, men were violated sexually. Before the mayhem, Mungiki youths, majority of whom were unemployed, lurked around the public service transport termini extorting money from bus operators. In a very real sense, therefore, Kenya was reaping the fruits of ignoring its youth.

High unemployment rates in Kenya had given rise to a disillusioned youth, who resorted to drugs and gang fare, and murderous groups like the Mungiki among the Gikuyu and Taliban among the Luo. These groups, fuelled by a spirit of 'the country owes us', had morphed into organized crime units. By the time the elections came, these groups were a gun-for-hire for the politicians, who funded them to wreck mayhem. In the week during the post-election violence, Kibera and the rest of the country witnessed how disillusioned youth can easily be bought and deployed to wage war.

By the end of the week, I moved back to my flat in Langata. My flat overlooks the Kibera slums, barely 400 metres way from the hyacinth-filled Nairobi Dam that demarcates Langata from Kibera. At night, I could hear screams, shouts, and the horrifying sounds of iron sheets being pulled down. I would peer from my balcony and see whole sections of the slums being set ablaze. Balkanization of the slums was being brutally enforced. The Gikuyus in Luo zones were being kicked out, and the Luos in Gikuyu zones of Kibera were being kicked out. The screams by women were horrible; I don't think we shall ever know the scale of rape that went on there. Even the entrances to Kibera were manned by the two groups: Mungiki controlled the Laini Saba main entrance, while the Taliban had controlled the entrance from the Langata side.

By day, hundreds of youth would sit on the tarmac on Mbagathi way just idling, but the moment a truck with the word 'Press' emblazoned on it came towards them, they would yell and go into a frenzy shouting blood-curdling war cries and burning tires. Again, characteristic of Kenyans, the youth were playing a murderous circus to the international press, instead of addressing their issues. In the power corridors, our leaders too were not doing anything; they would sit down and wait for the international press to come to them. Then they would issue ultimatums that Kenya was headed for doom. It is no wonder then that when African leaders flew in to mediate, our politicians refused to give them a chance. After all, Kenyans are 'international'; we extend our begging bowls to the Western world and only they, it seemed, could help us.

But the problem of Kibera was not just a problem caused by Raila and Kibaki. Kibera has unresolved historical issues that have long been simmering and frequently erupting. The election crisis offered these problems a major fissure to finally explode. Kibera land was originally given to Nubian soldiers who had fought in the Second World War for the British immediately after the war ended. Though never officially given title deeds till decades later, these Nubians gained control of the government land and settled in. They built rental houses which offered cheap housing to hundreds of migrants flocking from upcountry to the city in search of jobs. Over the years, the land was grabbed by politicians, and some of it sold in unscrupulous deals to other people. With the high rural-urban migration coupled with corruption, the Nubians found themselves a minority, and couldn't even gain economically from their land. Over the years they have faced the wrath of migrants who feel that they oppress them by charging high rents, and others who feel that the land is 'free for all.' In recent years, there has been a push by residents, encouraged by political leaders, to refuse to pay rent to the landlords. When the post election chaos erupted, most of these landlords found it an opportune time to cleanse people 'from their houses, their land,' further complicating the violence. Just like the Rift Valley and Coast Provinces where land ownership, land grabbing and corruption were fuelling the clashes, Kibera's historical issues were combining with the election dispute to ignite the fire that was burning the slum down, literally.

Weeks after The Panel of Eminent African Personalities headed by Kofi Annan managed to make Kibaki and Raila agree to a power-sharing formula that put an end to the physical fighting in Kenya, Kibera and the country had not healed from the wounds of the skirmishes. Every morning and evening, hundreds of casual labourers walking from Industrial Area had to walk an extra ten or so kilometres to use the Lang'ata side in order to get into their Kibera home. They couldn't use the Laini Saba side since it was controlled by the militia. Most of the casual labourers from Kibera who offer laundry and house cleaning services to the flats on the Lang'ata side would swear never to move back to the areas of Kibera where they used to stay because the ethnic hostilities were still there. Many youths, having tasted the illicit sweetness of violence, still roamed in gangs engaging in acts of gratuitous violence. Years down the line, many women in Kibera still bear the mental anguish of the rape orgies they underwent during that period. Some of them were infected with HIV. All this for what purpose? For whose political agenda?

The truth lies in the daily reality of Kibera, which is also the daily reality of Kenya. That reality is that for long, we have chosen to bury our heads in the sand, and have got used to the lies that our lives are, chosen to let others to grow fat on our sweat. That for long, we have agreed to watch as things go from bad to worse.

Chapter 3

Sanctuary and Mayhem in Naivasha

Gakiha Weru

Naivasha owes its cosmopolitan status to its colonial heritage. At the turn of the last century, Naivasha attracted many settlers of British extraction due to its natural beauty, enhanced by the fresh water lake and warm weather all year round. It was the stop of choice for sons of the British aristocracy, such as Lord Delamere, Lord Errol, Sir Jock Delves Broughhton and Diana Caldwell who had migrated to Kenya at the beginning of the 20th Century. Some of them, like Lord Delamere, established farms around the lake and were instrumental in setting up Naivasha town. Their proclivity for a life of endless debauchery than serious farming gave Naivasha the name, "Happy Valley". The presence of the settlers created employment opportunities for indigenous Kenyans who had been forced to venture from their homes to look for work, primarily to be able to pay various taxes imposed on them by the colonial government.

In *Taxation without Principles: A Historical Analysis of the Kenyan Taxation System,* Kenyan law scholar Attiya Waris records that Hut Tax of one rupee payable in kind or labour was imposed in 1901. It, therefore, followed that Naivasha had an influx of Africans looking for work as domestic servants and farmhands. They were invariably drawn from different communities including neighbouring central Kenya and as far as Nyanza. Marginalized and shunted to a peripheral existence in designated African areas, the community of servants had everything in common, and though many of them were interacting with members of other communities for the first time, they all lived in harmony.

Some of the settlers such as Lord Delamere made huge success out of farming with lucrative large scale holdings that – to-date – remain major players in the dairy industry. It is such holdings, coupled with boat riding and fishing, that gave Naivasha the impetus to grow into a commercial centre. After independence, thousands of Kenyans, who were either investing in various businesses or who found some form of employment, settled in the town. At independence, when many colonial settlers opted to return to Britain, some of the farms were acquired by locals, mainly Kikuyus through land-buying companies that were formed in the 1960s.

The presence of a large number of Kikuyus in the proximity of Naivasha accounts for their predominant settlement of the town, even though it is situated in the Rift Valley.

In addition to local entrepreneurship, post independent Naivasha saw the establishment of tourist class hotels that continued to hire personnel from diverse ethnic backgrounds. The lake had abundant fish that attracted fishing communities such as the Luo, who made homes for themselves and their families here. However, it is the flower industry which has flourished in Naivasha in the last one decade that has spurred growth of the town as a vibrant commercial hub. The multi-billion flower industry has attracted both skilled and unskilled labour from all parts of Kenya. At more than 50,000, the workers employed by the flower farms around the town have created a demand for housing, leading to growth in real estate. While the flower farms are mostly owned by foreign companies, the presence of a large number of workers makes it difficult for politicians to ignore them.

However, like elsewhere in Kenya, migrant workers prefer traveling to register and vote in their ancestral homes, leaving the constituency politics to the locals and their parliamentary hopefuls. Like in other urban centres in Kenya, residents of Naivasha share the same rental blocks irrespective of their ethnic backgrounds. Naivasha too has its urban poor. Karagita is a sprawling slum where the poorest of the town live. Though the majority are Kikuyus, other communities are represented here. The large gainfully employed community has in turn created more opportunities for small businesses such as tailoring, cobbling, domestic work, motor garages and small entertainment ventures. All these again, have attracted members of many different communities. While ethnic violence in many parts of the Rift Valley started in 1992, areas such as Maela have witnessed skirmishes between Maasai pastoralists and Kikuyu farmers since the 1980s. This was often during times of drought when pastoralists moved their animals to areas they believed to be their ancestral lands, but now occupied by migrant agriculturalists.

Naivasha town and its immediate environs had remained peaceful until towards the end of January 2008, while many parts of the country were already engulfed in ethnic violence following the disputed 2007 presidential elections.

When violence hit Naivasha, the unexpected and chilling atrocities that were committed in the town in just two days of mayhem captured headlines around the world. All along, residents of this town had assumed that its cosmopolitan nature, which they believed had ensured calm even as other parts of the Rift Valley burned, would continue to guarantee peaceful co-existence.

However, even as peace prevailed, something was happening in the town. The violence raging in the rest of the country had led to mass displacement of hundreds of thousands of people fleeing to safety. For the fleeing Kikuyus who had difficulty tracing their roots in central Kenya, Naivasha was just the perfect sanctuary. Throughout the month of January 2008, they converged in the town in their thousands.

A local resident, Evans Njoroge, says that while the town remained calm, the arrival of traumatized men, women and children had a disturbing effect on the resident Kikuyu community that naturally sympathized with their kinsmen. "Day in day out, hundreds of families were being ferried to the town and dropped at various points. Local residents would gather around them and listen to the gory stories of death and destruction that had been meted on them in their former homes in the sprawling province," recalled Njoroge. Tears were plenty as the now internally displaced people narrated their encounter with marauding gangs, stories of death, nights of hunger, and crying children who had lost their parents. This was the typical scene every other day as the fighting raged. Emotions were slowly building up as more hungry families were dropped in the open by Kenya Army lorries which were evacuating them from various flash points within the Rift Valley. Local residents struggled to provide them with food before NGOs could put in place measures to ease their suffering.

Multiple interviews reveal that though there was mounting anger every day, most residents expected the peace to continue holding. When violence erupted exactly a month after fighting first began elsewhere in the country, most residents were caught unawares. That something sinister was afoot became apparent on Saturday January 26th 2008 when word from an un-determined source went round that all shops should remain closed. Matatu operators were also asked to keep off the road to allow a protest march through the town the following day. At the time, the complaint was about the high-handed nature of some prison officers who had been deployed in the town to boost security at night due to the population explosion occasioned by thousands of IDPs camping in the town. The protestors were to march to the provincial administration offices to air their grievances about the alleged harassment by the prison officers. The march to the provincial administration offices was peaceful. It was while a senior provincial administration officer was responding to their grievances that sounds of gunfire forced everybody to scamper to safety. A seemingly drunk prison officer had shot in the air as the meeting was in progress. And with that, pandemonium broke out. Hundreds of incensed youths started barricading roads along the busy Nairobi-Nakuru highway, and before the security personnel could react to the unfolding scenario, the situation was rapidly getting out of control.

On the face of it, the violence appeared spontaneous and triggered by the officer who fired in the air. But the organization with which the mobs went about their destructive activities would indicate that prior plans for the mayhem had been made. Though it was difficult to establish the accurate version of events, there are suggestions that the prison officer was part of the ploy. The mob stopped all public service vehicles headed for upcountry and started vetting passengers. The targets of the mobs were members of Kalenjin, Luo and Luhya communities. They were removed from the vehicles and beaten to death with the lucky ones escaping with serious injuries. The swiftness of the violence caught security officers flatfooted and it was clear they lacked the manpower to deal with the mobs. As security personnel battled those spreading terror on the highway, other mobs were going from door to door looking for people from 'wrong' ethnic groups.

Some members of the targeted communities had gotten information of the impending violence and had managed to escape, while scores of others were holed up in their houses. Being a Sunday, many people were at home, others had gone to church. Information availed by locals reveals that the ring leaders of the attacks were local members of the outlawed Mungiki sect who were joined by fellow sect adherents from elsewhere. It is believed that strangers had moved into the town the previous night. The attackers swelled their numbers by forcing local Kikuyus to join them in carrying out the violence. As pointed out earlier, Naivasha has several slums where the poor live. Jobless youth from those informal settlements were only too willing to join in the mayhem.

Jane Njeri was washing clothes outside her house in the compound where she lived when a gang of young men entered through the gate. "They first enquired if there was anybody from other communities who was staying at the residence. Later they asked me to abandon my work and join them and help in barricading the roads in the estate. In some areas, we were forced to remove the property of some members of the Luo community who had fled from the houses. They were then placed in the middle of the estate streets and set ablaze."

Many other members of the Kikuyu community found themselves in a similar situation. By midday, the situation had turned ugly. One gang of attackers torched a house where a family of several children and women had sought refuge. The more than 10 bodies recovered had been burnt beyond recognition and only the husband of the two women escaped unhurt. The violence continued throughout the night and by the following Monday morning, estate streets were littered with bodies, and despite attempts to beef up security, the fighting continued. Greetings were used to identify non-Kikuyus at the roadblocks erected on the highway and estate streets. When this writer drove into the town on Monday the 28th January 2008 he was able to get through the road blocks because he could speak Kikuyu which is his mother tongue.

A senior manager at one of the flower farms found herself in a peculiar situation. She is a Kikuyu while her husband is a Kalenjin. "My husband had travelled home to Koibatek a day before the fighting broke out. My problem was that our 3-year-old has a Kalenjin name and I was scared the mobs would kill him. I had to relocate to my parents' home in Murang'a for safety," she recalled. At Karagita Estate there was a standoff between the targeted group and their adversaries as police officers stood between them without any attempt to disarm the adversaries who were armed with machetes and other crude weapons. The officers were clearly overwhelmed by the sheer numbers of the attackers. Even the arrival of Internal Security Minister George Saitoti did little to calm the tempestuous situation. As he addressed a meeting in the town centre, the gangs retreated to the estates where they continued to unleash more violence. It took the deployment of army men to bring the situation under control on Tuesday. Using two helicopter gun-ships backed by ground personnel, the soldiers managed to scatter the mobs who had blocked the roads.

Members of communities under attack had in the meantime sought refuge at Naivasha Police Station. Others were camping at GK Prison in the town without adequate food, shelter and sanitation. It was from those refugee camps that they would be later evacuated to their ancestral homes. From investigations, it was clear that members of the Luo community bore the brunt of the violence in Naivasha. There is a concentration of them working in the flowers farms and as fishermen in the lake.

Like most members of his Luo community living in Naivasha, David Kilo made a living as a fisherman on the lake. On that black Sunday, he had woken early because he had a fish consignment to deliver to his clients in Nairobi. "Before I could get to Nairobi, I received numerous calls from friends back in Naivasha. They informed me that there was serious trouble in Naivasha. I toyed with idea of returning to Naivasha but decided to drive on to Nairobi because at that time there were no signs of trouble on the road, " he said.

The magnitude of the violence hit home on his return journey. Gangs of attackers had virtually taken over the Nairobi-Naivasha highway, where they were flushing non-Kikuyu from public service vehicles and beating some of them to death. Through communication with friends back in Naivasha, he diverted to the Maai Mahiu-Naivasha road which was trouble free at the time. He managed to get to Naivasha where he was shocked by the scale of the violence. "It was clear that I was in grave danger so I immediately took my boat and rowed to the deepest end of Lake Naivasha, where I felt safe. I could not spend another second on dry land. It was too dangerous for me," Kilo said.

Though the seasoned fisherman was safe, his family was stilled holed-up with friends in the town and he could not figure out a way of reaching them without endangering their lives or his own. Eventually he managed to get hold of a police officer friend on phone and requested assistance in evacuating his family. The police officer hired a cab and transferred the family to the shores, where Mr. Kilo picked them up and retreated to the depths of the waters. The family spent the night in a boat watching out for hippos which could easily capsize the boat. Venturing to the town to buy food was out of the question. The hungry children were traumatized by the events that were clearly way beyond their comprehension. They had witnessed people being butchered by marauding gangs and his assurances that all would be well did little to reduce their terror.

The following day brought little solace to the family. However, with the children getting desperately hungry, Mr. Kilo rowed to the shores and sneaked into a hotel, bought some food and dashed back to the boat and into the lake. As the violence continued, the family had no choice but to spend another night in the lake. Mr. Kilo continued monitoring the situation via his cell phone. On the third day, he received information that his belongings had been set ablaze by gangs of attackers. "Property worth close to Ksh. 3 million went up in flames. They burnt everything I owned, including spare parts for my commercial motorboats with which I used to ferry tourists for sightseeing in the lake. I was instantly reduced to a pauper," he said.

After a third night in the waters of the lake, a Kikuyu friend agreed to host the family on condition that they remained indoors at all times. The friend later arranged an airlift for them to Wilson Airport from where they were flown to Kisumu and hence to the safety of their ancestral home. After spending close to a month in his native rural home, Mr. Kilo decided to return to Naivasha to pick up the pieces of his broken life. He was brought up in the town and it was where he felt he could make a comfortable living. With a steaming cup of hot coffee already placed on the table, Kelvin Owour was ready to have his breakfast. A Bible and a keyboard were the other items on the dining table. Being a Sunday morning, the family was all set to attend the morning service and thank God for a peaceful past week and pray that the lakeside town would remain calm as many other parts of the country went up in flames. They never made it to the house of worship.

Before his family could settle down for breakfast, hell broke loose. People were running in all directions, attracting the attention of the God-fearing family. "As I stood at the window on the balcony of my house, my cell phone rang. My friends were worried about my family's safety, saying violence had erupted and the Luo community was being targeted by roaming bands of attackers," he remembered. He hurriedly called his wife and told her to rush to the Naivasha police station with their 18-month-old baby. He remained behind with a friend and together they weighed their options.

As violence escalated the duo decided they had to move if they hoped to stay alive, "We were badly outnumbered and finding our way out of the mayhem was a big challenge," he recalled. All the roads leading to the town had been barricaded by the machete, *rungu* and *panga* wielding mobs. They vetted all the people who were leaving and entering the town. Before Mr. Owour and his friend left their house in Kabati area, he remembered his Bible and the keyboard. He carried the Holy Book with him while the friend carried the keyboard.

Fear stricken, they made their way out of the estate. Their decision to carry the Bible and the keyboard made the difference between life and death. The mobs they encountered showed some reverence for the word of God and let them through when they explained they were on their way to spread the gospel. They managed to get to Mr. Owour's business premises in the centre of the town where he had a tailoring business. The town was by now a virtual war zone with police outnumbered by the rampaging mobs. For hours, Mr. Owour and his friends continued to follow events in the streets from the safety of the shop. The situation was getting worse by the hour and it was clear they had to move sooner rather than later.

Fortunately for them, a mob broke into a nearby soda depot, thereby creating a distraction. As the youths scrambled for drinks, Mr. Owour and his friend slipped out. They were spotted by two policemen on patrol who escorted them to Railway Police Station where they found his wife and child. Mr. Owour and his family were to spend a week at the police station. Eventually, he managed to secure transport to take him and his family to his rural home. At the time, he was only too keen to see the last of Naivasha. "All I wanted was to get back to Homa Bay," he said.

After staying at home for five months, another reality struck home. He was never going to find any meaningful work to do. He realized his destiny was irrevocably linked to Naivasha, the town where he had witnessed untold brutality visited upon his kinsmen. By this time, fighting in all parts of the country had ended. Mr. Owour packed his bags again and headed back to the place he had called home for many years. Upon arrival, Mr. Owour realized life was never going to be the same again. Not for a long time. The stock he had left behind had been looted. His household goods too had been destroyed. It was starting life all over again.

Since his return, peace has prevailed. However, any slight tension in the town leaves him a frightened man. The events he witnessed in January 2008 will live with him for years to come. While the violence in Naivasha was targeted at non-Kikuyus, it touched even members of the community.

Ms. Ann Mburu recalls spending a peaceful Saturday and by the time she retired to bed at night, there was nothing to indicate that the following day she would witness events she had never contemplated in her life. On Sunday, she was supposed to be on duty at the school where she taught computer classes. She had plans to join her students for mass in the morning. After stepping out of her house, she was taken aback by seeing people clustered in small groups, talking. It was immediately clear that something was in the afoot. Since she had overslept, she did not stop to talk to the people gathered in the streets, but proceeded to her place of work where she found mass was already in progress. "We were in the middle of a song when we were interrupted by the sound of gunfire. Terrified students ran out of the room and scattered in different directions in confusion," she remembered.

It was only when the gunfire persisted that Ms. Mburu and her colleague realized that something was seriously wrong. Investigations at the school gate revealed the town was engulfed in violence and there was pandemonium everywhere. The teachers feared that the gangs running wildly around the town would attack the school. They, therefore, shepherded the students into their dormitories and locked them up. When some semblance of order returned to the school, Ms. Mburu secured an armed escort back to her house. Everywhere, there were security men battling with mobs. People carrying their belongings were streaming towards the police station in search of safety. After walking for some time, she realized that as long as she could speak Kikuyu, she was relatively safe. After spending some time in her house, she decided to check on her friend at Site and Service Estate.

Though members of her community were not under attack, many people felt it was safer to stay together if only for comfort. She wasn't surprised, therefore, when she found many other people in her friend's house. Ms. Mburu recalled that it was a restless lot that huddled together in her friend's house. The violence was now full scale and venturing out of the house was too dangerous. Since her friend's house was near the police station, she decided to stay there until the violence subsided two days later. When she eventually left the house, she was shocked by the destruction. Many houses had been burnt down. Shops had been broken into and goods worth millions of shillings looted.

In some streets, she came across the smoldering remains of household items such as beddings which had been removed from the houses of people who had fled to safety. What shocked her was coming across dead bodies lying in the streets. "Police were driving around collecting them. I hope I will never again witness such wanton destruction of life." Since all shops had closed down, those who did not have enough food stocks in their houses were on the verge of starvation.

It was only after two days of full-blown violence that things settled down. This was after the intervention of the military which was deployed to help the police who had been overwhelmed by the scope of the violence. By now, at least 40 people had been killed in the fighting. When sanity was finally restored, residents realized that the town was virtually under the control of the Mungiki. The next few weeks, women were banned from wearing trousers and a good number of them were stripped naked or whipped. It was only after police started rounding up Mungiki suspects that life returned to normal.

Life in Naivasha has returned to normal and different communities are once again living together. The suspicions that led to the fighting linger on. What is disturbing though is that many Kikuyus in Naivasha approve of the killings that took place and believe it was the reason why the military was called in to help stop the killing of their kinsfolk elsewhere in the Rift Valley. The general feeling on the ground was that the killings were necessary to remind other communities that Kikuyus too can fight back with equal brutality. "Since 1992, other communities had developed the idea that anytime there was a political problem, all you needed was to kill Kikuyus to resolve it," said Maina Ng'ang'a.

The 72-year-old resident who grew up in the town said fighting in Naivasha reminded Kikuyus that they are not that helpless. "I think in future, other communities will think twice before they can attack us. Everybody now knows that nobody is safe when one community is under siege," he said.

Chapter 4

Anger and Violence in Kisumu

William Oloo

Introduction

Kisumu, Kenya's third largest city, has had a turbulent political history connected to the country's post-independence period. The town's propensity for protest politics and violent reactions to political developments and government decisions that appear to marginalize the Luo and Nyanza Province can be traced to the events immediately after independence. The town, which is the administrative and political headquarters of Nyanza Province, has been a hotbed of politics since the 1960s. After independence, the city gained prominence due to the political activities of Kenya's first Vice President, the late Jaramogi Oginga Odinga, and more so after he quit the position and government in March 1966 to found Kenya's first post-independence party, the Kenya People's Union (KPU).

Odinga quit his position in government following irreconcilable ideological differences with Kenya's first president Jomo Kenyatta. Anger built up in Nyanza Province generally among Odinga's Luo community who felt that their son had been frustrated out of government by Kenyatta and a powerful clique around him, with the connivance and active input from Tom Mboya, then Economic Planning Minister and ruling Kanu party Secretary General.

Odinga's new party, the Kenya People's Union (KPU), was viewed as a threat by the Kanu establishment as it threatened to paralyse government business in parliament as a number of those who were dissatisfied with the government crossed to join the party in the opposition benches. Unfortunately, the law was quickly changed to stop the apparent depletion of the Kanu side, which now required those crossing to the opposition to resign their parliamentary seats and seek fresh mandate from the public. This stopped a number of legislators from crossing over. By the time the law came into being, a significant number of legislators had already joined KPU. This necessitated what was to be referred to as the "Little General Elections of 1966". Only a handful of those who had resigned, including Odinga, made it back to parliament. The government was heavily accused of harassing the KPU team and even helping to "rig out" most of those who had resigned and tried to reclaim their parliamentary seat on a KPU ticket.

The stage was set for violent confrontations between KPU supporters and the rest of Nyanza and those of Kanu and by extension Kenyatta's government. Although the government generally harassed KPU supporters across the country, in Nyanza it became more pronounced as it was the bedrock of KPU and Odinga's support.

In 1968, a senior Minister in Kenyatta's government, Argwings Kodhek, a Luo, died in an accident considered to have occurred under suspicious circumstances. This heightened the tension between the Luo and the government. But it was the assassination of Tom Mboya, then Minister of Planning in July 1969 that brought matters to a head. The country generally and Nyanza particularly boiled with rage. The Kenyatta government was blamed for the assassination of Mboya. There were anti-government demonstrations and violence, which targeted the Kikuyu and other communities from the Mount Kenya region.

When three months later President Kenyatta visited Kisumu to officially open the New Nyanza Provincial Hospital, the town residents went into an anti-Kenyatta frenzy, pelting the presidential motorcade with stones after a public quarrel between Kenyatta and Odinga at the opening ceremony. Kenyatta's presidential security guards are reported to have literally shot their way out of Kisumu and the hostile crowd, in the process killing hundreds of people who had lined up along the Nairobi route up to Ahero, 24 km away. Odinga and several KPU leaders were immediately arrested and detained and the party banned, setting the stage for decades of strained relations between Nyanza and the central Government. Both the Kenyatta and the Moi regimes were often accused of sponsoring or imposing parliamentary candidates in Luo Nyanza constituencies, which over the years contributed to resentment towards the government. Under both the Kenyatta and Moi regimes, Odinga was repeatedly put under house arrest at his Milimani Home in Kisumu. Residents of this lakeside city always identified with Odinga's tribulations which they blamed on the government. Most residents and indeed many Luos often narrate these episodes with a lot of anger and pain and with such authority and clarity one would think successive generations were all there when these events happened.

The country's return to multi-party politics from 1991 opened up space for the residents to vent their anger on the government and pro-establishment politicians' from Nyanza. Indeed, any politician believed to be overly supportive of the government or viewed as anti- the Odingas often avoid the city altogether clandestinely. Such politicians face the wrath of residents who confront them in the streets either asking embarrassing questions or being outrightly hostile to them. The long lists of politicians who have been so confronted include among others, former Ministers Raphael Tuju and the late Odongo Omamo. Not even Anyang' Nyong'o, The Minster for Health Services and James Orengo, The Minister for Lands have been spared this embarrassment, each time they have been seen as being on the opposite side of Raila Odinga, now the Prime Minister. The loyalty accorded to Odinga in Kisumu is total and unwavering.

Kisumu and the post election violence

The scenario described above gives the context within which the violent scenes witnessed in Kisumu following the disputed presidential election results can be explained.

As the 2007 General Elections approached, it was generally expected that Kisumu City would experience some reaction whichever direction the results of the presidential elections went. Either, the city was expected to erupt into joyous ecstasy if the Orange Democratic Movement (ODM) won the elections or riots and orgy of violence if the party and its presidential flag bearer Raila Odinga lost. To many people in Kisumu, and indeed many ODM supporters across the country, Raila's victory in the 2007 General Elections was a foregone conclusion. They could not entertain any thought of electoral defeat for the Orange party and its flag bearer. It could only be through rigging that ODM and Raila could lose and they were prepared to resist this at all costs.

During the campaigns preceding the polls, the town experienced calm except for a few skirmishes between ODM supporters during the party nominations. But tension rose and some violence was also witnessed a few days to the General Election after some groups of people said to have been security personnel, mostly Administration Police, were reported to have been ferried to various parts of Nyanza in buses to act as poll agents of the President Kibaki's Party of National Unity (PNU).

Residents of Kisumu and indeed Nyanza quickly mobilized and blocked roads, searched buses and hunted for the "PNU party agents", flushing out some from hotels they had booked. By the evening of December 26, several of these "strangers" had been beaten and a number reported killed at Ahero on the outskirts of Kisumu, Homabay and Mbita townships in Nyanza. Journalists and other eye witnesses saw some of the "agents" who sought refuge at police stations and were later that day escorted out of Kisumu and other parts of the province under heavy police guard.

Persistent reports of planned rigging of the elections had been expressed through various channels, including through short text messages (SMS). ODM politicians had also made numerous allegations about the possibility of rigging and residents were on "high alert". PNU politicians dismissed the rigging claims by their ODM rivals, arguing that the Orange party had sensed defeat and was getting ready to reject the poll results. The claims and counter claims over the possibility of electoral fraud became the subject of discussions in nearly every corner, bar and other public places in Kisumu.

By the time suspicion started building up that something was indeed afoot with the presidential results, self-acclaimed "political analysts" were all over the place giving various interpretations to the events, inflaming passions that reached fever pitch on December 30, 2007.

The wealthy business class in Kisumu, most of them Asians and a few others from outside the Luo community, especially from Central Province, who were to later bear the brunt of the violence, destruction and looting, had been under some sort of surveillance by the more rabid supporters of ODM. There were reports, before the elections which gained ominous prominence as the dispute over presidential results raged, that a section of this wealthy business community were supportive of the PNU and had even made generous donations to the party during the "One Million a plate" dinner party in Nairobi as the elections approached.

As the major town in Western Kenya, Kisumu has attracted large numbers of migrants, most of them youths from both Nyanza and Western Provinces looking for jobs or other means of livelihood. While a significant number have been absorbed in the informal sector, including the thriving "boda boda" (bicycle and motorcycle taxi) business, many more are idle and those who get temporary employment within the Indian business sector are badly exploited. There has been growing resentment among the local population over the increased domination of the town business sector, not just by the Indians who started settling in the town in 1901 with the arrival of the railway from Nairobi, but by other communities, notably the Kikuyu and the Kisii. Moreover, the local people accuse members of the two communities of largely being alienated from the rest, often buying or procuring most services from among themselves and mostly patronising the social places belonging to their kin. Indeed, as the political situation became tense with clear political divisions among Kenyans, members of the two communities were believed to be holding night meetings at which they were thought to be strategising for PNU's infiltration of the area.

One enduring complaint from those casual workers in Kisumu has been mistreatment and low wages by the business owners. There have been frequent layoffs which local labour officials have done very little to stop. The labour officers are accused of being in the "payroll" of the business community. Statements like: *"Abonyo gi kod jorabuon ochayo ji"* (These Indian and Kikuyu business communities look down upon locals) were not uncommon before the elections. Employees who had been sacked for one reason or another had a story to tell about their previous employers, and they seemed to be particularly influential in mobilising public opinion against sections of the business community considered "exploitative, racist and ethnic."

In the 1990s, it was believed that the then powerful Nyanza Provincial Commissioner Joseph Kaguthi facilitated a number of Kikuyu business people to acquire prime property and start thriving businesses. It was even rumoured the PC was in joint partnerships with some of the business class from Central Province who were generally seen to be "taking over". The Kimwa Grand and Kimwa Annex Hotels which were burnt by demonstrators during the post-election violence represented the face of perceived Kikuyu domination. In the upmarket Milimani area, the owner of Kimwa, thought to be in partnership with the former PC, had acquired the four storey Gulf Stream Hotel after it was put under receivership. The hotel was built by a prominent Luo family, but was for a long time under receivership before its acquisition by the Kimwa Hotel chain owner. The same businessman was said to own Motherland Hotel which was a favourite of Kikuyu business transporters to Western Kenya and Uganda. In the 1990s, his other hotel business venture at Nyamasaria "KEUTA Hotel", previously operating under the name "Silicon Hotel" was burnt down by youths for what was suspected to be politics. It has remained a gaping ruin on the Kisumu-Nairobi road.

A growing number of Kisiis have bought land and increasingly run thriving businesses in Kisumu, with a significant settlement in the Nyamasaria area. In this city, politics matter to people and each time there is a political contest, especially at the national level, all communities are monitored in terms of which political direction or parties they associate with.

Members of the Kisii community were not particularly in danger as there was a general swing by large swaths of Gusiiland towards ODM, with a feeling that the community's pre-eminent leader at the time and former cabinet minister Simeon Nyachae had had his influence so significantly reduced, that PNU would be lucky to get any seats among his community. Emerging Kisii politicians, led by Omingo Magara, the then ODM treasurer and the repackaged former Minister Chris Obure were expected to lead a determined onslaught against Nyachae and his KANU colleague, Sam Ongeri. Indeed both Obure and Magara went ahead and secured their parliamentary seats on the ODM ticket and got appointed to the cabinet in the Coalition Government.

The attack on William Ruto and Omingo Magara of ODM at a function in the latter's constituency during the campaigns by pro-Nyachae youths made the Kisii in Kisumu and other parts of Luo Nyanza to be looked at a bit suspiciously. But it was known most of the young generation of Kisiis were in ODM and even in Kisii, a number of them were openly supportive of the Orange party.

The Luhya were largely considered to be in ODM while the Kikuyu and other communities from outside Nyanza who were believed to be supportive of PNU, were largely treated with derision for supporting the "losing side", and were expected to conform or submit themselves to an "ODM government".

The business people from Central Province were expected to continue with their business without any hustle after an ODM victory, unless something went terribly wrong. To most ODM supporters in Nyanza, their party's victory was almost a *fait accompli* and they felt there would be no need to bother with anybody. But they were resolute that any attempts at rigging would be resisted. This was the scenario in Kisumu and most of Nyanza, with slight variations from one part of the province to another. It must be pointed out that prevailing opinions and attitudes in Kisumu often significantly influence the rest of Nyanza.

However, the elections were largely peaceful and there was an air of great expectation from residents of this lakeside town as they looked forward to what – in their opinion – was an obvious victory for their preferred party and its presidential candidate Raila Odinga, who hails from Nyanza. They looked at this as Raila's best chance to get to the leadership of this country, which had eluded his late father Jaramogi Odinga from the 1960s, and more painfully in 1992 on the return of multiparty politics, and to put paid to decades of exclusion of the Luo community from national leadership. It was going to be their chance to have a voice to influence the distribution of national resources which, in the opinion of many Nyanza people had — since independence- – been given to them, either in small quantities and often grudgingly, or not given at all, by successive governments. The foregoing scenarios among other dynamics appear to explain why residents went wild in their protest against the delay and bungling of the presidential elections results.

Kisumu represents the nerve centre of Luo politics and thinking about national issues, and there is a level of political consciousness that manifests more flamboyantly than in many other Kenyan towns and appears unmatched even by Kenya's capital, Nairobi. There is also what psychologists describe as "communal trauma" among the Luo community. During any political disturbance or riots in which the Luo feel aggrieved, it is not uncommon to find youths aged less than 15 years literally mourning the killings or assassinations of key Luo political figures by previous regimes.

During public demonstrations against the government, the youths mourn and loudly curse those who allegedly assassinated the then Economic Planning Minister, Tom Mboya in 1969 and a former Foreign Minister, Robert Ouko, in 1990. The deaths of Owiti Ongili (a former MP for Gem Constituency in Siaya, found murdered in 1985) and his predecessor Otieno Ambala (who died mysteriously at Kodiaga Remand Prison after being arrested and charged with Ongili's death) also often form the basis of loud wails in town.

"Ne ginego Mboya, gilodho wang' Ouko kendo pod gidwa lal gi Agwambo? Wang'ni ok nwayienegi! (They killed Mboya, gorged out Ouko's eyes and now still want to assassinate Agwambo [Raila)]? Not again! We shall not allow it!)

This statement came from a youth of about fifteen years who wailed in the streets of Kisumu after rumours emerged that Raila had been arrested in Nairobi at the height of the dispute over the presidential election results in December 2007. Coming from a youth who was born long after Mboya and Ouko had died, clearly explained how communal history and trauma were passed on from one generation to another, and how deeply some of these painful memories were etched into the minds of people.

On December 27 2007, as people trooped to polling stations, reports emerged, which were later confirmed by the then Electoral Commission of Kenya, of confusion and inordinate delays in the start of voting in Raila's Langata constituency. When reports further emerged that Raila's name was missing from the ballot papers, the town was on edge and the tension was palpable. To the town residents, this was confirmation that PNU had not only planted their candidate Stanley Livondo in Langata, but was determined to rig out Raila at all costs. Angry residents gathered in huge groups and threatened to block roads unless ECK clarified and corrected the anomaly. Residents briefly clashed with the police at Kondele, on the Kisumu-Kakamega highway and at Kachok on the Kisumu-Nairobi highway.

Kondele is normally the epicentre of any form of agitation, and it is where demonstrators congregate before moving to the town centre. This highly populated suburb – whose population is continually fed by the neighbouring slums of Manyatta and Obunga – is located 5 km from the town centre. Satellite settlements such as Riat Hills, Mamboleo, Kibos, and Kiboswa can only access the town from Kondele, and when it is volatile, huge numbers of people gather here to gauge the situation before marching into the town centre or fleeing if there is danger.

The increasingly shrinking open space between Kondele, the New Nyanza Provincial Hospital and Tom Mboya Estates often forms the battleground on which the police engage with crowds in an attempt to bar them from accessing the town centre. Anybody attempting to judge the mood of the town or politicians desirous of addressing impromptu rallies come to Kondele for instant crowds. Anti-Raila politicians avoid Kondele by all means.

The other hotspot is Kachok on the main exit from the city to Ahero, Nairobi and Kisii. In the event of any displeasure with anything, crowds from Nyamasaria, Nubian, Manyatta Gonda, Pand Pieri and Nyalenda estates gather here and block access or exit from the town centre. On the Busia-Uganda, Bondo-Usenge route are populated areas of Bandani, Otonglo, Kodiaga and Usoma which generate crowds that often play hide and seek with the police on the Western exit from town. To the North lies the Riat and Nyahera Hills which are not easily penetrable and to the South and South West are the airport, Pipeline and the waters of Lake Victoria through which no one can easily escape in the event of trouble.

Although the situation cooled somewhat following media reports that the then ECK chairman himself, Samwel Kivuitu had gone to Langata and ordered for a new printout of a voters' register which now included Raila's name, allowing him to vote, it was clear trouble could break out anytime now if anything else went wrong.

By the end of the following day, there was an air of ecstasy as results from different parts of the country pointed to an apparent ODM victory in both parliamentary and presidential results. Residents started elaborate preparations to celebrate what they considered a sure victory. Despite a heavy police presence in all parts of the town and in the restive Kondele, Obunga, Manyatta, and Nyalenda estates, all seemed well throughout December 28. But activities in Kisumu were being closed -- the business community not taking any chances. Based on past experience, they knew that whichever way the results went, there would be chanting crowds in the streets who could easily start looting, either out of anger if something went wrong or in celebration if their party won. Although everybody was on edge, the situation remained calm throughout December 28 and in the early morning of the following day.

The scenario began changing rapidly on December 29 before final presidential results were announced when protestors invaded and burnt the provincial water officers where they also torched 9 GK vehicles. Another group stormed the Kenya Broadcasting Corporation premises in Milimani area and burnt five motor vehicles. The following morning, full-scale violence broke out when demonstrators blocked the roads at Kondele and Kachok and began marching to the city centre to protest delays in announcing the results. Kisumu was teaming with huge numbers of police in riot gear who immediately clashed with the demonstrators. As people watched the radio and TV transmissions from the ECK tallying centre at the Kenyatta International Conference Centre (KICC), anger was building up exponentially. How could results from areas as close to Nairobi such as Juja and other parts of Central Province be delayed when those from Busia, Mombasa and other far places had been relayed? This was a major question on the minds of the crowds who ceaselessly debated the scenarios.

The police and the media were out, alert and monitoring the tension. By the end of the day when the Electoral Commission of Kenya Chairman Samuel Kivuitu announced the results and President Kibaki was hurriedly sworn in for a second term, tens of bodies lay dead in the streets, some of them shot dead by the police as they tried to quell the violence. December 30 2007 effectively marked the beginning of large scale violence, destruction and looting. It was a stampede as hundreds of people from different communities, mostly the Kikuyu and the Kisii, fled from their houses and sought refuge at the local police station. By the evening of December 30, New Nyanza Provincial Hospital mortuary was bursting at the seams with over 70 bodies brought in from the streets, most of them shot in the back by the police as they fled.

Many more were being brought in with serious injuries from different parts of the town by the Red Cross and the police. Many others succumbed to their injuries later, as the facilities at both the district and the provincial hospitals were overstretched. The show of police might was massive, comparable to but surpassing the deployment in 1990 when the body of the then Foreign Affairs Minister Robert Ouko was discovered in a thicket in Got Alila in Muhoroni. The anger that followed the announcement of the presidential results was overwhelming. It was mayhem. All roads into and out of the city were barricaded by rampaging youths chanting, "Haki yetu! Haki yetu! (Our rights! our rights!); No Raila, No peace; Kibaki must go!" Although it has been argued that youths were incited into violence in many parts of the country, the violence appeared largely spontaneous and self-directing, taking different forms and increasing in intensity at different places.

Out of the crowds, leaders emerged to take command. Elected leaders, both civic and parliamentary, were nowhere to be seen. Many had fled and were in hiding from the angry crowds. Most of the elected leaders were fatigued and broke after the campaigns and feared the youth would demand money from them. From the evening of December 30 2007, the situation quickly deteriorated and degenerated into uncontrolled chaos with massive looting of targeted property, burning of vehicles and barricading of roads. Conservative estimates put the figure of those dead at about 100 people, mostly shot dead by the police. Hundreds of others were left nursing various forms of injuries. The Waki Report into the post-election violence put the figure at 64, way below the number killed. Reports from civil society groups estimated that over 200 people died in Kisumu during the violence. The violence was devastating in scale and the city lay in ruins. Many business premises were looted, vandalized or burnt by rampaging mobs of largely youthful people who were protesting what was widely considered a rigged presidential poll.

Public transport was paralyzed. The only vehicles in the streets were those of the police, the Red Cross and other relief organizations and ambulances.

Streets were littered with tonnes of papers, polythene bags and other pieces of looted merchandise. Among the looted, vandalized or burnt down businesses were Ukwala Supermarket, Format, Kimwa Grand Hotel and Annex, automobile and electronic shops, guest houses and other hotels. Initially, the looting and destruction was mainly in the town centre along Oginga Odinga Street, Obote Road, Kakamega and Kondele Roads and a few others. But as the violence became more uncontrollable and police brutality increased, looting and destruction spread to the estates, targeting the houses and property left behind by those who had fled. These mostly belonged to the Kikuyus and Kisiis who were by then camping at the local police stations.

Kisumu's social and economic fabric was devastated and may take a long time to recover. The informal sector on which many locals depended was also badly affected, and in the post-election period, there has been panic selling of property by those who fear recurrence of violence.

The Waki Report indicated that at least 50 commercial buildings and 200 residential houses were destroyed. The Kenya Broadcasting Corporation building and broadcasting equipment, South Lake Water Offices, provincial public works offices, Kondele chiefs office and 32 government offices were destroyed or burnt. Those who fled and went to camp at police stations were eventually moved out of town and ferried under heavy police escort to Nakuru, Naivasha, Nairobi and Kisii. Others were moved to Kisumu West where temporary transit camps were established. The police and the provincial administration led by the then District Commissioner Jamleck Baruga facilitated the hiring of vehicles to ferry those fleeing from Kisumu and Nyanza to different destinations.

Initially, anger was directed at the government and its installations which led to the burning and destruction of vehicles at the provincial water services offices among others. The protestors had been remarkably restrained in their treatment of non-Luos and their property. Leter reports from Nakuru, Nairobi, Naivasha, Nyeri, Thika and other places indicated that Luos and Luhyas had been brutally evicted and some killed or burnt alive and this stoked anger that led to an orgy of destruction and violence that was to see virtually all houses in the estates and property belonging to perceived PNU sympathisers completely destroyed. Although it was difficult to verify, killings by citizens were hardly reported, but a number of people were injured. There was anger when reports emerged that Ugandan security personnel had been sighted in Imbo Usenge,

Bondo, Busia, Muhuru, Sori and Sindo beating up people. One woman I interviewed claimed the Ugandan soldiers even helped her brother who was fleeing from Eldoret to make a distress call home from the edges of Riat Hills where the family arranged to pick him and take him home to Kisii.

There were websites immediately after the post-election violence with YouTube video clips showing images of security personnel deployed to quell violence in Kisumu who were significantly different-looking from the Kenyan police. The Provincial Administration led by the then Nyanza PC Paul Olando, provincial police Chief Grace Kaindi and Kisumu OCDP Simon Kiragu all dismissed claims that any external soldiers were deployed. They were later to tell the Waki Commission that what the local people claimed were detachments of the Uganda People's Defence Forces were the Rapid Deployment Unit (RDU), a section of the Kenyan Administration Police who donned unique uniforms and gear (red helmets with green coats) . But those were crazy times and it will take long to uncover the truth.

At some point, it appeared that the Kenya police action was not well coordinated with different units of the security forces exchanging fire. There were claims that the local police bosses were not briefed about additional deployment of security personnel. At the time, it was difficult to focus on what kind of uniform or jungle fatigues security personnel were wearing. The events were so overwhelming that even seasoned journalists paid little attention to uniforms and claims of confusion among the police. What is not in doubt is that the police response to the protests against the presidential election results debacle was brutal and led to the death and maiming of hundreds of people.

During the interdenominational prayer meeting at the Moi Stadium in Kisumu attended by ODM leaders, including Raila, sections of the crowd demanded to be given guns. This was in response to the breakdown of law and order, and what the residents believed was the need for self protection. Traditionally, Luos are averse to shedding blood and that explains why even at the height of the protests, and despite the degree of hate, there were no large scale killings. Some killings did occur like in the case of the "PNU agents". In most cases where killings were reported, it was the work of mobs. Few Luos would want to be the ones who "finish off an individual" for fear of being haunted.

Of course traditions are wearing thin, and these traditional safeguards against arbitrary taking of life are losing their effectiveness. There are now more criminals in every community than was the case before and urban life is producing many heartless people who are not averse to murder. At the height of the post election violence, criminal gangs in some sections of Migori Town were reported to have pulled out their weapons: deadly homemade guns and modern AK-47 rifles, which they threatened to use against the police, and would probably have, had the violence escalated. It is important to understand that there were hardly any functional government systems in this region, the entire government apparatus having virtually collapsed. The police, who were also divided along ethnic and party lines, maintained control in the city centre only and a few pockets of the town.

Prior to the elections, there were transfers of a number of senior police officers who were replaced by largely Kikuyu officers. This brought suspicion about the intentions of the government and fuelled tension. That is why additional and heavy deployment of security, whether from Uganda or Kenya, raised temperatures. It was known the police were under special instructions and had a duty to quell the violence, even if it took brute force. Reports in government circles at the time indicated that in the event of rigging, the rest of the country would react feebly save for Kisumu and Kibera in Nairobi, hence the deployment of special police units to deal with perceived "trouble makers".

The police pursued people into the estates using parastatal vehicles or under cover. The special unit, coordinated from the provincial office became particularly brutal after it appeared that the regular police were being overwhelmed by the demonstrators. One of the most graphic images of police brutality was that of a policeman shooting a young boy in Kondele area and then kicking him as he lay dying. Karama Baraka, the journalist who covered the incident, was threatened by the police and had to take cover for a long time.

The police officer was later taken to court following a public outcry but was eventually acquitted. But many of his colleagues who killed in similar fashion and who were not captured in camera continue to walk scot free. After the media failed to declare the results, media people were treated with suspicion by protestors who became very hostile. Many journalists worked under threats, making it difficult to cover the violence. There were chilling threats from individuals to journalists both directly or indirectly, with some callers giving graphic descriptions of where the journalists lived. Reporters from the state owned Kenya Broadcasting Corporation were particularly in danger after their station was invaded and property burnt. The station was accused of "misleading the people" with their broadcasts of proceedings both from the ground and the election tallying centre at KICC. All journalists had to be careful where they went , as there were many no-go areas , either controlled by frenzied and hostile mobs or the police who did not want to see any journalists at all.

Journalists in most of the violence hit areas were deeply traumatised by what they witnessed as they covered the violence; the shootings, hundreds of bodies (some decomposing in the mortuaries, streets and estates); brutal beatings and killings; the destruction of property and the daily threat to their lives. Some of the traumatising experiences journalists went through are contained in a booklet "Healing the Messenger": A *Journalists Trauma Hand book* (2009), published by International Media Support (IMS), who worked with the Kenya Correspondents Association (KCA) and the Kenya Association of Photographers and Illustrators and Designers (KAPIDE). The two media organizations, with support from IMS, worked with a team from Kenyatta National Hospital to offer trauma counselling to more than 140 field-based correspondents across the country who covered the violence.

Although the Waki Report on the Post-Election Violence, which largely relied on police reports, put the death toll at 64 in Kisumu and the whole of Nyanza at 107, residents, journalists and other groups agree this was a gross underestimation. The New Nyanza Provincial Hospital Mortuary had more than 100 bodies, including women and children, most of who had been shot in the residential compounds. More than 250 people were admitted to the hospital with serious gunshot wounds. Many others who were injured later died both in residential areas and at various hospitals due to delayed or lack of medical attention. Tens of bodies were also uncollected from deep in the slums for a long time or completely decomposed within the two months that violence raged.

The police and the Kenya Red Cross Society, the two agencies that were intervening, were clearly overstretched. Attention was also turning to the Internally Displaced or returnees who were arriving from other areas. After some time, attention turned to the thousands of desperate returnees at the transit camps at the Moi Sports Ground, the Anglican Church and several other centres established in Manyatta, Nyalenda and other areas to deal with the humanitarian crisis. The two transitory camps alone handled more than 250,000 IDP/returnees. Many others returned home without necessarily passing through the camps and were, therefore, not captured in government and the civil society databases.

Government response to the post-election crisis appeared poorly coordinated and discriminatory. This became a source of dissatisfaction among the people and other players, and residents and leaders from Nyanza openly grumbled about what was seen as favouritism and discrimination. Competition and rivalry among civil society organizations also undermined the intervention efforts, as some people or organizations sought to turn the whole humanitarian crisis into a money-minting venture.

There were claims that the provincial administration and security agencies largely helped evacuate those who were fleeing from Nyanza and other areas through government organized transport and escorts. It was also believed the government acted with partiality in the evacuations from the Rift Valley where the government mobilised the army and National Youth Service to ferry mainly people from Central Province to safety to Nakuru, Nairobi and Central Province. However, those from Nyanza evicted from parts of the Rift Valley, specifically Naivasha, Nakuru and from towns in Central Province such as Nyeri, Juja ,Thika, Tigoni and Nyahururu, among others, had to hire their own transport or rely on the trucks sent by leaders and well wishers from Nyanza. The returnees came home with bitter tales of death, injuries, loss of property, rape by Mungiki sect members, and complaints of partiality by most government officers in the areas they lived.

"It was a crisis and when we learnt that Nyanza people were not being helped to get out of danger, it was our responsibility as local leaders to mobilize resources and intervene, including organizing transport for them to come home," said Chrispine Owalla, a civil society official.

A number of local civil society actors, including the Kenya Red Cross Society were deeply involved in the evacuations, setting up transit camps to receive the returnees. Once they arrived from wherever, the returnees would then be helped to trace their way to their rural homes. For most of the returnees, once they were out of the danger zones, it did not matter where they were headed.

"For us, the most important thing was to get out of danger in Naivasha and get to any part of Nyanza which we knew was safe," said John Opiyo, whose home was in Kadem, more than 250 km South West of Kisumu. He could not wait for direct means of transport through Kisii to reach home because he felt he could not stay in Naivasha any longer. Many others like him had harrowing tales of how they escaped death. Some of those fleeing brought with them remains of their loved ones, either in Polythene bags or parts of the bodies in coffins. These stories added to the feeling of bitterness among the residents, leading to more protests.

The police were not only blamed for the killings of innocent people, but also for facilitating the looting and destruction of property. Some of the security personnel were said to have actively participated in the looting of property and money, often shooting doors open, picking money or goods before calling on the demonstrators and looters to go in. There were also reports that some senior police officers who were involved in controlling the crowds in the streets would telephone big business owners in town and demand to be paid to protect their premises from looters. It was claimed the police actively encouraged looters to invade the premises of business people who had declined to play along. Some of the premises that were burnt down in Kisumu were said "to have been set on fire by police tear gas canisters or bullets that shattered gas cylinders or ignited other inflammable materials." Reports of police involvement in looting were widespread in many parts of Nyanza. In Migori, for instance, some police officers were reported to have rented houses and hired pick-up trucks to ferry looted goods which they kept and later sold after the violence subsided. The looting of the National Cereals and Produce Board depot in Migori was said to have been facilitated by the police. But these claims were difficult to verify.

The post-election violence and destruction was later to degenerate into a sort of class struggle, with the propertied people, including Luos being attacked and their property looted. Criminal elements took advantage of the situation and went on a looting and robbery spree. It was no longer a case of violence or protest against election rigging. Classic Hotel near Dunga Beach, worth more than Ksh15 million was completely burnt down. It belonged to a retired Luo teacher. Reports later linked the burning to the fact that his wife, a lecturer at Egerton University, was a Kikuyu.

Hundreds of youths were arrested and locked up in police cells for a long time. Many were tortured and some have not been accounted for. Some were charged with violence and looting and jailed at Kodiaga Prison.

Civil society organizations in Nyanza have conducted surveys and analyzed trends that show the causes of the violence went beyond ethnicity, race or politics and the situation can erupt now or in future if nothing is done to create jobs for the many jobless youths in the city. According to the Waki Report, an estimated 40,000 people fled from Nyanza. Although these figures are not verifiable, it is often claimed that the province received back from other parts of the country more than 200,000 returnees.

The role of leaders

There have been widespread claims of incitement of people, particularly the youth, to violence with regard to the post-election situation. However, it appeared spontaneous and leaders of whatever category were largely absent. Leaders had been fatigued by the campaigns and many of them retreated to their houses during the violence, while others, especially parliamentary candidates and later MPs-elect, travelled to Nairobi to reinforce the ODM national leadership's claim of victory. The youth were uncontrollable and any leader who attempted to reason or pacify them at the time risked being accused of betrayal. Moreover, the youth were hungry and would have demanded handouts from the leaders whose resources had been virtually depleted by the campaigns. In fact, the media found it difficult to reach leaders for comments on what was going on as most of them hid away from the youth and the violence. As violence escalated, the leaders also feared arrest by the police.

While it is difficult to rule out political incitement, it must have been subtle, perhaps using modern technology such as the mobile phone. Text messaging had started prior to the elections. One of the text messages alleged that a senior ECK official had travelled to London where he was to meet a "renowned Nigerian election fraudster" who was to help rig elections in Kenya. Another text message claimed the ECK official was in Brussels, Belgium, and gave details of a hotel next to the city's cemetery where he was reportedly holed up with those who were to help him with the rigging plans. The graphic descriptions claimed the fake ballot papers he had gone to print would be flown back to Kenya through the Eldoret Airport for use in selected parts of the country. Such text messages and many more alarming ones made the rounds, adding to the anger that led to the violence and destruction of property. However, remarks by ODM leaders during campaigns which suggested that they would not accept the outcome and calls for mass action to protest the outcome gave impetus to the protests.

But as the riots progressed, it appeared the leaders were losing control of their supporters. At the height of the mayhem, ODM Secretary General Anyang'

Nyong'o and Raila's wife Ida Odinga flew to Kisumu to try to calm the crowds. The riots went on unabated for several weeks despite their pleas. The demonstrators shouted them down and demanded that they ask the police to stop killing people, that the security personnel withdraw from the streets and the PNU side concedes defeat before they could vacate the streets. These were top leaders whose pleas should have made a difference, but did not. The crowd was not friendly and both had to leave at some point. Had the mayhem continued even for a few more days beyond February 28, 2009 when the National Accord was signed, increasing hooliganism and crime would not have been easy to control for a long time to come.

Alternative leadership is emerging among ordinary people in Kisumu, with groups of people convening under what they call "Bunge La Wananchi" [The People's Parliament]. Since the post-election violence, there are at least ten such "Bunge La Wananchi" groups debating the outcome of the elections, assessing the performance of the Grand Coalition Government and elected leaders in Nyanza. The "Bunges" are increasingly powerful platforms for mobilization of the people of Luo Nyanza, and will influence the politics of the region significantly. The platforms offer critical analysis of the social, political and economic situation in the province. The "bunges" are often no-go zones for most leaders whose loyalty or disposition do not resonate well with the demands of the local population. In some cases, the forums have been very critical of the Coalition Government and the Principals - President Kibaki and Prime Minister Raila Odinga.

When the Kilaguni Lodge talks between PNU and ODM meant to iron out issues in the Grand Coalition collapsed, these platforms quickly mobilized the town population and were in a state of readiness for fresh riots. The same platforms were again ready and waiting to "deal with" the current Speaker, Kenneth Marende, if he had ruled in favour of PNU in the matter of the Chairman of the House Business Committee. President Kibaki had written to the House Speaker that the Vice President Kalonzo Musyoka be the chair while the Prime Minister Raila Odinga also staked a claim to the seat, creating a stalemate that heightened temperatures in the Coalition Government.

The afternoon Marende was to give his ruling was tense after members of the Luhya community residing in Kisumu were warned that if the speaker ruled in favour of Vice President Kalonzo Musyoka, they would have to leave town.

"We have never engaged Marende meaningfully. Let us wait for him over this ruling!" That was the message from the town residents who planned to block Marende from passing through the town to his Emuhaya home in the event that his ruling favoured PNU. The tension only subsided and the Luhya in Kisumu got back to their businesses after Marende ruled that he would hold the chair of the House Business Committee on an interim basis until the coalition partners sorted the matter out.

In August 2009, Agriculture Minister William Ruto had to sneak in incognito from the airport to open the Agricultural Show, with no ministerial flag flying on his vehicle after intelligence reports indicated that residents of the town were planning to confront him on his criticism of the PM over the Mau Forest issue. At the show grounds, he had to tone down his strident anti-Raila stand in his remarks. He even appeared conciliatory. But the youth still blocked the route from the showground at Kondele and Ruto and his security detail and local police had to make a detour to avoid confrontation. Ruto has for a long time been leading a group of Rift Valley MPs critical of Raila over the Mau Forest issue, demanding that all those with title deeds be compensated irrespective of how they acquired the forest land. Such is the growing power of youth in the town. They do what they want to do without prompting and this can be for good or for bad.

Many of these are jobless with nothing to lose in the event of mayhem, except their lives. They live from hand-to-mouth and can be mercenaries for hire. Although the dreaded Baghdad Boys of the 1990s who fought pitched battles with their FORD Kenya faction rivals–The Raila-Kijana Wamalwa wars and later the Raila – Oile (then a mayor aligned to Wamalwa and later Kanu) wars - are no longer visible, new and perhaps more dangerous players have taken over the city.

The reconstruction

The people and the town suffered greatly. The roads and other forms of infrastructure were destroyed, the town's informal economy which supported hundreds of thousands of people was ruined and investor confidence shaken. Crime soared and government offices remained shut for a long time. On the political front, ODM brought in a seasoned businessman Sam Okello from Mombasa to head the Council as mayor, and meetings were held by the local politicians and the business community to try to reconstruct the town.

Initiatives such as Nyanza Economic Forum and Nyanza Recovery Forum later came to try to diagnose the problems and prescribe cures. However, some of these initiatives, spearheaded by Nairobi-based entrepreneurs, academicians and bureaucrats who flew in for one-day sessions have not dramatically changed things. To some extent, a number of Nyanza people living in Nairobi have started investing back home and the town is experiencing a residential housing building boom. Many more people are now buying plots on the outskirts of the town on Riat and Nyahera Hills, Kanyakwar and other areas.

The post-election violence saw the city lose most of the entrepreneurial skills, capital and skilled labour in such areas as education and health among others. But a new spirit of entrepreneurship among many local people has emerged, with many people, including some of the youth, taking up the space left by those who fled to provide some of the services that collapsed. Some of the burnt business premises have been repaired, but some have not. The business community had disagreements with their insurance firms which refused to compensate them for the losses, forcing many businesses to just close completely.

The IDPs/Returnees compensation

It is estimated that more than 350,000 "returnees" came back to Nyanza from different towns. As noted earlier, the government did little to facilitate their return and it was left to the local leaders, civil society, business community and religious groups to organize means of transport from wherever they were stuck in various police stations, camps and church compounds. Most of these came back destitute with nothing to fall back on and with no homes to go back to. Some had been away for between 15-30 years, having chosen to settle in other parts of Kenya. Their kin were brutally murdered using crude weapons while some were shot dead by the police in Nairobi and elsewhere. The IDPs/returnees face socio-economic challenges having lost everything they had saved over the years. Some came back as third or fourth generation immigrants who had left decades ago ago to work in plantations, tea and coffee estates and construction sites.

Most of these returnees are skilled and socialized to working in urban centres and have not been able to integrate well in their rural villages where they settled at the height of the violence. The rural economies are overstretched and can hardly absorb the returnees. Facilities such as schools and health services are not adequate and are often distances away. Sick returnees who were living with HIV and who were on Anti-Retroviral Drugs (ARVs) faced serious difficulties accessing the drugs. Due to the difficulties in rural areas and lack of facilities, most of the returnees have opted not to return to their rural homes and have settled in towns, overstretching the meagre amenities of slums such as Nyalenda, Manyata, Obunga, Bandani and Kaloleni.

Other Nyanza towns such as Migori, Homabay, Oyugis, Siaya, Bondo and Mbita have experienced similar surges in their populations, resulting in serious challenges which include a rise in crime. There are a number of pull factors that have made the returnees to prefer urban centres. These include the need to break away from constraining social and cultural set-ups, as well as escape from drought and floods and competition for resources such as land.

Returnees in Nyanza have not been compensated by the government. This has bred new grounds for protests in Kisumu and other towns. The mapping of returnees has been poor and the situation has not been helped by erroneous claims by government that the returnees have "re-integrated" with their kinsmen.

There have been frequent and violent demonstrations pitting the returnees against the government. In other towns, the protests have not been as violent but have nevertheless remained visible with many demonstrators camping at government offices demanding compensation. In Kisumu, the returnees have found support from civil society groups who have helped them to remain visible and demand compensation from the government.

It will be remembered that hundreds of IDPs confronted the Prime Minister Raila Odinga at the Tom Mboya Labour College in May 2009 demanding compensation. Raila's security guards and the local provincial administration tried in vain to avoid them. In the end, Raila was forced to address them and make promises about compensation which have not been fulfilled months later. The immediate former Nyanza PC Paul Olando had several nasty encounters with IDPs as they demonstrated and camped next to his offices demanding compensation. The PC's relationship with the returnees was strained until he was replaced as PC after he was quoted in the media as saying that most returnees had reintegrated in their communities and compensation money for some of them had been withdrawn after the government failed to trace them.

The returnees, led by civil society activists Betty Okero and Joshua Nyamori of the NGO Network, demonstrated against the PC's remarks and accused the government of discrimination. The two officials have led the civil society in

Kisumu and the rest of Nyanza in putting pressure on the government to urgently compensate the IDPs.

A number of issues have emerged over the IDP compensation issue:

- Very few IDPs in Nyanza have been compensated and the vast majority do not appear to be on the government's radar. Data on genuine IDP/returnees has been very poor.

- In the few attempts at compensation, there has been corruption and discrimination, leading to replacement of the names of genuine IDPs with fake ones, some of them friends and relatives of government officials.

- The IDPs in Nyanza have an ongoing battle with the provincial administration which has declared that those agitating for compensation are "fake", while the IDPs claim the government has ignored the genuine ones and has fabricated a list of fake ones to facilitate misuse of the compensation money.

- While IDPs from other areas have been compensated and resettled or attempts made to do so under the Operation Rudi Nyumbani, those in Nyanza have largely been forgotten and the common reasoning from government officials is that they have "reintegrated within their communities". The truth is that they continue to live in squalor and deprivation in Kisumu and other towns in the province.

- While ministers, MPs and other politicians have been vocal about the issue of compensation for IDPs and returnees in their areas, those from Nyanza have largely remained quiet over this matter.

- Debates on the non-compensation of IDPs have been going on over the FM stations in Nyanza, making it a big agenda. The level of bitterness is rising and this will create explosive bitterness as the country moves towards the next general elections.

- The delay to compensate IDPs/returnees in Nyanza has generated different interpretations with feelings that the government is more concerned with Kikuyu IDPs than the other Kenyans who also suffered. These feelings have implications for the future.

The Media depiction of violence in Kisumu

Kisumu has always provided the media with rich stories. The town never lacks drama, especially of a political nature. Most media outlets always expect a story each day. The town dwellers are also avid consumers of media products; print and electronic. However, this does not mean that people necessarily agree with the media and how they portray events in Kisumu and Nyanza. The people are very conscious of the fact that the major media outlets are not owned by people from the region. This is reflected by how they relate to the media products and even journalists who work for the various media organizations.

In the run up to the 2007 General Elections, The Standard was generally favoured because of its obvious pro-ODM coverage, and it was the newspaper of choice for Kisumu and Nyanza residents. The same can be said of KTN TV. Nation Media Group products – print and electronic – were read or watched for cross referencing purposes and because they have a wider reach in Kenya. But the Nation Group is only tolerated and during the campaigns and the post-election crisis, the media organization was viewed as pro-PNU and largely anti-ODM. Nation has often made efforts to project a fair and balanced coverage but people still find (by reading through the headlines, placement of pictures, watching its television coverage and listening to its radio news) enough reason to pick a quarrel with its coverage of issues in the city and region.

The Royal Media Services stable of Citizen TV and radio and its Dholuo FM station Ramogi were, between 2002 and 2005, highly regarded as alternatives to the Nation and to some extent, the Standard. However, Royal Media lost this trust significantly after its media outlets supported the 'Banana' side during the 2005 referendum. Ramogi FM, which had hit Nyanza with a bang, and was for a while , thought to have shareholding from the region, was so badly hit after 2005 that it could hardly raise any funeral adverts. The entire Royal Media Services stable comprising Citizen Radio, TV, Ramogi FM and the defunct *Leader* newspaper were generally viewed as anti-Raila, Luo and the Orange team from 2005.

There were obvious commentaries in some of the outlets that rubbed the people and the Luo community the wrong way. Waweru Mburu's radio commentary was and still is particularly hated even if he sometimes appears to be critical of both sides in the political divide.

There was a degree of respite for Royal Media Services thereafter when it adopted a more moderate approach. Its media outlets won back a significant chunk of listeners and viewers when it adopted a moderate approach coupled with aggressive marketing, and programmes that resonated well with the local crowd. But Kisumu and Nyanza people still saw a clear leaning towards PNU and this pushed them more and more to the ODM-leaning Standard newspapers. Not that The Standard was the perfect choice. To them, it was a choice between unpleasant alternatives, because they knew that the latter was associated with retired President Moi who was supporting PNU, and under whose regime they suffered.

As for the Kenya Broadcasting Corporation, very few Kisumu and Nyanza people bother to listen to its radio news bulletins or watch its TV news, except where the reception of all the others are extremely poor. The establishment of other radio stations in the lake region including Radio Lake Victoria, Radio Nam Lolwe, Radio Sahara and Kisii-based Radio Star have also offered alternatives to the people in this region and broken the dominance of Nairobi-based media outlets.

During the campaigns and immediately after the elections, there was focus of both local and international media on the province. The violence attracted attention and, to some extent , the people felt that their voices were heard. Some were able to interact with various outlets through call-in sessions and others through interviews both on radio and television. Nyanza generally offered a big market for media products.

However, there is a worrying degree of disenchantment with the media in Nyanza. The big media particularly bear the brunt of this disaffection. In the post-election period, people wanted to speak to the rest of Kenya and the international community on various issues, notably, the contested presidential election results, police brutality and killings, non-compensation of IDPs and so on.

Kisumu, for a while during the post election period, remained in the limelight then it disappeared from the headlines. The rest of Nyanza experienced a blackout for over two months as the violence raged. After the violence, media coverage, as with other services, collapsed in the region. No newspapers came, the radio stations and the TVs did not have news from the region and the people felt marginalised. Disturbing reports about media complicity in the rigging of the elections, the ban on live coverage during the height of the violence and partisan positions by senior media editors and managers all contributed to growing suspicion of the media.

During the post-election violence period, text messages went round alleging that the Nation newspaper distribution vans were being used to ferry weapons for the Mungiki sect members who had killed many people in Nairobi, Nakuru and Naivasha. The text messages gave even car number plates and urged people in Nyanza, Western and Rift Valley to block roads and intercept the vans. It is not clear where this anti-Nation campaign originated from or the veracity of the claims, but the information hit Nation and its products in the region badly. Some analysts have alluded to the possibility that the claims may have originated from a competing media hound.

For months after the nation resumed distribution, few people touched its print product and even the TV station and radio suffered. In an apparent bid to win back the people of Kisumu and the entire Western region, the NMG top cream led by Linus Gitahi came for a highly publicised public relations bash. Virtually all media products from all media outlets are again being consumed in this region, albeit with different levels of acceptance.

In Central Kenya, the Standard newspaper, frowned upon during campaigns for its pro-ODM stance is hardly being displayed in the streets and KTN, its television wing, is not enthusiastically embraced even after the Standard group cleaned from its editorial and management ranks those considered pro-ODM, and significantly toned down its anti-PNU streak. Of course Standard and KTN understand their market segment and though striving to tread the middle path, have been struggling to please and retain the niche it curved in the pre- and immediate post election media consumers. The argument among media consumers in Kisumu and Nyanza generally is that the media have focussed on Nyanza generously during times of political crises and violence, but are not enthusiastic or supportive when they want to articulate other issues, particularly complaints against the government and even elected leaders from Nyanza.

A section of Kisumu and Nyanza residents have serious issues with the coalition government and their elected leaders, and would like to address them through the media, but they claim media outlets are not interested. "They wait for violence to rock before they cover issues here," said an angry resident at a forum convened in June 2009 by a civil society organization to discuss what people claim is media bias and failure to focus on the post election situation in the city.

Journalists operating in Nyanza are merely tolerated and the common belief is that they are working for a media largely hostile to Nyanza and, even where this is not the case like in the case of local FM stations, the thinking is that journalists are compromised. The three top Dholuo FM radio stations are Ramogi which is part of Royal Media Services, Radio Lake Victoria (owned by a Non-Governmental Organization OSIENALA-a dholuo acronym for Friends of Lake Victoria) and Radio Nam Lolwe, associated with Gem MP, Jakoyo Midiwo.

There is a marked hostility towards journalists in general while for various reasons, some journalists are potential targets of various groups in the city, either because of their own personal dispositions or because of the media organizations they work for. In the event of any public political agitation, including demonstrations and riots, journalists are often obliged to be more careful as they do their work and in the manner they package stories.

On the one hand there are sections of local leaders who would want to issue critical statements against the perceived failing of the Coalition Government and the ODM leadership, including Raila Odinga. But the journalists know very well there is the other wing, the pro-Raila forces who would want nothing negative to appear in the media against their man and party. It is a tight rope for journalists and the media.

Other hot spots in Nyanza during the post election violence

Migori/Rongo/Nyatike

As indicated earlier, the post election violence paralyzed everything in Nyanza, including the media. From January 1, 2009 violence escalated across the province and other parts of the country. In the larger Migori District, now split into Rongo, Migori, Uriri and Nyatike Districts, there was widespread violence, destruction of property and killings that the media did not capture. There were widespread demonstrations, lootings, police brutality and killings that went unreported because the media framework collapsed.

Roads and bridges were barricaded. The Kuja Bridge between Rongo and Awendo was blocked for a long time using welded rods. Others were blocked using logs, scrap metal containers and boulders. Rowdy youth set-up illegal tax collection centres on all roads, including in villages, and harassed everybody irrespective of ethnicity. More than 100 people were admitted to various hospitals with gunshot wounds and other injuries sustained from police brutality.

In Nyatike, all the District Officers fled from their stations and all the chiefs were rendered "jobless" and replaced by local people, including bicycle taxi (boda boda) operators. In one incident, an Assistant Chief had to flee to Tanzania with his family after his home was invaded by demonstrators who slaughtered all his animals and burnt his home. Nyatike was particularly affected by the violence because 7 councillors on the PNU ticket went in unopposed after their ODM counterparts were time barred at the nominations in December, 2007.

After the declaration of results and following the dispute over the presidential election results, they became targets of attacks for being in league with those who had "rigged ODM out of victory." They fled to Tanzania where they stayed in exile for three months and were brought back for swearing in under police escort. Their homes were vandalized and property looted. They and local PNU agents are yet to be fully accepted back into the local community, and relationships in the constituency are still very strained. The government goat multiplication farm at Macalder was raided and all the goats slaughtered by rampaging youths who also raided and slaughtered animals belonging to perceived PNU supporters. More than 15 people were shot dead in Nyatike Constituency.

In Migori, the police shot dead at least 12 people, among them women and children. Tens of others were admitted to the local hospitals where others died eventually. At least 13 houses, both residential and commercial, were destroyed and the local National Cereals and Produce depot was looted completely. About ten people were shot dead in Awendo and Rongo where demonstrators also blocked roads, looted and destroyed property. Some protestors threatened to set Sony Sugar cane farms on fire. Members of the Kikuyu community residing or doing business in Migori fled to Isebania and Tanzania while those in Rongo fled to Kisii from where others later went to Nakuru, Nairobi and Central Province.

Initially, the violence was fairly muted, restricted to demonstrations in the streets and some small-scale looting. However, when reports of the killings, evictions and burning of members of the Luo community filtered in, the local people went berserk and were unrestrained by any pleas from religious leaders, civil society officials and other leaders who attempted to intervene. In Homabay, more than 5 people were shot dead and property including 12 government and private vehicles and tractors worth more than Ksh10 million were destroyed. Scenes of violence looting and destruction were also witnessed in Bondo, Siaya, Ugunja, Oyugis and Kisii. The first reported case of killings after the elections was in Kisii town. The scale of violence and destruction varied from one town to another and the police response was predictably brutal, leading to the deaths and injuries of many people.

Peace building and reconciliation efforts

Peace building and reconciliation efforts have been going on meaningfully in Nyanza. The level of bitterness and the feeling of being cheated out of victory abound. The atmosphere is as if people are preparing for the next round of violent engagement.

The Government put together some ineffectual district peace committees that have fizzled out. Civil society organizations in the region and at the national level have also made efforts and continue to do so. At least ten community-based groups have been funded by UNDP under the Civil Society Democratic Governance Facility Emerging Issues Fund to handle peace and reconciliation efforts in Kisumu, Siaya, Nyando, Oyugis, Kisii, Migori and Suba Districts. There are a total of 45 such civil society groups funded by UNPD across the country handling peace and reconciliation issues. The peace and reconciliation projects are expected to go on beyond 2012.

Many people believe violence is unavoidable unless fundamental issues, including inequalities, land issues and constitutional and institutional reforms are undertaken and electoral processes reviewed. IDPs have used the peace and reconciliation forums to articulate their grievances about neglect and non-compensation by the government. Others have used them to pour out their grief over the death of loved ones and indicated the possibility that given a chance, they will revenge.

However, many others have called for tolerance and the building of a united and democratic Kenya in which all citizens feel safe and valued; where the right to associate and participate freely in governance is guaranteed, and where elections do not lead to grief and the kind of suffering that many Kenyans went through in 2008.

Chapter 5

Lest We Forget

Gitau Warigi

On New Year's Day, 2008, at around 11 o'clock in the morning, a makeshift church in Kiambaa farm near Eldoret was surrounded by a baying mob of Kalenjin youths armed with a variety of weapons. Dozens of Kikuyu women and children had taken refuge there in the wake of the December 27, 2007 General Election when word travelled fast via mobile telephones saying that Rurigi Farm had fallen to Kalenjin youths and Kimuri, Ngeria and Kiambaa were soon to be attacked. The Kiambaa people hid in the Church on the assumption that they would be spared the madness that was happening elsewhere because, with the exception of an ugly Muslim-Catholic encounter in Nairobi's South B area in 2000, houses of God in this country are largely considered inviolable.

They were wrong. From witness accounts, the attackers sprinkled a combustible liquid on the church's mud-and-wooden walls and lit up the structure. They then pressed against the walls the mattresses the victims had brought to the church to sleep on so as to make the flames flare stronger. Many of those who somehow managed to escape from the entrapped church show, up to this day, the machete and arrow scars they suffered as they took flight from the attacking mob. Twelve or so were killed outright within the church environs as they desperately tried to flee. Then there were those who got trapped inside the church, about thirty frightened souls. They all perished in the inferno.

Among the inferno victims was a widowed and crippled grandmother who died strapped to her wheelchair. Margaret Wambui Njau, for that was her name, had been a popular lady of the Kiambaa community because her disability never affected her cheerfulness nor her determination as she struggled to educate one son through university and another through the Eldoret Polytechnic. The streams of visitors who later came to bear witness at the shrine would find the wheelchair, rusted from the fiery soot of the fire, just as it had been left.

Amid the subsequent national and international revulsion at what had happened there, Peris Simam the MP representing this Eldoret South constituency, made the outrageous remark that perhaps the fire had been caused by an exploding gas cylinder. Astonished survivors were not sure what to make of the deeply insensitive remark. Well-wishers who poured in to help the victims pointed out that the remark signified the kind of unrepentant mentality that has marked Rift Valley as the cradle of impunity ever since the multi-party era began[1].

For one, metallic gas cylinders cannot be burnt into indistinct embers but will be left fairly intact as evidence at the site of the explosion in the same way that Mama Njau's sooty wheelchair remained. It is pointless to seek to give credence to Mrs. Simam's revisionist theory, but it should be pointed out in passing that both relatives and investigators who returned to the site to try and identify the charred bodies never saw any exploded gas cylinder. One presumes, also, that a gas cylinder explosion does not ordinarily inflict machete and arrow wounds such as those suffered by many who were running to escape from the inferno.

At the beginning when I set out to revisit the events and the lesson of Kiambaa, a pernicious narrative that was being relayed in some media commentaries and by some civil society groups boiled down to this question: Why should Kiambaa be different from the other cases of post-election violence, such as the people who were shot by police in Kisumu, for instance? Or, even, as some dared to ask, from those killed in retaliatory or other violence in the Rift Valley? Indeed, whenever a round-table presentation began with these words: "We really don't mean to trivialize what happened at Kiambaa…," you were being primed to sit back and expect precisely that – a revisionist belittling of a brutal fact. There is little doubt that Kiambaa remains one of the defining moments of the evil committed in the post-election aftermath. Looking through the *Kenya Burning*[2] photographic exhibition, one sees many horrifying images of stark brutality but whatever is conjured up by the mere mention of the words "Kiambaa Church" stands out as one of the defining images of our collective failure to evolve into a nation.

In Kenyan political parlance, commentators prefer using the word "communities" as a cover against identifying specific ethnicities. In the ordinary course of political life, this is fine. But when we talk of atrocities, that definition is an inexcusable cop-out. It amounts to a refusal to deal with truth in all of its dangerous surprises. It hides the stark lessons that Kenyans must learn about each other, the antagonisms underneath, the suspicions, hatreds and fears, all of which must be laid bare if a recurrence is to be avoided. It is a cop-out that suggests that it is easier to keep truth hidden than to fight for its exposure and preservation. In all the readings of the 1994 Rwanda genocide, the reality that 800,000 Tustis, and Hutus perceived to have been their sympathizers, were massacred by Hutu extremists is not something that can – or should – be shrouded in the amorphous phraseology of "communities."[3]

The question of whether an electoral dispute – even one as emotive as rigging – can justify the level of atrocity witnessed in Kiambaa is the crux here. One of the more bizarre re-tellings of the events of that time suggests that the so-called warriors were only peacefully demonstrating against what they claimed to be a stolen election. The manner in which they went about that business gives a huge lie to this excuse. It doesn't even start to answer the contradiction of why the North Rift was the bloodiest theatre of the violence compared to other regions like, say, Nyanza which had more legitimate grounds for special outrage if only because the Orange Democratic Movement (ODM) presidential candidate in whose name the violence was being carried out comes from there. Why, therefore, would the Kalenjin feel they were owed anything special just because the ODM party had been declared the loser? The answer is: because the violence and the hatred were about something else.

Kiambaa sits some dozen or so kilometers away from Eldoret town. It can be accessed from either the Eldoret-Kapsabet road or the Eldoret-Nairobi highway. Either way, the killers had made sure outside help for the cornered residents would not immediately be forthcoming as they had thrown boulders and dug ditches to block access roads before commencing with the business of killing. When I travelled there in February 2008, the trenches were still there and I had to use some knowledgeable locals and a circuitous route to reach the site of the burnt-down church.

The topography of the land is generally flat, sub-divided into small plots of land worked by peasant families. In that locality, it is easy to distinguish a Kalenjin homestead from a Kikuyu one simply by looking at the vegetation and tree cover. The former prefer to sprinkle their plots with wattle and the occasional gum tree which are prevalent in the area.[4] The Kikuyu homesteads are littered with banana plants and the *grivella robusta* tree ubiquitous in Central Province and which may have served to memorialise an ancestral land the migrants had left behind long ago.

Anybody coming to Kiambaa after the atrocity was committed could immediately see the settlement was a sitting duck, a tragedy waiting to happen. It is ringed on three sides by Kalenjin-populated farms, the exception being the fourth outlet where it adjoins a smaller farm called Kimuri, also occupied by Kikuyu farmers. The two farms are boxed in such a manner that escapees had to endure a considerable distance through hostile territory before they could reach the nearest highway for help. When the killings started, the inhabitants of both farms found themselves hopelessly outnumbered and thus suffered a shared fate.

Originally, Kiambaa was a 600-acre wheat farm owned by a white settler. In 1965 groups of peasants from faraway Kiambu teamed up together to purchase the farm when they learned it was up for sale. These peasants were from what is today Kiambaa constituency in Kiambu District. That is how the farm they purchased came to be known as Kiambaa. Initially, the company did not sub-divide the farm. They ran it as a single entity from which they drew dividends. The sub-division and settlement of individual shareholders on their allocated parcels did not happen until the early 1980s following the then president Daniel Arap Moi's directive that all such farms be sub-divided. Many of the original shareholders of the Kiambaa farm never actually moved to the site. During the subdivision process, they sold their shares to other Kikuyu migrants.

One of the fall-back arguments that seeks to give excuses for the recurrent violence in Rift Valley province is the transplanting of ancestral names. When the attackers descended on the Kiambaa farm, one of the first things they did was to knock down the sign-post of Kiambaa Primary School which they replaced with another reading *"Kipnyigei."* In the Kalenjin dialect, it translates to the name of the age-group that the attackers belonged to.

There were several reports in the daily press about similar renaming of places in the North Rift that had previously been inhabited by Kikuyu people. These acts of renaming were seen as the culmination of the Kalenjin quest to repossess "stolen" lands. The county edition of the *Daily Nation*[5] reported that a primary school in Kiambaa had been renamed "Kipnyigei Primary" and on its hastily reworded signpost were the words: "success through war".

Perhaps unbeknown to the Kalenjin, the transplanting of ancestral names is a practice as old as the time when human beings started migrating from one place to another. It gives a sense of community through the enactment of shared memories. When the English first sailed away to America and Australia, they brought along to these New Worlds names that were familiar to them like (New) London, (New) South Wales, (New) York and so on.

Likewise, Asian migrants to Kenya built schools and social clubs with names from their original communities and regions in the Indian sub-continent, names like the Oshwal and the Arya Samaj. African communities have never been static, rooted in one place. Individuals seeking opportunities for their families have fanned out all over the country, and you may encounter a shop in, say, Trans Mara which bears the name of a village somewhere in Gucha, or a hotel in Malindi named after a town in Murang'a. In the same way, in many large towns outside Nyanza where the Luo have settled, there is invariably a suburb called Kisumu Ndogo.

But it appears that in the world view of the Rift Valley "warriors," names like Kiambaa somehow legitimized the Kikuyu claim to the land and sought to disinherit the Kalenjin, who it is in fact argued were never the original claimants in some of those parts of the Rift Valley as is historically borne out by names such as Uasin Gishu, Eldoret, Kipkaren, Sirikwa and Eldama Ravine[6].

When I first visited Kiambaa, accompanied by a colleague, our mission being not so much to gather the strands of whatever happened there but more so to get some meaning, some idea, of what reason drove this fateful act of arson. All the residents of Kiambaa had fled to the sprawling and extremely squalid tented Internally Displaced Persons (IDP) camp at the Eldoret town showground. All over the land they had left behind you could see the burnt-out shells of what were once homesteads. Anything of value in those houses, we later came to learn, had first been looted, starting with the iron-sheet roofing. Anomalous as it sounds, iron-sheet roofing happens to be one of the overt distinguishing marks of "affluence" between Kikuyu and Kalenjin peasant homesteads. The Kikuyu insist on using iron-sheet roofing for their houses; many of the Kalenjin peasants have grass-thatched huts. In the recurring instances from 1992 when the Kikuyu have been attacked in the Rift Valley, these iron sheets are always the first to be looted.

There was no sign of life anywhere when we arrived in Kiambaa; no sounds of happy children playing in the compounds, or women chattering as they tilled the fields. Only an eerie silence. There was not a single bird in the sky, no cats running around, no cow or goat, though we could see enough evidence from the abandoned homesteads that the inhabitants had kept livestock. It had all been driven away by the attackers. A ghostly pall hang over the surroundings. Even the barking of dogs and the loud cackling of chickens, common sounds in a typical peasant farm, were absent.

In one of the abandoned *shambas,* a few metres from the burnt-out church, we met a man nonchalantly scavenging for building posts from the shell of a burnt house. Another was lazily grazing his cow on an abandoned plot which had sprouted green shoots of grass. None of the interlopers wanted to meet our gaze. No-one approached us or spoke to us even from a distance.

Kiambaa Primary School, with its hastily scrawled new name, had of course been closed down. We drove on to the sacred plot – where the desecrated Kiambaa church had stood. Nothing much remained of the building, save for the rubble of collapsed mud walls and chunks of leftover wooden poles. The collapsed walls were baked soot black, a sign of the intensity of the fire that had razed the building.

The wheelchair of the disabled woman had since been removed. An unknown 2ww built a semi-permanent house. She also owned a clothes shop at the junction of the Eldoret-Nairobi highway.

Jane Wambui voted early in Cheplaskei because she was travelling to Nakuru with her daughter to spend the New Year holiday with friends there. At the polling station she noticed that other people queuing to vote gave her odd stares. She recognized plenty of the people around, some of who were her fellow teachers and some her former pupils. On that day, however, they did not seem keen to talk. She started getting a strong feeling of foreboding, which increased when she took an Eldoret-bound matatu and a fellow passenger remarked: *"kwani kabila hii ni nini?"* (after all, what is this tribe worth?)

Two days later, on 31st December, while in Nakuru she received an alarming phone call that Kikuyu houses had started being torched in Kimuri farm, adjacent to Kiambaa. Her worst fears came flooding in. She knew Kiambaa would be next. She had left all her documents in her house there, not to mention all her household goods including electronic gadgets. But she knew going there now would be courting real danger. There was nothing to do other than wait and see.

At some point, she thought of phoning a policeman she knew who was stationed in the Eldoret area to keep an eye on her property until she returned. But he offered little help other than to utter a strange remark: *"Hii shida haingekua ikiwa kura haikuibwa.*" (this problem would not have arisen if the votes had not been stolen). Those among her Kalenjin workmates who she had considered to be friends were not helpful either. Many months later, after she had relocated from what she thought of as the God-forsaken place, some former workmates would call her and claim that they had not warned her early enough because they did not have cell phone credit at the time. "I wish they didn't bother calling me with such stupid excuses," she says.

When Kiambaa was finally attacked, Wambui's house was one of the few that were not torched. The reason was simple: It made better sense for the attackers to loot the house first because they knew she owned a TV set and other electronic valuables. They also knew she stored in her house the valuable stock of the clothes that she sold at her highway shop.

After everything was stolen, the house was vandalized including doors and window frames. A couple of livestock she owned were the first to be driven away. The argument by Kalenjin politicians that the Kiambaa attack had been "spontaneous" is one she and her neighbours have no patience with. If indeed they had been spontaneous, they should have commenced the moment the presidential results were announced, not a full 40 hours after the Kibaki swearing-in ceremony.

When Jane Wambui returned on January 11th, the first thing she did was to take photographs of her vandalized house. When this writer encountered her in February 2008 at her plot, still dazed and emotionally wrung, the evidence of the Biblical quotations that she had fretfully scrawled on the walls of her house was still legible:. Luke 24:50 and John 16:1amongst others.

Wambui eventually got a transfer to Nakuru where she tried to piece her life together again. Prior to the transfer, she volunteered to teach at the IDP Eldoret camp where many of her Kiambaa friends and pupils were confined. These same children would talk with their teacher about people who attacked their farms, who included their fellow pupils and grown-up neighbours.

The violence did not spare Kikuyus who had married Kalenjins. Joseph Ngaruiya, 36, and his Pokot wife Agneta, 35, had built their home next to the doomed church. He was a popular figure in the area, and ran a well-stocked shop which served Kikuyus and Kalenjins alike. When the attack on the church happened, his wife and two young children were hiding inside the church itself, and it is only by a miracle that he managed to remove them from the building before it was set aflame. Everybody ran helter-skelter in different directions. But he has something to show for it. He broke a leg which did eventually heal but his face remains marked with a nasty scar running across the bridge of his nose down to his cheek; eternal evidence of the machete slash he sustained as he fled. The attack left him unconscious, which was perhaps lucky since his attackers presumed him to be dead. He had no idea how he was taken to hospital, or where his family had vanished to. And as this was happening, Agneta was heavily pregnant and struggling to run alongside her two children. She lost track of the older girl.

Ngaruiya's situation is poignant because in the immediate aftermath of the chaos the family had trouble getting refuge because both the Kikuyu IDP camps and the Kalenjin households distrusted them. Agneta first sought refuge at St. John's Catholic Cathedral in Eldoret town but after a few days of trying to bear the resentment of the refugee Kikuyu women, she moved to the Happy Church congregation where she stayed for a while. The Happy Church pastor received threatening messages telling him to move the Kikuyus IDPs to the Eldoret showground camp.

Meanwhile, Agneta had no idea where her daughter and husband were. From the Happy Church, she would hear stories they were dead. She had already visited the Eldoret Referral Hospital several times, where she failed to find her child among those admitted. On the first visit she fainted on imagining that they could be dead. It so happened that her husband was in the same hospital but she could not recognize him among the patients because his face was so swollen and almost completely covered in bandages. In fact it was Ngaruiya who first recognized his wife when he heard her voice.

Their family was finally re-united in full when her daughter was found at Langas Police station, together with other children who had either been orphaned or separated from their parents. A third child had joined the family at Happy Church, where Agneta had given birth.

Before their lives were turned upside down by post-election violence, Ngaruiya and Agneta were a prosperous couple by Kiambaa standards. They used to sell *mitumba* clothes in Eldoret, where they actually first met and later became man and wife. While the husband kept their new shop in Kiambaa, he would send his wife on errands to Malaba to buy shoes and curtains which they would re-sell in Eldoret. They lost everything in the mayhem. Typical of the amazing resilience of the Kiambaa victims, Ngaruiya and Agneta have restarted their lives all over again, first by going back to that plot right next to the burnt-out Pentecostal Assemblies of God (PAG) church, building a small house and re-opening a small shop on one side of the house. They admit that their only customers these days are Kikuyus.

The couple also describes the on-and-off reconciliation process as a sham. At joint meetings organized by churches, the local administration or mediated by donor agencies, the Kalenjin elders like to say that it was "the Devil" who was behind the chaos. It is never explained how this Devil always materializes during election cycles, and how come it is always one side made to suffer. The other claim the elders are fond of making is that the Kiambaa attack was carried out by "outsiders." The Kikuyu side finds this difficult to believe. They have the names of most of the attackers, and these are local names of neighbours they knew well and interacted with. And if by chance the attackers had been outsiders, how come they were so precise in pinpointing the "foreigners" homes for destruction?

There should be a two pronged approach to the violence: criminal elements must be punished and reconciliation efforts be pursued in earnest. Those who committed crimes must own up and seek forgiveness.

However, many post-election violence victims are convinced the culprits have no desire to own up, nor are their leaders urging them to. Their children, too, show the same mindset in school. Asked why they and their parents attacked their neighbours, they say it is because "they (Kikuyu) had stolen our land." The whole narrative about "stolen" land is a (sub)version of history that Kalenjin peasants have been poisoned with over the years by politicians whose overriding interest is to ethnically cleanse the Kikuyu from the Rift Valley. The way the narrative goes is that Jomo Kenyatta settled "his" Kikuyus in the land of the Kalenjin in the Rift Valley.

From the start, there is willful blindness to the fact that Kikuyu settlement in the Rift Valley started long, long ago when colonialism took root and in any event, the Rift Valley had not even been designated as such and people migrating through Kijabe, Nyandarua or Laikipia had no sense of entering a new province. Colonial migration was prompted by white settlers who had not only annexed prime lands in Central Kenya, but who also needed labour for their newly-acquired farms in the White Highlands. This process was helped along by the colonial imposition of a tax which then forced the "natives" to sell their labour and earn the capital to pay taxes.

In "The Lie of the Land: Evictions and Kenya's Crisis", Horace Gisemba (2008) has traced four distinct patterns of Kikuyu settlement in the Rift Valley. Amongst them is one of the most deliberately misunderstood land transfer developments in post-independence Kenya – the Settlement Fund Trustee (SFT) through which the Kenyan government acquired former settler farms for re-distribution to Africans. The scheme was financed through British and World Bank settlement programmes.

The important thing to note was that the SFT land did not come for free. And though a tiny African elite from all the main farming communities took advantage of the scheme, the vast majority of the beneficiaries who paid up were ordinary Kenyans, again from the main farming communities like the Kikuyu, the Luo, the Kisii, the Luhya and, in the case of the Rift Valley, even the Kalenjin.[7]

The land Kenyatta allocated directly was actually insignificant comparatively, and in places like at Burnt Forest where he gave away a piece to one Nyakinyua Women's Group, it was shared equally with a Kalenjin women's group. Many of the Kikuyu in the Rift Valley do not even own land because of the STF. They purchased their plots directly from emigrating settlers by pooling money through co-operative societies. That is how the Kiambaa land came to be under Kikuyu ownership. Many other Kikuyu bought land directly from Kalenjin (and Maasai) owners though willing-seller-willing-buyer deals. Much as the Kalenjin who sold their land this way did so without any coercion, their politicians continue to incite with the cry that the land was "stolen."

Is it possible that one community has found justification to attack the other using distorted facts over the land issue? According to Bishop Cornelius Korir land is the cause of the enemity. "The new enemity, politics wakes up the old enemity, ethnic competition over land."[8] In fact, land has always been the excuse rather than the reason local politicians routinely find expedient to unleash the "Kalenjin warriors" against their neighbours. It is a matter of no passing interest that the pogroms against non-Kalenjins in the Rift Valley, especially those directed at the Kikuyu, always coincide with electoral cycles when the two communities stand opposed in different political camps. That was the case in 1991/92, 1997 and 2007. The only reason the attacks were not repeated in 2002 was because, under Daniel Moi's influence, the Kalenjin were largely supporting a Kikuyu presidential candidate, Kanu's Uhuru Kenyatta.

More to the point, in spite of the attacks being usually clothed as spontaneous outbreaks of inter-communal violence incited by malcontents on both sides, truth-evaders have never succeeded in covering up the fact that they are highly organized by vested political interests. Successive high-level inquiries like the Kiliku Commission, the Akiwumi Commission and, lately, the Waki Commission, have all attested to this fact.

Lucy Wanjiru, 30, a mother of three girls, is one of the Kiambaa victims who came out alive from the ordeal. But one of her little daughters was not so lucky. She was hacked to death as Wanjiru tried to save her. Another daughter, who was barely eight years old, was brutally raped. The mute way she keeps to herself is testimony that she will remain traumatized for the rest of her life.

Lucy explained to me how the attackers behaved when they came upon her and a group of older women. Ordered to hold up their hands, they were forced to repeat: "*Sema waKikuyu ni wezi! Sema wewe ni mwizi! Sema muliiba kura! Sema ODM ilishinda!*"[9] Was this an attempt by the attackers to assuage their own conscience?

Lucy and virtually all her Kiambaa neighbours have no illusions whatsoever that the attack would have happened anyway even if the ODM had won the election. In fact, they are convinced the attacks would have had more intensity had that been the election outcome. All of them report an air of quiet intimidation from their neighbours weeks before voting day. Just days to polling day, Kalenjin youths, pretending to be drunk, would openly mutter that "*lazima makwekwe warudi kwao uchaguzi ikiisha.*"[10] Makwekwe, which is a kind of weed, was one of the many epithets employed against the Kikuyu and given wide circulation and currency by vernacular radio[11].

The fact that reconciliation remains a mirage was displayed in the most stark manner during the heartbreaking funeral service for the Kiambaa victims on May 14, 2009. Not a single Kalenjin member of parliament attended, certainly not even area MP Peris Simam of the "gas cylinder" fame. One of the MPs claimed they had not been "invited." It was left to one of the mourners to eloquently respond in the media that nobody in civilized cultures gets invited to funerals[12]. Genuine mourners come at no behest.

The same virulent political forces had desperately tried to block the mass funeral. At the onset local Kalenjin leaders strongly objected to initial plans by civil society sympathizers to erect a monument at the site. They even objected to the burial being within the church compound, which is where the Kiambaa community and the Kenya Assemblies of God (KAG), who owned the destroyed church, insisted the dead must be laid to rest and memorialized at that very site. In the meantime, work on a new and permanent church on the site begun almost immediately. The money came from well-wishers outside of the Kiambaa community.

The opposition to these plans, especially regarding the monument, was clearly a function of communal guilt. A clergyman of the ACK Eldoret Diocese betrayed the feelings at work of those in opposition with these words: "The local community (meaning the Kalenjin) fears that by allowing the monument to be built, they would be accepting guilt over the burning of the Kiambaa church. That is why there is so much resistance to the idea." These words expressed publicly were not solitary: they were shared by many others.

A measured response was offered by the KAG minister, Pastor Stephen Mburu: "What happened in Kiambaa is not a secret. A monument will always be a reminder to generations to come of what intolerance did to us and as a warning to what it can do."[13] It was an apt reminder that those who are not forced to confront their wrongs will show no compunction in repeating them. That is why Jews and the Tutsis of Rwanda, who singularly understand mass atrocity, unite in saying: "Never again!" And Anti-Semitism laws were instituted globally precisely to avert the kind of revisionism that rewrites history by denying the fact of ethnic cleansing.

In any case, it would be ridiculous to say that the memorials that dot Rwanda today are an impediment to Hutu-Tutsi reconciliation, or that those in Germany commemorating the Holocaust are an affront to the German population. If anybody felt affronted, that would be all the more reason for the memorials since they are meant to convey to him a certain vital lesson.

Tragedy had stalked the Kiambaa victims even in death. On January 7, 2008, authorities at Moi Teaching and Referral Hospital attempted to bury the bodies secretly without informing the victims' families. The badly burnt bodies had remained in the hospital's mortuary for months awaiting DNA identification. Hospital authorities claimed that preserving the bodies was consuming too much space – and electricity. The crude plan to dispose of the bodies at Kiplombe public cemetery before DNA tests (which were done in South Africa) were completed was physically thwarted by the victims' families when they got wind of it. The drama left many who watched it on Kenya Television News (KTN) evening news shocked and outraged at the pictures of wailing women and a menacing earth mover preparing to drop body bags into an already dug mass grave.

So far only four suspects have ever been charged in court over the Kiambaa atrocity. On April 30, 2009, Justice David Maraga of Nakuru set free Stephen Leting, Emmanuel Lamai, Clement Kipkemei and Julius Rono, dismissing the case for "lack of evidence." The judge ruled that the police had carried out "shoddy" investigations. In Kiambaa, the Kikuyu were stunned and felt deeply aggrieved by the outcome. As if to further dramatize the ongoing rift in Kiambaa, the Kalenjins celebrated and organized a loud homecoming party for the freed suspects. They were joined by a few of their prominent politicians.

The political hypocrisy that Kenyans have perfected cannot obscure the fact that the immediate post-electoral holocaust throughout the country was directed at ordinary Kikuyus – in Eldoret, in Kisumu, in Busia, in Narok, in Mombasa, in the slums of Nairobi. Later, a full four weeks after Samuel Kivuitu had declared Mwai Kibaki the winner, Kikuyu gangs organized themselves to retaliate – mainly in the same Nairobi slums, and in Naivasha and Nakuru – using more or less the same vicious methods of forced eviction, machete killings, as those employed in the first wave of post-election violence.

Did the Kikuyu disproportionately bear the brunt in what was a culmination of a hate-filled national political campaign that went under the code-name of "Forty-one versus one" (denoting 41 ethnic communities against the Kikuyu)? The Centre for Strategic Studies, an NGO which did an extensive survey of the entire Rift Valley province immediately after the bloodbath, estimated that about 31,000 houses had been torched, most of them Kikuyu-owned.

Thousands of women were raped by gangs. Over 300,000 victims – again mainly Kikuyu, were displaced. This figure covers those who were accommodated in IDP camps, not the thousands of others who chose to relocate for good or temporarily with relatives in Central Province and other safer areas. Needless to add, cows and goats and other livestock which are dear to every peasant were stolen and driven away by the attackers. In all, billions of shillings worth of property accumulated over lifetimes instantly went up in smoke.

The case of Kiambaa is made special not because it is the Kikuyus who were the victims there. In fact, neither is the other parallel atrocity in Naivasha, where a whole family was burnt inside a house by a Kikuyu mob, made special because Luos were the victims in that instance.

First and foremost, the victims of Kiambaa were not combatants in the inter-ethnic mayhem that was raging all over the province. These were innocents who had taken refuge in a holy sanctuary, but who ended up in the worst of circumstances purely because of their ethnic background – and because they were presumed to have voted for PNU candidate Mwai Kibaki.

Political killers who violate holy sanctuaries have always had a special place of infamy throughout history. It is no accident that the majority of memorials to the ghastly 1994 Rwanda genocide are dotted in compounds that once used to be churches. It did not help matters when a top ODM leader gave a misinformed interview to an international media outlet, just as the gravity of what had happened at Kiambaa was sinking in, suggesting that the attackers were reacting to rumours that the priest in charge had allowed people to stockpile weapons inside the church. [14] Among its many errors was Raila's assertion that the Kiambaa Church was headed by a Catholic priest. Pastor Stephen Mburu was the man in charge at the evangelical Kiambaa Pentecostal Assemblies of God.

Second, it is obscene to compare an atrocity such as this committed inside a church with the shootings by the police of a varied crowd of demonstrators, rapists and arsonists who were roaming all over the North and South Rift scrawling "Kipnyigei" - the name of their age-sect - in places such as the signposts of the primary schools they had burnt down. There can be absolutely no moral equivalence between the killing of a child and his mother hiding in a church and the shooting by a policeman of the thug who is threatening to occasion the death of that child. By the same token, there can be no moral equivalence to actions taken by law enforcers to restore calm and order and those by self-declared "warriors" intent on killing and raping as many people as possible.

I use the words "warriors" in quotes deliberately, for as I will later endeavour to show, the term is a false affectation when applied to the Rift Valley violence since all it does is to attempt to give a valorous and respectful character to acts of pure and premeditated political gangsterism.

One of the attempts at downplaying the significance of what happened at Kiambaa is a narrative that says that the Kalenjin who were shot by police in the environs of Eldoret were more than those who died in the church. Trying to re-calibrate who suffered most by drawing parallels between the fate of some of the "warriors" and their victims is basically a fool-hardy exercise, even assuming that the figures quoted are real. In the end, guilt is not determined by actual body counts. More Nazis actually died in World War II than the Jews they eliminated.

We live in a country where tribalised hatreds have reached such low depths that even moral outrage over mass killings will not be forthcoming unless it is weighted on some 'equalised' scale of ethnic suffering. What we learn from Kiambaa is that speaking of death in terms of such 'equity' is obscene when the case is about deliberate mass atrocity. Even the law grants distinctions between pre-meditated killing, manslaughter and slaying in self-defense.

In the course of discussions about the post-election violence, one strand of argument has been that we should let by-gones be by-gones and build a fresh Kenya. I have always found this argument incredible, perpetrated as it were by people who have something to hide, or feel there is too much for them to lose if the skeletons are exposed. Not even the Kofi Annan team pretended that this cathartic reckoning could be ignored. In clear terms, that is why it advocated for a local tribunal to punish the perpetrators, failing which the International Criminal Court at The Hague would take over. Attempting to throw the ball away by equating the necessary pursuit of justice to revenge will not do.

A slightly less crude approach than the let bygones-be-bygones mantra is the one about apportioning blame 'equally' across the 'combatants'. This argument is couched in the plea that this is the only way to build "trust" in the future. But it is a false and ultimately indefensible argument. The Kiambaa people were simple folk who had merely exercised their right to vote. The majority of them may indeed have voted for Kibaki. That alone is the crime their enemies thought they committed. They were not party to rigging at polling stations or the virulent election dispute, whose drama was being played out 300 kilometres away in Nairobi.

As Philip Gourevitch writes in *We Wish to Inform You That Tomorrow We Will be Killed With Our Families*, his classic study of the Rwandan genocide, reconciliation can never happen in a vacuum. Atonement and forgiveness will only follow when those who kill in a mindless frenzy own up that they did wrong. Guilt in this context is very much a prerequisite for reconciliation. The shame it induces is indeed therapeutic. It is what leads to remorse and repentance. Gourevitch's words should serve as a powerful tonic for the Grand Coalition government which has taken the completely wrong path of imagining reconciliation can happen when there is no justice.

It is a testament of the tenacity of the human spirit that the survivors of Kiambaa are back on their farms and intent on reconstructing their lives. Though for the time being they remain encamped in a so-called transit camp, they spend the days tilling their fields and starting all over again with the small, homegrown businesses that once made them self-sufficient. Occasionally, something that causes a little joy happens in their lives, like one day when a stolen cow strolled back to its owner's plot on its own volition after sensing she had returned. The thief who had stolen it, and who must have left it grazing somewhere unattended, did not have the stomach to come and reclaim it.

Yet the Kiambaa people know life will never be the same again, not after what they went through. They know this when they watch young Kimunya limp along with a hoe held in his withered arm which was scarred so irreversibly when he fell on a mattress as he fled the fire in that church. His mother is the iconic face of the Kiambaa fire, her brightly coloured sweater an incongruous contrast to the burnt shoe in her hand, the nearly audible wail from her mouth and the smoke and shell in the background. Something of the dreams Kimunya, his mother and all the others must have had in their previous life was snuffed out forever. But they soldier on with the consolation, as shared by an old Igbo proverb, that 'no condition is permanent.'

Postscript

The following are the names of those who died inside the Kenya Assemblies of God Church, Kiambaa:

1. Margaret Wambui Njau (Cucu was Kahia) – who died on a wheel chair. She was a heroic woman who used to till her own *shamba* despite being crippled. One of her twin sons, John Njau, a student at the University of Nairobi, sustained serious burns and cuts from the raiders. Njau had tried to remove his mother from the burning church but when the raiders saw this they came and hacked him, thus preventing him from rescuing his mother from the flames. He was taken to hospital with lost memory where his twin brother, Stephen Njau, student at Eldoret Polytechnic, was taking care of him. Their younger brother, Joseph Irungu, had just cleared KCPE.

2. Benson Njoroge– twelve years old, formerly of Kiambaa primary school and brother to Rachel Mwihaki

3. Dennis Kuria – a child of about 10 years

4. Njihia (the other name unrecorded) - a brother to Esther Njeri who was in class two

5. Edith Mumbi Githuku (Mama Waithira or Mama Sammy who died with young Sammy on her back)

6. Sammy Githuku (died on his mother's back)

7. James Mwicigi popularly known as Gathee (an elderly man)

8. Naomi Ng'endo (adult woman)

9. Joyce Njoki Harun (child)

10. Mama Eunice (an old woman popularly known as 'Matha')

11. Peter Gradson (child)

12. Ben Mutahi Macharia (youth)

13. Mary Gathoni (adult woman)

14. Peter N. Mwangi (youth)

15. Miriam N. Mwangi (woman)

16. Mary Wangui (adult woman popularly known as 'Wachoma')

17. Samuel Kiong'o (old man)

18. Gitahi Rubia (old man)

19. Peter Kung'u (old man)

20. Daniel Mwangi Kung'u (youth)

21. Joseph Kimani (adult man)

22. Kim (the other name unrecorded)

23. Simeon Gitau (child)

24. Mary Wanjiru (child)

25. Miriam Ng'endo (adult woman)

26. Peter Ng'ang'a (child)

(*Names of five other victims unrecorded. Complete list remains with Pastor Stephen Mburu*).

At least 51 people suffered serious burns. Many were hospitalized like Rachel Mwihaki's mother, Anne Macharia, who was admitted at the Nairobi Women's Hospital. Below are some survivors:

1. George Karanja
2. Charles Muraguri
3. Pastor Stephen Mburu
4. Joseph Kamande
5. Esther Njeri
6. Eunice Kamau
7. Anne Macharia
8. Rachel Mwihaki
9. Jane Kamau (4 year old)
10. Peter Kamau (6 years old)
11. Joseph Njuguna

In addition, several teenaged survivors got so badly disfigured that they were ultimately flown to the US for reconstructive surgery. They were Mercy Wanjiru, Mary Wahito, Mary Kariuki and Anthony Njoroge. They were admitted at Shriner's Children's Hospital for Burns in Sacramento, California on April 15, 2009. The Kiambaa fire was a defining moment in Kenyan political and social history.

Notes

[1] Kipchumba Some. *Daily Nation* January 3, 2009.

[2] This exhibition opened at The Godown Arts Centre, Nairobi April 19, 2008. Under the theme "Never Again, Never Forget" the curators, Joy Mboya and Judy Ogana, sourced hitherto unpublished photographs of the 2007 election and post-election period as a way of triggering public debate on the question of Kenya's nationhood and (in)humanity. The exhibition has since been published as a book completed with excerpts of testimonies from victims, aggressors compiled by Kwani Trust and translated into Kiswahili by Twaweza Communications Ltd.

[3] Philip Gourevitch (1999). We Wish to Inform You That Tomorrow We Will be Killed With Our Families: Stories from Rwanda. New York: Picador.

[4] The former Lonrho-owned EATEC farm and its wattle plantations, which have since been cut down, is only a shouting distance away.

[5] Jonathan Komen (2011) "The Kalenjin want Kiambaa renamed Kipnyigei, which is an age group in Kalenjin between 16 and 23 years... the age set that provided the youths who fought in the post-election violence" in *Daily Nation*, April 7, 2011, County Edition/E.

[6] Horace Njuguna Gisemba (2008) "The Lie of the Land: Evictions and Kenya's Crisis". *Africa Policy Brief* No. 2, February 2008 an abridged version of which appeared as "Bad Politics Fuelled Clashes in the Rift Valley" in *The Sunday Nation* February 17, 2008.

[7] *See* also Alfred K. Nyairo, "Land Resettlement Programme Was Grossly Misrepresented", The *Daily Nation*, November 23, 2009, p.13.

[8] *See* "Kenya's Disputed Elections Awaken Warring Tribes Grab for Land" *www.bloomberg.com/apps/news. See* also Karl Maier in *www.ogiek.org.*

[9] Say Kikuyus are thieves; say you are a thief; say your people stole the votes; say ODM won.

[10] All weeds must go back to their ancestral homes once this election is over.

[11] Twaweza Communications media monitoring report *Meddling with the Message.*

[12] Rift Valley MPs say they were not invited for the Kiambaa burial, Uploaded NTV Kenya on 16th May 2009 *http://wn.com/kiambaa. See* also *The Standard* online edition – skewed mourning won't heal Kenya by Okech Kendo h*ttp://www.standardmedia.co.ke/archives/oddnews/inside page.*

[13] Vincent Bartoo, "Not even church was refuge enough". The Standard online edition, January 1st 2009 *www.standardmedia.co.ke/archives/...inside page.* (Accessed on March 7th, 2011).

[14] Excerpts of this Raila Odinga BBC interview were aired on several radio stations on the morning of 17 January, 2008 YouTube-Raila Odinga Hard Talk, *http://www.mashanda.com/forums/politics/14203 - shocking-bbc-tape-raila-defending-burning-alice-children-kiambaa-church-3.html* and carried verbatim in the Nairobi Star. Among its many errors was Raila's assertion that the Kiambaa Church was headed by a Catholic priest. Pastor Stephen Mburu was the man in charge at the evangelical Kiambaa Pentecostal Assemblies of God. Hard Talk Raila Odiinga 2 BBC World News *http://www.youtube.com/watch?v=k_vhoiDmHmU&feature=relmfu* 2:53. (Accessed on March 8, 2011).

Part Two

Resolving The Crisis

Chapter 6

Putting Out The Flames: The Kenya National Dialogue and Reconciliation Process

Kimani Njogu

Background to the negotiations

Kenyans went into polling stations in millions to elect the President of the Republic and Members of Parliament (MPs) on 27th December 2007 after a gruelling campaign mounted by two key protagonists: Mwai Kibaki, the incumbent and presidential candidate for the Party of National Unity (PNU), and Raila Odinga, the candidate for the Orange Democratic Movement (ODM)[1]. The third presidential candidate Kalonzo Musyoka of ODM-K, though with a substantial following, was not likely to win but would be a factor in the size of the final margin between the two heavy weights and the subsequent formation of the coalition government. As polling came to an end, and contestants eagerly waited for the final results to be announced by the Electoral Commission of Kenya (ECK) as required by the law, the country was tense and anxious. All indications were that voters would turn out in large numbers and the Presidential results would be very close.

Meanwhile, there were claims of rigging of the results and occasionally the Chairman of the ECK, Samuel Kivuitu, appeared on national television shifting blame on his returning officers. At one point, Kivuitu casually pointed out that some of his officers in rural constituencies had 'switched off' their mobile phones and he could not reach them. He went on to suggest that he had even contacted the police to help trace the returning officers[2]. The claims of possible rigging and the casualness of the ECK chairman and unprofessionalism at ECK headquarters created an atmosphere of doubt among voters about the overall integrity of the results and served to heighten emotions among the electorate. Matters were not helped by the delay in the transmission of results and the analysis at the ECK headquarters. In addition, some of the results at headquarters had significant alterations which were not explained to the satisfaction of voters and politicians. Although the alterations may have been a consequence of the provisional nature of the results received from polling stations, the fact that they existed introduced doubt on their integrity in this high stakes election[3] . Moreover, the fact that most of the results from ODM presidential candidate strongholds were received and announced through the media earlier than those from President Mwai Kibaki's highly populated strongholds – and no explanation was offered for this action – led to major expectation of victory among Raila supporters. Furthermore, in many ODM and PNU strongholds, there were unrealistically high voter turn-out, discrepancies in the votes cast, and imprecision in some election reporting documents, notably Form 16 A – which was filled at the polling stations before transmission to the constituency polling centre where results were recorded and tallied on Form 17A before the constituency results were announced. The transfer of data from Form 16A to Form 17A suffered from 'low level of precision and reliability'[4] and this compounded the national anxieties.

Interestingly, although the discrepancy between turn out in Presidential and parliamentary elections was interpreted as evidence of rigging in favour of Mwai Kibaki by some observer groups, certain members of civil society and ODM, the Independent Review Electoral Commission's (IREC) 'analysis of counting and tallying in ten constituencies with huge voter turnout discrepancies demonstrate[d] convincingly that the discrepancies were probably due to human error and general incompetence.'[5] The Report also cites other possible causes for the discrepancies including difficult working conditions at the constituency tallying centres, pressure from Kenyatta International Conference Centre (KICC)-based ECK staff on returning officers to provide fast results, pressure from candidates and incumbents who wanted to know the results, lack of training and poor communication. Assuming that the Kriegler Report presents the 'correct' picture with regard to the elections, claims to massive rigging at ECK tallying centre by a section of the political elite and the drama witnessed glaringly at the KICC may have served to legitimize violence on voters viewed as having cast their ballot differently. If the view that some of the post election violence was organized months before the polling day as reported by the Commission Investigating the Post Election Violence in Kenya (CIPEV) and the Kenya National Commission for Human Rights , then the drama by certain politicians at KICC may have been a communicative signal to the 'troops' to be on standby.

Indeed, is it possible that by stating unequivocally in the media that rigging was taking place at the tallying centre the political elite was providing a coded message for violence to be unleashed? Knowing the chameleonic nature of the Kenyan politician, this proposition which is guided by the findings in the IREC and CIPEV reports principally, is not far-fetched. But again, knowing the stakes involved in the acquisition and maintenance of power, it is equally conceivable that some rigging, not identified by IREC, may have occurred at ECK headquarters (*see Muli, this Volume*) and that the loss of life and anarchy witnessed in Kenya may have been a consequence of spontaneous anger occasioned by frustration due to shattered hopes. Whatever the case, events following the polling on 27th December 2007 were depressing and are a clear manifestation of what greed for the maintenance or acquisition of political power can do to an emerging nation-state. It is a statement of the extent to which a corrupt and unaccountable leadership can go in the violation of the citizenry.

The symbolic verbal and physical confrontations at the Kenyatta International Conference Centre (KICC) from where results were being announced on live radio and television were to be directly mapped viciously and ruthlessly within communities around Kenya. Without doubt, tension was further exacerbated by public declarations made by a number of international observers that the results were not free and fair. The European Union (EU) publicly questioned the presidential results released by ECK, doubting the credibility of the vote tallying process. A visibly angry EU Chief Observer Alexander Graf Lambsdorff made reference in particular to discrepancies noted in the Molo presidential votes and which were not addressed by the ECK; the 'identification' of Molo Constituency as a site of rigged elections was volatile considering that the area has been an epicentre of violence at election time since 1992. It could be argued that the public statements, whether valid or not, served to provide additional armour to those who may have been 'planning violence' no matter the results, especially because the claims were not accompanied by calls for restraint, accommodation and non-violent options to the crisis. The emotional gestures, expressed publicly by foreign missions and national leaders, inadvertently gave 'legitimacy' to the violent actions that took place around the country. An aura of potential state collapse pervaded the country.

There was desperation in the air and the future of the country was quite bleak. But even as the violence was taking root, the ECK did not help matters.

On 30 December 2007, five Commissioners – Jack Tumwa, Alfred Ndambiri, Samwel Arap Ng'eny, Jeremiah Matagaro and Joseph Dena – spoke in their private capacities and called for an independent inquiry into whether any of their colleagues tampered with presidential election results before they were announced. Apparently, the figures received from polling stations did not tally with those announced. The five commissioners named Molo as one of the constituencies where the presidential elections could have been manipulated. Tellingly, after the Coalition government had been formed, IREC headed by Judge Johannes Kriegler argued that the discrepancies in the Molo votes were insignificant and that ultimately it was not possible to establish the causes of the delays or that they formed part of a comprehensive plot. IREC could not determine any numerical consequences of the anomalies.

Regarding the integrity of the results, IREC concluded that the *conduct of the 2007 elections in Kenya was so materially defective that it has been, and will remain, impossible for IREC to establish true and reliable results for the presidential and parliamentary elections.* Whether the elections were rigged or not remains immaterial because 'we will never know.' If IREC's final assessment is correct, is it possible that the invocation of 'manipulation of results' in certain constituencies was meant to add fuel to public anger at not only the regime in power but also those perceived to have supported the incumbent? But again, some rigging may have taken place though not seen as significant by the Kriegler Commission.

In an interview with Jeff Otieno (*Daily Nation January 3, 2008*), ECK Chairman conceded that he was under immense pressure at the time from different quarters. Asked if he released the results under duress, he retorted:

"What duress? I was only being pressured by foreign diplomats and Maina Kiai [Chairman of the Kenya National Commission on Human Rights] to postpone announcing the results of the elections until proper investigations were complete on rigging claims. Then ODM-K and PNU were pushing me too on the other hand to announce the results. But I decided to go ahead given the tension that was there in the country. Some people also came to me saying they had come to collect the document (Certificate) and I said I can never do that…Yes I delivered it. Because I had declared him the President, so what was wrong with delivering it to him?"

Despite the pressure not to announce, ECK did not postpone declaring the outcome of the polls because there was immense tension around the country which could have been exacerbated. Instead, on 30th December, 2007 the Chairman, Samuel Kivuitu, made the announcement that Mwai Kibaki had won. If the announcement was meant to deter election related violence, it did not. In fact, the declaration exacerbated violence on sections of the citizenry. Kenya was on a path towards self-destruction.

The calls for national dialogue

Following the announcement and the subsequent swearing in of Mwai Kibaki by Chief Justice Evans Gicheru, the country experienced unprecedented large scale violence as citizens were killed on account of their real and perceived ethnic identity, women raped, communities forcefully deported and property destroyed. The political elite did not come out strongly to condemn the violence, at least in the initial stages and Kenya, previously viewed as a beacon of hope for the African continent, was on the brink of total disintegration. In a Commentary on the violence, the *Daily Nation* (January 1, 2008) called on Mwai Kibaki and Raila Odinga to stop the mayhem. The editor told the two leaders:

> Never, since 1982 [after the attempted coup by the Kenya Air Force], has there been so much fear and uncertainty in the country. Never has there been so much animosity between people who have lived as good neighbours for many years. And the rights of Kenyans are slowly being squeezed, movement restricted and some broadcast rights suspended. Kenyans are dying, their property is being looted, and livelihoods are being destroyed. There is absolutely no doubt in the minds of Kenyans that this is the fault of your political parties. The chaos we are now experiencing is the handiwork of the tribal, economic, and political elite, which identify with you. The simmering power struggle between your two camps, which has been waged since 2002, has brought Kenya to the verge of a complete melt-down."

The newspaper editorial correctly observed that the violence was not just about the presidential results; it was the culmination of a protracted power struggle between two camps seeking political and economic power. Considering the benefits accruing from the acquisition and retention of executive power at the level of the presidency, none of the protagonists sought to genuinely address the violence. They were unmoved by the deaths, destruction and mayhem even when all mainstream media carried the headline on January 3 2008: "*Save our Beloved Country*". Affirming that 'there is no cause and no right more valuable than the right to life,' Kenyan media called on political leaders to stop the violence, lest they lose all credibility. Clearly, newsrooms in mainstream media viewed the political elite as able to call a halt to the crimes against humanity that were taking place around the country. There was subtle inference that politicians were 'in charge of the destruction' and could stop it if they chose to do so. They did not.

Right from the beginning, the country was in a serious stalemate which had the potential of being protracted and metamorphosing itself into a civil war with telling consequences. Kenyan journalist, Macharia Gaitho, reflecting on what was going on at the time wrote:

> ...who will save Kenya from the brink? Mr. Raila Odinga may be rightfully aggrieved at the election outcome. He may be enjoying the paralysis facing the newly-installed President, and salivating at the prospect of an Orange Revolution that will run the President out of town and pave the way for his own triumphant entry into State House. But this should be the time for statesmanship, not brinkmanship. Mr. Odinga may well have been robbed of electoral victory but this is the time to demonstrate leadership in the interest of the nation. Nobody right now is better placed than Mr. Odinga and his key ODM lieutenants, Mr. William Ruto and Mr. Musalia Mudavadi, to do what the government is unable to do – save the country from total destruction, and President Kibaki's people from the threat of genocide." (*Daily Nation, January 1, 2008*).

This journalist's view, though contestable, was that Raila Odinga was best placed to save the country by accepting the results as announced by the electoral body and paving the way for resumption of 'normalcy'. But many within ODM argued vehemently that the onus lay squarely with Mwai Kibaki because the results were being violently contested and the judiciary could not be trusted to arbitrate objectively, given its perceived proximity to the executive. The ODM leadership called for prayer meetings and 'peaceful' rallies and there were threats of making the country ungovernable. PNU argued that Kibaki had been declared winner by the ECK and he would not give up power. The country was in an extremely precarious situation and the moment was ripe for third party mediation.

The violence was ethnically pointed and citizens were targeted on the basis of an identity for which they had no choice. During the first twenty one days after the announcement of the results, three forms of violence can be discerned: spontaneous violence resulting from anger and frustration at the announcement of results perceived to have been rigged and directed mainly at members of the

Gikuyu and Kisii communities who were viewed as having voted for the incumbent; organised and systematic violence aimed at deporting particular communities notably the Gikuyu and Kisii from their land and dwellings especially in the Rift Valley in order to deprive them of economic opportunities and livelihoods; and excessive use of force directed at ODM supporters notably the Luo especially in Kisumu by government security agents. Later, as internally displaced persons flocked to safer zones, especially in Naivasha and Nakuru, swift and vicious retaliatory violence was meted by certain members of the Gikuyu community on the Luo and Kalenjin communities in late January 2008. Whereas most of the violence in January and February 2008 took an ethnic dimension, in certain parts of Nairobi, notably in Kibera, Mathare and Huruma, there was a class dimension to the conflict as tenants violently took over rental houses from landlords, perceived to have voted differently. But even in the latter case, ethnic considerations were at play.

Wide ranging attempts were made by local and international actors to try and resolve the crisis. One early effort to prepare the ground for dialogue was by the Concerned Citizens for Peace (CCP) who sought a local solution to the conflict from their meeting room at the Serena Hotel. But CCP mainly composed of peace activists including Ambassador Bethwel Kiplagat, George Wachira, Brigadier Daniel Opande, General Lazarus Sumbeiywo and the late Dekha Ibrahim among others was not trusted by sections of the political elite and was generally dismissed as a waste of time, especially by ODM. But in fairness, CCP had made the first move in calling for national dialogue and creating a space within the Serena Hotel for civil society actors to converge and share their feelings about the national catastrophe at a time that emotions were extremely high and the political elite were not willing to give way. Soon after, Kenyans for Peace, Truth and Justice (KPTJ), initially housed by the Kenya National Commission on Human Rights (KNCHR), congregated around the importance of factoring in 'justice' in the peace efforts.

Evidently, CCP had paid more attention to creation of 'calm and stability' and not asserted the centrality of 'justice' for sustainable peace. That was their initial approach to the conflict. But how are citizens to respond in a time of violent political crisis? Do they put out the fire and then seek to understand who lit it in the first place or do they chase the arsonist later come to marvel at the damage? Is there a pursuit that is more superior than the other? The answer to these questions will help us understand the dilemma of civil society in Kenya in January 2008. Disturbingly, well intentioned civil society organizations lost precious time as they jostled to understand the intricate relationship between 'calm, peace and justice' within the context of a disputed election.

Whereas some viewed 'calm' as a necessary condition in the pursuit of peace and justice and appeared to downplay the pursuit of electoral justice during the violent crisis, others argued that 'calm' was diversionary and that electoral justice ought to be pursued if the country was to be peaceful in a sustainable manner. Most in the latter group wanted matters related to the integrity of results resolved before pointed conversations about peace could be held. But in situations of extreme political divisiveness, notions of justice and fairness while not accompanied by calls for peace and the laying down of weapons and violence enhancing rhetoric are likely to exacerbate conflict by creating divergent rather than convergent expectations of the results. In such circumstances, conceptions of justice become arenas for contestation with each party taking the view that their position is the most ' just' and 'fair'. This could lead to delays in negotiations and consensus building and increase brinkmanship and extreme positions as strategies of maximizing benefits from the conflict. The complexity of the relationship between peace and justice is best played out in the protracted struggles in the Middle East. In our own case the over-used slogan "Haki Yetu" (Our Right) in Kenya during the political crisis was viewed by some as having traces of impunity especially in circumstances where it was accompanied by criminal activities. Despite this complex relationship between peace and justice, it cannot be denied that sustainable peace is impossible without justice.

Lacking consensus and clarity, civil society could not, at least in the initial stages of the violence, present a united perspective on how to deal with the violence and the political elite took advantage of this split as ordinary citizens died on account of the ballot. In addition, the positions taken by different groups served to weaken civil society because the tensions generated suspicion and mistrust. If civil society hopes to provide leadership in violent situations, more clarity on the interaction between peace and justice needs to be sought and shared widely.

Equally disturbing was the lukewarm reaction by faith based organizations. It was expected that faith based organizations would have provided leadership in resolving the political crisis given their role as neutral arbiters in Kenya's political history. However, during the 2005 Referendum on the proposed constitution and the run up to the 2007 elections, religious groups were deeply divided along ethnic and regional lines and the Muslims were split on the basis of a Memorandum of Understanding (MoU) allegedly signed by Raila Odinga and their leaders. Lacking legitimacy and credibility, local religious groups could not be mobilized to unite the nation and it was left to international ecumenical groups to call for peace. It is within that context that Archbishop Desmond Tutu, chair of the African Elders Forum, arrived in Kenya under the umbrella of the All Africa Conference of Churches (AACC). The short visit, rebuffed by sections of the political elite, was crucial because it opened the path for religious groups to participate in the negotiations. Urging the protagonists to accept an internationally mediated process, Archbishop Tutu heightened international interest in the humanitarian and political crisis.

Another earlier effort was by President Yoweri Museveni of Uganda, who was also chair of the East African Community. Although Museveni's call for restraint and return to normalcy was welcomed by President Kibaki and PNU, it was rejected by Raila and ODM in view of the fact that he had earlier on congratulated Kibaki on his re-election. Moreover, there was concern over rumours that Ugandan soldiers had been sent to Western Kenya to assist the government in quelling violence. There were also calls for restraint and compromise made by the United Nations. UN Secretary General Ban Ki Moon, in a statement from his office, urged that peaceful means be embraced in the resolution of the conflict. Recognizing the overzealous nature of the Kenyan police in dealing with demonstrators, he called on Kenyan security forces to show utmost restraint as they deal with the perpetrators of violence. For the Secretary General at the time, political leaders 'could resolve their differences peacefully through dialogue and making full use of the existing legal mechanisms and procedures.' (Ki Moon, 2008). Apparently, Ban Ki Moon was not aware that the legal option he was proposing was not being considered by the ODM leadership because the judiciary was viewed as compromised and lacking independence and integrity and could not therefore be a neutral arbiter. In any case, the 1992 and 1997 were contested in court but judges ruled against the opposition. A repeat scenario was being imagined in this high stakes election.

In addition, Western powers, notably the United States and the United Kingdom, weighed in and called on the African Union and the Commonwealth to help reconcile President Kibaki and Raila Odinga. Drawing on statements from the European Union observer mission that the electoral process had fallen short of international standards, Prime Minister Gordon Brown said that he wanted to see talks that would lead to reconciliation and unity; a situation in which Kibaki and Raila would 'come together in government,'[6] (*See BBC January 1st, 2008*).

The rapid response to the crisis in Kenya by the international community and leaders on the continent led to the establishment of the Panel of Eminent African Personalities (PEAP) by the African Union to help find a peaceful resolution to the stalemate. The Panel led by Kofi Annan, former Secretary General of the United Nations, and comprising of Benjamin Mkapa and Graca Machel brought PNU/Government and ODM into the Kenya National Dialogue and Reconciliation (KNDR) process as a forum for political engagement and resolution of the violent conflict. The goal of the process was to achieve sustainable peace, stability and justice through the rule of law and respect for human rights. Over a period of 41 days of negotiations at the Serena Hotel (Cana Room), under the leadership of the two Principals, the Negotiators (Martha Karua, Mutula Kilonzo, Samuel Ongeri and Moses Wetangula–representing PNU/Government and Moses Mudavadi, William Ruto, Sally Kosgei and James Orengo – representing ODM – signed a raft of major Agreements on 1st, 4th, 14th and 28th February, 4th March and 23rd July 2008. The Agreements sought to address the immediate and root causes of the national crisis, including what needed to be done to end the violence, the humanitarian problems, how to address the presidential election dispute and measures aimed at engaging historical concerns such as poverty, unemployment, land and constitutional reforms.

Through a range of mediation tactics[7], the Panel engaged the Principals and the Negotiators towards a power-sharing arrangement and the formation of a coalition government. The agreements were transformative because they set on course a number of key national instruments critical for political, economic, legal and social reform. The peaceful referendum on the Constitution on 4th August 2010 and promulgation on 27th August 2010 of a new Constitution with a devolved system of government and an extensive Bill of Rights was revolutionary. It remains a major accomplishment considering that within two years of signing the KNDR agreements a new Constitution was passed yet for over two decades constitutional reform had stalled.

The role of the African Union in the negotiations

Although the UN Charter has a provision against interference in the domestic affairs of member states, except under enforcement measures stipulated in

Chapter VII – the Constitutive Act of the African Union has a wider spectrum of engagement ranging from mediation to use of force in order to intervene in specific cases. Indeed, Article 4 (L) of the Constitutive Act mandates the "right of the Union to intervene in a member state pursuant to a decision of the Assembly in respect of grave circumstances, namely: war crimes, genocide, and crimes against humanity."

The African Union has a formal mandate to engage in mediation as part of peacemaking on the continent. This mandate is derived from three instruments:

- The protocol relating to the Establishment of the Peace and Security Council of the African Union (2002)
- The ECOWAS Protocol Relating to the Mechanism for Conflict Prevention, Management, Resolution, Peacemaking and Security (1999)
- The SADC Protocol on Politics, Defence and Security Cooperation (2001)

During the Heads of State Summit in January 2008, the African Union "expressed deep concern at the prevailing situation, stressed the need for those involved to be held accountable, called on restraint by all parties, [and] strongly urged the parties to commit themselves to a peaceful resolution of the crisis through dialogue and in conformity with the rule of law," (African Union, 2008). The Summit also urged the parties to support the Panel of Eminent African Personalities. The need for speed and single minded focus on Kenya had earlier been expressed by the then Chairperson of the African Union Commission (UAC) former President of Mali, Alfa Konare. When addressing the Executive Council, Konare emphasised that "Kenya is a country that was hope for the continent… if Kenya burns there will be nothing for tomorrow… Today if you look at Kenya, you see violence on the streets. We are even talking of ethnic cleansing. We are even talking of genocide" (Konare, 2008).

It is likely that the African Union chose Kofi Annan to lead the process because of his moral authority, political contacts and experience as General Secretary of the United Nations. As General Secretary he was instrumental in the formulation of Responsibility to Protect Policy, launched at the World Summit in 2005. As an official of the UN, he had witnessed many tragedies around the world and understood the urgency of the Kenyan situation. When he was rushed to hospital on 15th January 2008, the day he was due to fly to Nairobi, many Kenyans hoped that he would quickly recover in order to start his immense task of convening and coordinating the process of dialogue and reconciliation. While in hospital for a week, he was able to reflect on the task ahead and get the commitment of the international community[8]. In an interview with Martin Griffiths.

Annan said that his mandate was broad –

"I had a mandate which was quite unusual, and very short – almost one line – which is sometimes good. I also felt, as it was an AU mandate, we were going to need strong support from the international community, and I felt I had to organize it before I got in: get them to understand how I was going to approach the problem, what sort of support I needed from them, and how we should coordinate. Because I know that sometimes, when these things happen, lots of people rush in and sometimes different mediators come in and it leads to confusion. So I wanted to get it right from the beginning – that we should speak with one voice, and that I'm going in to do my best and there should be [just] one mediating process." They all agreed and said, 'We fully support what you are going to do.' (*The Prisoner of Peace*, Geneva, 9 May 2008, p.5)

In resolving the Kenyan crisis, the AU led initiative showed that it is possible for the continental body to contribute to peace through well coordinated and pointed local, regional and international collaboration. The Kenyan crisis was resolved because different institutions, supported by the Kenyan people, came together to address it, guided by the Panel of Eminent African Personalities. In a sense, therefore, a convergence of factors contributed to the resolution of the conflict. First, was the clarity of the framework for national dialogue under the umbrella of the AU, identified early on during the crisis. Second, was the role played by civil society organizations, media, private sector, religious groups and other stakeholders in Kenya in putting pressure on the political elite to engage in dialogue. By getting fully engaged in the national dialogue, Kenyans owned the process and buttressed the Panel of Eminent African Personalities (PEAP) who became facilitators in the peace process. Third, was the stature and calibre of the Panel. The three Panel members are respected and trusted locally and internationally. This translated into greater confidence on their ability to be neutral, listen to both sides and build bridges across political divides. The fact that they are African cannot be under-estimated: there is a sense in which "foreign interference" and impositions can be resisted by both sides in a political conflict. Fourth, there was immense local and international pressure exerted through the PEAP on Mwai Kibaki and Raila Odinga to avoid brinkmanship and reach consensus for the sake of the country. These factors created a sense of urgency to anchor national dialogue and ensure that Kenya did not degenerate any further.

Laying the ground

Prior to the KNDR process, important ground work had been prepared to cool off political temperatures. On January 2nd, 2008 Nobel Peace Laureate Archbishop Desmond Tutu arrived in Nairobi. Although Desmond Tutu had the moral authority to facilitate the dialogue, the protagonists were not yet ready to engage with each other. Raila Odinga insisted the election had been stolen and Mwai Kibaki argued that he had been declared the winner constitutionally and the only recourse open to the aggrieved party was through the courts. Both did not believe that their political destiny was dependent on their willingness to work together; because the country was split down the middle. Desmond Tutu brought international attention to the crisis in Kenya and legitimized the involvement of religious groups in its resolution but left without having made a significant impression on the political elite. The US Secretary of State for African Affairs, Jendayi Frazer, arrived immediately thereafter, followed on January 8th by four former Presidents: Tanzania's Benjamin Mkapa, Mozambique's Joachim Chissano, Botswana's Katumile Masire and Zambia's Kenneth Kaunda. They travelled to Eldoret, the epicentre of the post election violence, to assess the situation and were shocked by what they saw. That visit was transformative because it vividly underlined the gravity of the crisis.

The President of Ghana and the then Chairman of the African Union, John Agyekum Kufuor, was in Kenya between 8-10th January 2008 and held face to face engagement with Mwai Kibaki at State House and another with Raila Odinga at the Intercontinental Hotel. His verdict was that both sides had agreed that "there should be an end to the violence" and that "there should be dialogue" to be facilitated by a Panel of Eminent African Personalities. Earlier, British Prime Minister Gordon Brown had appealed to President Kufuor and former Sierra Leonean President Ahmad Tejan Kabbah to intervene. British Foreign Secretary David Milliband and US Secretary of State Condoleezza Rice issued a joint statement calling for restraint and intense political dialogue. Considering that it was not clear who won in view of the irregularities on both sides, these leaders called for Kenya's political leaders to take responsibility, stop the violence and find common ground for the country (*Reuters* January 2,

2008). These earlier efforts in pursuit of dialogue and reconciliation were significant in a number of ways. They provided important background information to the PEAP which was instrumental in the development of the strategy and approach to the process of dialogue. Throughout the period, one thing was clear: the country was divided and neither PNU nor ODM could claim ability to rule effectively without involving the other. A political solution, in the direction of power sharing, had to be sought.

But at what point was the idea of a coalition government in Kenya mooted? Was it during the National Dialogue and Reconciliation (KNDR) process or earlier? On January 16, 2008 the Centre for Strategic and International Studies (CSIS) organised a teleconference on Kenya: Assessing the Political and Humanitarian Crisis. The teleconference was moderated by Jennifer Cooke, Co-Director, African Program and the speakers were Michael Ranneberger (US Ambassador to Kenya), David Throupe (Senior Associate CSIS), Mark Bellamy (Senior Fellow-in-Residence, CSIS), Burkard Oberle (World Food Programme) and Sam Kona (Specialist in Conflict Media). In his contribution to the discussions, Ranneberger said:

> "At any rate, I was saying that our own running of numbers, both that are available from public sources and that we have privately, comes out with a sort of – we ran it six ways, and three of the ways Kibaki wins from anywhere by 50,000 to 150,000 and three of the ways Odinga wins by about the same margin, depending on how you run it. And, so you know, at any rate that led us to conclude that you know, half the people voted for one guy and half the people voted for another, and the only realistic thing to do was to push for some kind of a power sharing arrangement..." (*CSIS teleconference transcript* pg.4).

Thus almost at the outset, the USA took the position that there should be discussions which would lead to a power sharing arrangement and a commitment to an agenda for institutional reform related to elections and the constitution and a stoppage of the violence. Furthermore, the USA took the view that the violence was both spontaneous and organized, particularly in the Rift Valley. Recognizing that the international community would not support its demands indefinitely and that mass action could not be sustained for long, ODM was willing to participate in dialogue. On its part, PNU realized that it could not govern alone given the humanitarian and political crisis in the country. As a result, a way had to be sought to bring the key protagonists to a negotiating table and to reconcile the country. According to Ranneberger –

… we're trying to push them, obviously, towards dialogue. Privately, I will tell you that both Odinga and Kibaki have looked us in the eye and have said they're willing to engage in dialogue without preconditions, although with one precondition: Kibaki's not prepared to accept that he would step down, past apart from that, they both claim that discussion is wide open (*CSIS teleconference transcript* pg. 5).

Apparently, whereas in mid-January 2008 Mwai Kibaki and Raila Odinga were privately ready and warming up to the possibility of a coalition government, in public their supporters took extremist approaches with one group wanting to make unilateral decisions and the other calling on international pressure and pushing the government security apparatus to the limits through mass action. When ODM won the Speaker's seat in parliament on 15th January 2008, the need for a national dialogue became even more imperative for the government, if it was going to push through crucial legislation.

By the time Kofi Annan started the KNDR process under the mandate of the African Union, informed discussions about a political solution and a coalition government were on the table. However, major hurdles had to be surmounted by the Panel in order to reach consensus. Whereas the government under Mwai Kibaki believed the crisis could be resolved internally through dialogue, the opposition ODM wanted a mediation process guided by a foreigner acceptable to both sides. Raila Odinga insisted from the beginning that the election had been rigged and the presidency "stolen" from him. He maintained that his preconditions for dialogue would begin with Kibaki's resignation, a rerun of the presidential election, the formation of a transitional government, and an agreement to undertake comprehensive, legal and constitutional reforms. The ODM strategy was to maximally use the national dialogue and reconciliation framework to get concession before participating in the process. Meanwhile, Kibaki was strengthening his position as President. He delayed meeting Kofi Annan on 22nd January 2008 in order to hold discussions with President Yoweri Museveni, Chairman of the Heads of State Summit of the East African Community. Throughout, Kibaki affirmed his willingness to enter into dialogue with Raila Odinga but on condition that ODM accepted his presidency as legitimate, having been declared winner by the Electoral Commission of Kenya and sworn in constitutionally. He was not ready to negotiate on his presidency.

The process itself

The National Dialogue and Reconciliation process began in earnest on January 22nd, 2008 three weeks after the post election violence erupted across the country. It was led by the Panel of Eminent African Personalities, consisting of former President Benjamin Mkapa of Tanzania, former South African First Lady Graca Machel and former UN Secretary General Kofi Annan as Chairperson. The Panel relied on international diplomatic support and the technical support of the United Nations, including the Department of Political Affairs (DPA), the United Nations Development Programme (UNDP), the United Nations Office in Nairobi (UNON) and the Geneva based Centre for Humanitarian Dialogue (HD Centre). The Panel set up a secretariat and decided to make the KNDR process inclusive and transparent. As a result, civil society including religious leaders and community based organizations consulted regularly. The media were constantly briefed about developments. Despite the extensive consultations, Kofi Annan insisted from the onset that only one mediation team would be allowed; there should be no interference in the process; and the Chairperson would decide who to invite and when (*see interview with Martin Griffiths in "Prisoner of Peace"*). On 24th January 2007 Kofi Annan was able to bring the two leaders together and they shook hands in public, symbolically showing that they were willing to engage in dialogue.

The Agenda items

At the Fourth Session held on 1st February 2008 under the chairmanship of His Excellency, the Parties to the Kenyan National Dialogue and Reconciliation on the resolution of the political crisis and its root causes, namely the Government of Kenya/Party of National Unity and the Orange Democratic Movement, agreed on the following Agenda for the dialogue:

Agenda No.1: Immediate Action to Stop Violence and Restore Fundamental Rights and Liberties

After some deliberations, there was clarity from the Parties that resolving the national crisis through political engagement was a matter of immediate priority and a just and durable solution had to be sought as a matter of urgency. Discussions on Agenda No.1 were to be conducted to identify and agree on the modalities of implementation of immediate action aimed at:

- Stopping the wave of violence that had gripped the country since the announcement of the results of the Presidential Elections;

- Enhancing the security and protection of the population and their property;
- Restoring the respect for the sanctity of human life;
- Ensuring that the freedom of expression, press freedom and the right to peaceful assembly were upheld;

Agenda No.2: Immediate Measures to Address the Humanitarian Crisis, Promote Reconciliation, Healing and Restoration

Discussions were to be conducted to identify and agree on the modalities of implementation of immediate measures aimed at:

- Ensuring that the assistance to the affected communities and individuals was delivered more effectively;
- Ensuring the impartial, effective and expeditious investigation of gross and systematic violations of human rights and that those found guilty were brought to justice;
- Ensuring that the processes of national healing, reconciliation and restoration were started immediately.

Agenda No.3: How to Overcome the Current Political Crisis

Under this Agenda item, the Parties were to negotiate and agree on a solution *towards resolving the political crisis arising from the disputed presidential electoral results as well as the ensuing violence in Kenya.* The Parties appreciated that crisis revolved around the issues of power and the functioning of state institutions. Consequently, its resolution required making fundamental review to the constitutional, legal and institutional frameworks. The review would have the effect of redistributing power and ensuring more accountability and credibility in governance institutions.

Agenda No.4: Long-term Issues and Solutions

Poverty, the inequitable distribution of resources and perceptions of historical injustices and exclusion on the part of segments of the Kenyan society were viewed as constituting the underlying causes of the prevailing social tensions, instability and cycle of violence. Discussions under this Agenda item would be conducted to examine and propose solutions for long-standing issues such as, *inter alia:*

- Undertaking constitutional, legal and institutional reform;

- Tackling poverty and inequity, as well as combating regional development imbalances;
- Tackling unemployment, particularly among the youth;
- Consolidating national cohesion and unity;
- Undertaking a Land Reform;
- Addressing transparency, accountability and impunity

The Parties agreed that Agenda items 1, 2 and 3 would be resolved within a period of between seven (7) and fifteen (15) days from the date of commencement of the KNDR process while Agenda item 4 would be resolved within a period of one year after the commencement of the Dialogue (launched on 28 January 2008).

The Panel of Eminent Personalities decided to run a transparent process and provided regular updates to Kenyans through the media.[9] At the time of launching KNDR, hundreds of thousands of Kenya had been displaced from their homes, property destroyed and families rendered destitute, hundreds killed and others raped. Certain areas had been rendered ungovernable and State organs, notably the police, on many cases violated civil liberties, instead of protecting them. Citizen confidence in State organs was quickly being eroded and there were areas which the State had lost control to vigilantes and criminals. The country was on the verge of a standstill and this may explain why both parties may have agreed quickly on the need to end the violence and address the humanitarian situation, despite their disagreements on how to deal with the political issues. These initial agreements were strategic: by resolving the easier issues quickly, citizens were given confidence that the State had not fully collapsed despite the absence of law and order in many areas; much needed calm restored; and the space for dialogue expanded. Disturbingly, although relative calm was restored, the humanitarian crisis remained with hundreds of thousands of internally displaced people (IDPs) surviving on food aid and living in dilapidated tents around the country. Government support to IDPs was minimal, uncoordinated and half-hearted. Indeed, four years after the post-election violence, thousands of Kenyans are still living in tents even as political power struggles are entrenched and institutionalized. It seems likely that Kenya will go to the polls again before IDPs are resettled. The resolve to resettle them is not a priority to the elite.

Equally, thus far, there have not been well coordinated and impartial investigations of gross and systematic violations of human rights. Individuals who destroyed property, raped and murdered fellow citizens have not been brought to justice. This has created the impression that crime can be swept under the carpet and go unpunished. When impunity entrenches itself, it becomes quite difficult for the rule of law to be respected and this is fodder for anarchy. The involvement of the International Criminal Court (ICC) in the prosecution of leaders who bear the greatest responsibility for crimes against humanity during the post election period is only one step in the search for justice (*see Mbuthi Gathenji, this Volume*). The development of a culture of accountability for criminal actions committed is the responsibility of the Kenyan people themselves who must demand an end to impunity and the blatant abuse of citizens' rights by the political elite. If there was good will, some of the crimes committed could have been dealt with as envisaged in Agenda No.2 through existing legislation without recourse to a Special Tribunal. Surely, one does not need a Special Tribunal to prosecute individuals who committed arson, rape and murder.

Further, the political leadership has not participated fully in ensuring that the processes of national healing, reconciliation and restoration are taking place. The disparate efforts by the Provincial Administration, PEACE-NET, the Truth Justice and Reconciliation Commission (TJRC) and the National Commission on Integration and Cohesion (NCIC) and some civil society groups are not systematic and coordinated. The efforts can easily be subverted by the political elite through ethnic mobilization and manipulation. This reluctance to contribute in healing and reconciliation among communities may be a pointer that violence can again be used as a political tool.

The resolution of Agenda No.3 required a number of strategies, including a Retreat to the Kilaguni Lodge and the direct involvement of the two Principals. It is at the Kilaguni Retreat, away from the glare of media and the impatient crowd of supporters, that the idea of the Coalition Government was systematically explored. Although no agreement was reached on entrenching the post of Prime Minister in the Constitution, the Retreat allowed for a 'softening' of positions with regard to resolving the political crisis. In the final analysis, however, it is the Principals who agreed to power-sharing and Constitutional Amendment introducing a Coalition Government with a Prime Minister and two Deputy Prime Ministers. It took the Principals two hours with Kofi Annan, President Jakaya Kikwete of Tanzania (then Chairman of the African Union) and PEAP, to remove brackets from the contentious political issues, sign the National Accord Agreements and pave the way for fundamental reforms in the country.

Stakeholder engagement

The strategy of extensive consultations with civil society, religious groups, business and the media which had been adopted by PEAP right from the beginning of the negotiations was critically important in all the Agenda items but more significantly in identifying matters that needed to be addressed under Agenda No.4 on long-term issues.

Media played an important role in keeping pressure on the political elite to resolve the crisis. Granted there were moments of sensational journalism, but by and large the media sought to urge for an agreement and to get the country back on track. By constantly highlighting progress that was being made at the Serena negotiations, media reduced anxiety by keeping citizens fully aware of what was going on. It was easier for citizens to put pressure on the political elite to reach consensus.

The proactive involvement of civil society in the mediation process was immensely beneficial. First, right from the beginning of the crisis, civil society sought to look for solutions to the humanitarian crisis and the political stalemate. Groups provided material, and intellectual support to citizens in distress. Kenya driven humanitarian response was commendable: domestic contributions were mobilized and channelled principally through the Red Cross. Second, when extensive violence occurred in early January 2008 convenings of citizens in pursuit of peace prepared the ground for the eventual negotiators under Kofi Annan. Civil society actors took the initiative to monitor the elections and the violence, collect documents, record events and narratives, prepare possible scenarios for the resolution of the crisis and keep vigil on behalf of citizens. These initial actions had the effect of ensuring that the KNDR process had the critical background material it needed right from the onset and that it was locally owned. The third benefit for civil society involvement was the local demand for incorporation of truth and justice as necessary conditions for sustainable peace. In other words, in order for sustainable peace to prevail in the country it was necessary for truth about the elections and accountability for the violence to be addressed in the negotiations. Fourth, through wide ranging approaches including press statements, briefings to diplomatic corps, PEAP, the Africa Leaders Forum and the AU civil society provided much needed 'local legitimacy' for positions taken by international organizations about the crisis. Moreover, they served to buttress PEAP from accusations by the political elite. Finally, they worked closely with other groups including the private sector (through the Kenya Private Sector Alliance – KEPSA) to provide input into the Agenda items. Some of the input went directly to the recommendations for the National Accord and enriched it.

Civil society groups wanted certain concerns addressed decisively during the negotiations. These included a commitment to the enactment of a new constitution; judicial and police reforms; the disarmament of warring factions; demobilization and reintegration of armed groups and militias; focused action on youth issues such as employment; systematic analysis of the different forms of violence in order to show the various shades and categories of internally displaced persons (IDPs); legal protection for ethnic discrimination; land reform; measures to bring an end to impunity which had entrenched itself over the years; and legal and political accountability for the elections and the violence. Some of these concerns have been met but many more remain in unfulfilled. Fundamentally, the enactment of a new Constitution opened a path towards far reaching reforms. The promulgation of the Constitution was a revolutionary moment in Kenyan history.

Lessons learnt from the KNDR process

1. *Ensure quick, sustained and focused pressure before and during negotiations:* Normally, contending forces during conflict assume that peace efforts would wither out if they are dragged over time and frustrated. Patience is pushed to the limits in order to wear out the peace advocates or to gain maximum benefits from the crisis. That is precisely what happened in Kenya. Luckily, the African Union moved in quickly to assemble a team of seasoned Eminent Personalities that exuded confidence and had local and international legitimacy. PEAP did not tire but stayed focused until the National Accord was signed. Further, they maintained presence in the country and continued monitoring progress made on the Agenda items.

2. *Involve a credible intermediary:* The peaceful management of conflict may involve litigation, arbitration, negotiation and mediation. The last two require the involvement of an intermediary who is not party to the conflict, is credible, has integrity and can be trusted to be impartial. In situations where Parties consider their differences as irreconcilable, as was the case in Kenya, they tend to take extreme positions and a discourse

of non-negotiability is dominant. They distrust each other immensely and will try to reap maximum benefits from the negotiations. In the Kenyan context, the Party of National Unity (PNU) was of the view that they had won the presidential vote fairly, declared winners as per the Constitution. In contrast, the Orange Democratic Movement (ODM) believed that victory had been stolen from them. Whereas ODM did not trust the judicial process as a neutral arbiter and demanded that Mwai Kibaki steps down, PNU depicted Raila Odinga as a violent individual who is ready to use extra-judicial means to acquire power instead of following the constitution and seeking redress from the courts. With this type of extreme positions, an intermediary was needed to get the two sides to talk. Crucially, the intermediary had to be a *facilitator* of the dialogue.

On 29th February 2008 Mr. Oluyemi Adeniji was appointed to chair the negotiations in the absence of Kofi Annan. Mr. Adeniji had been Minister of Foreign Affairs of Nigeria from 2003 to 2008 and had served as a special representative of the Secretary General for Sierra Leone from 1999 to 2003. When he was brought to help address Agenda Item No.4, he was the Internal Affairs Minister of Nigeria. Despite his wide experience he did not command as much presence as Kofi Annan and therefore his engagement with the negotiators was low key. Working behind the scenes throughout the negotiations was the diplomat Amb. Nana Effah-Apenteng, Chief of Staff of the Kenya National Dialogue and Reconciliation Secretaria. The various leaders appointed by the African Union to resolve the Kenyan crisis appeared to command credibility and respect and this may partly explain how Kenya was saved from the precipice.

3. *Engage stakeholders deliberately and genuinely*: A major contributor to the success of the national dialogue was the deliberate involvement of the private sector, civil society, religious groups and the media. Although international bodies and development partners were also engaged, in the final analysis it is the Kenyan citizens who rallied behind the Kenya National Dialogue and Reconciliation process, owned it and gave it impetus. Through wide ranging submissions and interactions with the Panel and Negotiators, Kenyans ensured that the process remained on course. Indeed, the Panel would not have understood the root causes of the post election violence without this wide stakeholder engagement. When citizens own the process of conflict resolution the continue putting

pressure on the protagonists long after the Agreements have been signed. It is this resilience that has ensured that impunity is addressed and Agenda 4 items stay on the national radar screen, despite the lukewarm commitment by the political elite.

4. *Only one mediating team*: The fact that only the Panel of Eminent African Personalities were mandated by the African Union to lead the National Dialogue and Reconciliation process was instrumental in unlocking the impasse. The strategy ensured that there were no parallel negotiations. Further, it ensured that everyone was pulling in the same direction, there were no conflicting signals and that personal interests did not take precedence over national concerns.

The process of healing and reconciliation should be undertaken deliberately and rigorously. It should not be incidental. The invocation of community-based processes of truth-telling, healing and reconciliation driven by inter-ethnic dialogue and spirit of justice, tolerance and forgiveness is extremely important if we are to have harmonious coexistence. Culturally sanctioned narratives of forgiveness and show of remorse can be activated to address the contemporary problem. For example, amongst the Kalenjin the practice *Kebasta* in which communities donate livestock to aggrieved parties as a show of reconciliation and willingness to seek forgiveness should be considered in our pursuit of justice and reconciliation in the Rift Valley. Furthermore, the ritual practice of *Kianyiny* in which individuals are "sweetened" and "purified" after committing crimes so that they can be reintegrated into the community could also be considered on a large scale. These ritual practices of seeking forgiveness and showing remorse found in many cultures have the advantage of increasing community introspection and may contribute to sustainable peace. They should not however be seen as a replacement of the pursuit of justice for victims; they are symbolic expressions of the willingness to reconcile and seek forgiveness. They are also indicative of the human capacity to distinguish right from wrong. The pursuit of locally generated solutions to conflict is more lasting, even in a rapidly globalizing nation and should not be ignored. Even more urgent, is citizen education on non-violent expressions of dissent, entrenchment of the rule of law and an accountable and transparent leadership fully committed to democratic practice and social justice for all.

Agreements and Decisions

Public Statement

Kenya National Dialogue and Reconciliation
Mediated by H.E. Kofi Annan and the Panel of Eminent African Personalities

Feb 1, 2008

Preamble:

Goal:

To ensure that the National Dialogue and Reconciliation is carried out in a continuous and sustained manner towards resolving the political crisis arising from the disputed presidential electoral results as well as the ensuing violence in Kenya, in line with the agreement between His Excellency Mwai Kibaki and Honourable Raila Odinga, as publicly announced on 24th January and reaffirmed on 29th January 2008 at County Hall in Nairobi.

The final goal of the National Dialogue and Reconciliation is to achieve sustainable peace, stability and justice in Kenya through the rule of law and respect for human rights.

Noting with concern the situation of insecurity in the country;

We need to take the following steps to immediately halt the violence:

1. To the Police:

a) The police must act in accordance with the Constitution and the law and in particular the Police Act and the Force Standing Orders. While the police are entitled to use reasonable force to protect vulnerable populations and in case of self defence, live bullets must not be used on unarmed civilians in unjustifiable circumstances.

b) The security forces must carry out their duties and responsibilities with complete impartiality and without regard to ethnicity, political persuasion, or other partisan consideration.

c) The deployment of the security agents must at all times promote and reflect national integration and harmony.

d) In order to harmonise security activities at all levels, there is a need for the cross flow of information between administrative units and the leadership at every level.

2. To the Public:

a) All leaders should embrace and preach the peaceful coexistence of all communities and refrain from irresponsible and provocative statements.

b) Mobilise local community, religious, political, business and civil society leaders to hold joint meetings to promote peace and tranquility and stand up for justice and fairness.

c) All Kenyan citizens should stop acts of violence.

d) All illegal armed groups and militias should be demobilized and disbanded.

e) We appeal to all youths throughout the country not to participate in acts of lawlessness particularly those leading to harm or loss of human life and destruction of property.

f) We call upon the victims and those affected *by* violence to exercise restraint and avoid any acts of revenge or retaliation.

3. As to the restoration of fundamental rights and civil liberties:

a) Ensure that the freedom of expression, press freedom and the right to peaceful assembly are upheld. A suitable code of conduct on live coverage broadcasts, should be developed promptly by the Media Council in consultation with the Ministry of Information and implemented forthwith. This should include punitive measures against abuse.

b) Peaceful assembly as guaranteed by the Constitution should be protected and facilitated. Leaders and the public attending such meetings must ensure that meetings are peaceful, orderly and conducted in conformity with the law.

c) Impartial, effective and expeditious investigations on all cases of crime and police brutality and/or excessive use of force should be undertaken forthwith.

d) Enforce law and order to protect life and property, and to ensure that roads and railways are open and safe for people, goods and services. Major transit routes must be secured and safe passage on all internal road networks throughout the country be guaranteed.

e) All workers, both public and private, must be assisted to return safely back to their places of work. Reopen all institutions of learning and assist teachers and children to return in an environment of safety.

f) All internally displaced persons should be protected and assisted to return safely to their homes and places of work and their rights to reside anywhere in the country be upheld.

g) In order to promote food security, displaced farmers should be assisted to return to their farms. All farmers affected by the crisis should be assisted and encouraged to safely resume their farming activities.

h) Hate and threatening messages, leaflets, sms, or any other broadcasts of that nature must cease forthwith.

i) All criminal activities, particularly those of a violent nature, should be prosecuted forthwith.

Signed on this day, February 1, 2008.

On behalf of Government/PNU: On behalf of ODM:

_____   _____

Hon. Martha Karua   Hon. Musalia Mudavadi

_____   _____

Hon. Sam Ongeri   Hon. William Ruto

_____   _____

Hon. Mutula Kilonzo   Hon. Sally Kosgei

                                      _____

                                      Hon. James Orengo

Witnessed by:

For the Panel of Eminent African Personalities

_____

H.E. Kofi A. Annan

Chairperson

Public Statement

Kenya National Dialogue and Reconciliation
Mediated by H.E. Kofi Annan and the Panel of Eminent African Personalities

Feb 4, 2008

Preamble:

Goal:

To ensure that the National Dialogue and Reconciliation is carried out in a continuous and sustained manner towards resolving the political crisis arising from the disputed presidential electoral results as well as the ensuing violence in Kenya, in line with the agreement between His Excellency Mwai Kibaki and Honourable Raila Odinga, as publicly announced on 24th January and reaffirmed on 29th January 2008 at County Hall in Nairobi.

The final goal of the National Dialogue and Reconciliation is to achieve sustainable Peace, stability and justice in Kenya through the rule of law and respect for human rights.

1. With Respect to Immediate Measures to Address the Humanitarian Crisis:

a) Assist and encourage displaced persons to go back to their homes or other areas and to have safe passage and security throughout

b) Provide adequate security and protection, particularly for vulnerable groups, including women and children in the camps.

c) Provision of basic services for people in displaced camps:

  • Ensure that there is adequate food, water, sanitation and shelter within the affected communities - both those in displaced camps and those remaining in their communities.

  • Provide medical assistance with a special focus for women, children, and people living with HIV and AIDS and the disabled, currently in displaced camps.

  • Ensure all children have access to education. This will involve reconstruction of schools; encouraging return of teaching staff and provision of teaching materials, and assistance for children to return to their learning institutions.

d) Provide information centres where the affected can get easy access to information regarding the assistance that is available to them and how to access it, for example, support for reconstruction of livelihoods, or tracing of family members.

e) Operationalise the Humanitarian Fund for Mitigation of Effects and Resettlement of Victims of Post 2007 Election Violence expeditiously by establishing a bi-partisan, multi-sectoral Board with streamlined procedures to disburse funds rapidly.

f) The Fund is open to public contributions and all citizens and friendly countries, governments and international institutions to donate generously.

g) Ensure close linkages with the ongoing national and international assistance to enhance the effectiveness of delivery.

h) Ensure that *victims* of *violence* in urban areas are not neglected in the implementation of the *above*.

i) In order to promote food security, displaced farmers should be assisted to return to their farms. All farmers affected by the crisis should be assisted and encouraged to safely resume their farming activities.

2. With Respect to Immediate Measures to Promote Reconciliation, Healing and Restoration:

a) Joint peace rallies should be convened by all leaders of parties to promote peace and reconciliation.

b) Ensure that the freedom of expression, press freedom and the right to peaceful assembly are upheld.

c) Peaceful assembly as guaranteed by the Constitution should be protected and facilitated.

d) All-inclusive Reconciliation and Peace building Committees at the grassroots level should be established. The committees should *involve* the provincial administration, council of elders, women, the youth, conflict resolution/ civil society organizations.

e) Counseling support should be *provided* to those affected communities.

f) A national resettlement programme should be developed.

g) The law on registration of persons should be reviewed to remove the emphasis on ethnicity.

h) A Truth, Justice and Reconciliation Commission that includes local and international jurists should be established.

i) Welcome and encourage the United Nations High Commissioner for Human Rights investigatory team.

3. Recommendation to Parliamentarians:

Request the Speaker of Parliament to urgently convene a meeting of all members (Kamukunji) so that the Committee has the opportunity to inform Parliamentarians of the progress of the National Dialogue and Reconciliation.

4. Briefing on Progress to the Principals:

The Panel of Eminent African Personalities will provide periodic joint briefings to H.E. Mwai Kibaki and Hon. Raila Odinga.

5. Implementation of Recommendations:

Weekly progress reports on implementation of these and other recommendations to be made to the Committee by the relevant parties/institutions.

Signed on this day February 4, 2008.

On behalf of Government/PNU: On behalf of ODM:

_____   _____

Hon. Martha Karua   Hon. Musalia Mudavadi

_____   _____

Hon. Sam Ongeri   Hon. William Ruto

_____   _____

Hon. Mutula Kilonzo   Hon. Sally Kosgei

_____   _____

Hon. Moses Wetang'ula   Hon. James Orengo

Witnessed by:

For the Panel of Eminent African Personalities

_____

H.E. Kofi A. Annan

Chairperson

Agenda Item Three: How to Resolve the Political Crisis

Kenya National Dialogue and Reconciliation
Mediated by H.E Kofi Annan and the Panel of Eminent African Personalities

14 February 2008

I. Preamble:

Reaffirming the Goal of the National Dialogue and Reconciliation:

To ensure that the National Dialogue and Reconciliation is carried out in a continuous and sustained manner towards resolving the political crisis arising from the disputed presidential electoral results as well as the ensuing violence in Kenya, in line with the agreement between His Excellency Mwai Kibaki and Honourable Raila Odinga, as publicly announced on 24th January and reaffirmed on 29th January 2008 at County Hall in Nairobi.

The final goal of the National Dialogue and Reconciliation is to achieve sustainable peace, stability and justice in Kenya through the rule of law and respect for human rights.

Recognising under Agenda Item Three that, in large measure, the current crisis revolves around the issues of power and the functioning of state institutions, and also recognizing that its resolution may require adjustments to the current constitutional, legal and institutional frameworks, the parties negotiated and agreed on a solution *towards resolving the political crisis arising from the disputed presidential electoral results* as well as the ensuing violence in Kenya.

II. Regarding the disputed presidential electoral results, we examined the following options:

(a) Complete Re-count of the Presidential Elections

We agreed that any re-count, to be considered credible in the eyes of the Kenyan people, would need to be nation-wide, involving a ballot by ballot scrutiny of all of the more than 11,000,000 ballots cast on December 27th. We agreed that all ballots and electoral materials would have been made available at counting centres across the country before announcing a re-count. A re-count would need to be conducted under the full scrutiny of trained observers and party agents, who would have the right to scrutinize the counting and verify each and every ballot.

We agreed that a re-count would need to be overseen by a specially appointed independent body that enjoys the trust and broad support of all Kenyans.

We considered the timeline for a possible re-count. We agreed that the preparatory work required to make a re-count credible in the eyes of the Kenyan people and in keeping with international best practices could take up to three months.

We were concerned that a delay of several months could significantly increase existing tensions and delay resolution of the current crisis, and we recognize that the result of a re-count might not further Kenyan unity, and we therefore decided to review other options.

(b) Re-tally

We agreed that any re-tally, to be considered credible in the eyes of the Kenyan people, would need to be nation-wide, involving full scrutiny and re-tally of results sheets from all of the more than 27,500 polling station tally sheets and 210 constituency tally sheets.

We agreed that all forms would have to be made available across the country before announcing a re-tally. A re-tally would need to be conducted under the full scrutiny of trained observers and party agents, who would have the right to scrutinize the conduct of the process and the validity of each tally sheet, and would need to be overseen by a specially appointed independent body that enjoys the trust and broad support of all Kenyans.

While we agreed that a re-tally could successfully identify problems or irregularities in the tally sheets, a re-tally could not however identify the correct result in those stations or constituencies where problems or irregularities were identified.

For these reasons stated above, we decided to review other options.

(c) Re-run of Presidential Elections

We were not in agreement on the need for a re-run of the Presidential elections. We agreed however that, to safeguard the trust and confidence of the Kenyan people in the democratic process, the next election should take place only after electoral reforms, including but not limited to the reform of the Electoral Commission of Kenya, finalization of the work of the Independent Review Committee (see below), updating of the Voters' List, establishment and improvement of dispute resolution mechanisms and effecting measures to ensure enfranchisement of Internally Displaced Persons and refugees have been implemented.

We considered the timeline for these reforms, which would be essential to make the process credible in the eyes of the Kenyan people, and in line with international best practices, would be substantial and would take at least one year.

We recognized that Kenyans could not wait that long for a resolution of the crisis, and we therefore decided to review other options.

(d) Judicial Process

We agreed that a judicial process was no longer an option as the legal time limit had expired, and we therefore decided to review other options.

e) Forensic Audit

We considered a forensic audit of the electoral process. We agreed that an audit would have the advantage of investigating and making findings regarding the conduct of the 2007 election. We agreed that an audit will not reduce tension and violence and will not result in a solution to the crisis, and that the legal basis for such an audit was unclear.

We further agreed that the functions of a forensic audit would be best undertaken by an Independent Review Committee (see below).

f) Independent Review Committee

We agree to establish an Independent Review Committee that would be mandated to investigate all aspects of the 2007 Presidential Election and would make findings and recommendations to improve the electoral process.

The Committee will be a non-judicial body made up of Kenyan and non-Kenyan recognized electoral experts of the highest professional standing and personal integrity.

The Committee will submit its report within 3-6 months and it should be published within 14 days of submission. The Committee should start its work not later than 15th March 2008.

The findings of the Independent Review Committee must be factored into the comprehensive electoral reforms that are envisaged.

III. Regarding the need for a political settlement to resolve the current crisis, we agree on the following points:

We recognize that there is a serious crisis in the country, we agree a political settlement is necessary to promote national reconciliation and unity.

We also agree that such a political settlement must be one that reconciles and heals the nation and reflects the best interests of all Kenyans. A political settlement is necessary to manage a broad reform agenda and other mechanisms that will address the root causes of the crisis.

Such reforms and mechanisms will comprise, but are not limited to, the following:

- Comprehensive Constitutional reforms;
- Comprehensive electoral reform - of the electoral laws, the electoral commission and dispute resolution mechanisms;
- A truth, justice and reconciliation commission;
- Identification and prosecution of perpetrators of violence;
- Respect for human rights;
- Parliamentary reform;
- Police reform;
- Legal and Judicial reforms;
- Commitment to a shared national agenda in Parliament for these reforms;
- Other legislative, structural, political and economic reforms as needed.

We have only one outstanding issue under this Agenda Item, the governance structure, which is being actively discussed. Several options have emerged and the parties are going to consult their principals and leadership on these options and will revert to the Chair shortly.

We also agree that the issues in Agenda Item Four are fundamental to the root causes of the crisis, and are closely linked with Agenda Item Three. The implementation of the following reforms should commence urgently in concert with reforms of Agenda Item Three. However, these processes may continue beyond the timeline of the next election.

- Consolidating national cohesion and unity;
- Land reform;
- Tackling poverty and inequity, as well as combating regional development imbalances, particularly promoting equal access to opportunity;
- Tackling unemployment, particularly among the youth;
- Reform of the Public Service;
- Strengthening of anti-corruption laws/public accountability mechanisms;
- Reform of Public Finance and Revenue Management Systems and Institutions;
- Addressing issues of accountability and transparency.

We recognize that this settlement is not about sharing of political positions but about addressing the fundamental root causes of recurrent conflict, and we reaffirm our commitment to address the issues within Agenda Item Four expeditiously and comprehensively.

Milestones and benchmarks for the implementation of the reform agenda will have to be defined.

Signed on this day, 14 *February 2008.*

On behalf of Government/PNU:

On behalf of ODM:

_____

Hon. Martha Karua

_____

Hon. Musalia Mudavadi

_____

Hon. Sam Ongeri

_____

Hon. William Ruto

_____

Hon. Mutula Kilonzo

_____

Hon. Sally Kosgei

_____

Hon. Moses Wetang'ula

_____

Hon. James Orengo

Witnessed by:

For the Panel of Eminent African Personalities

_____

H.E. Kofi A. Annan

Chairperson

Acting Together for Kenya

Agreement on the Principles of Partnership of the Coalition Government

Preamble:

The crisis triggered by the 2007 disputed presidential elections has brought to the surface deep-seated and long-standing divisions within Kenyan society. If left unaddressed, these divisions threaten the very existence of Kenya as a unified country. The Kenyan people are now looking to their leaders to ensure that their country will not be lost.

Given the current situation, neither side can realistically govern the country without the other. There must be real power-sharing to move the country forward and begin the healing and reconciliation process.

With this agreement, we are stepping forwarding together, as political leaders, to overcome the current crisis and to set the country on a new path. As partners in a coalition government, we commit ourselves to work together in good faith as true partners, through constant consultation and willingness to compromise.

This agreement is designed to create an environment conducive to such a partnership and to build mutual trust and confidence. It is not about creating positions that reward individuals. It seeks to enable Kenya's political leaders to look beyond partisan considerations with a view to promoting the greater interests of the nation as a whole. It provides the means to implement a coherent and far-reaching reform agenda, to address the fundamental root causes of recurrent conflict, and to create a better, more secure, more prosperous Kenya for all.

To resolve the political crisis, and in the spirit of coalition and partnership, we have agreed to enact the National Accord and Reconciliation Act 2008, whose provisions have been agreed upon in their entirety by the parties hereto and a draft copy thereof is appended hereto.

Its key points are:

- There will be a Prime Minister of the Government of Kenya, with authority to coordinate and supervise the execution of the functions and affairs of the Government of Kenya.
- The Prime Minister will be an elected member of the National Assembly and the parliamentary leader of the largest party in the National Assembly, or of a coalition, if the largest party does not command a majority.

- Each member of the coalition shall nominate one person from the National Assembly to be appointed a Deputy Prime Minister.
- The Cabinet will consist of the President, the Vice-President, the Prime Minister, the two Deputy Prime Ministers and the other Ministers. The removal of any Minister of the coalition will be subject to consultation and concurrence in writing by the leaders.
- The Prime Minister and Deputy Prime Ministers can only be removed if the National Assembly passes a motion of no confidence with a majority vote.
- The composition of the coalition government will at all times take into account the principle of portfolio balance and will reflect their relative parliamentary strength.
- The coalition will be dissolved if the Tenth Parliament is dissolved; or if the parties agree in writing; or if one coalition partner withdraws from the coalition.
- The National Accord and Reconciliation Act shall be entrenched in the Constitution.

Having agreed on the critical issues above, we will now take this process to Parliament. It will be convened at the earliest moment to enact these agreements. This will be in the form of an Act of Parliament and the necessary amendment to the Constitution.

We believe by these steps we can together in the spirit of partnership bring peace and prosperity back to the people of Kenya who so richly deserve it.

Agreed on this date 28 February 2008.

_____
Hon. Raila Odinga
Orange Democratic Movement

_____
H.E. President Mwai Kibaki
Government/Party of National Unity

Witnessed By:

_____
H.E. Kofi A. Annan
Chairman of the Panel
of Eminent African Personalities

_____
H.E. President Jakaya Kikwete
President of the United Republic of
Tanzania
and Chairman of the African Union

The National Accord and Reconciliation Act 2008

Preamble:

There is a crisis in this country. The Parties have come together in recognition of this crisis, and agree that a political solution is required.

Given the disputed elections and the divisions in the Parliament and the country, neither side is able to govern without the other. There needs to be real power sharing to move the country forward. A coalition must be a partnership with commitment on both sides to govern together and push through a reform agenda for the benefit of all Kenyans.

Description of the Act:

An Act of Parliament to provide for the settlement of the disputes arising from the presidential elections of 2007, formation of a Coalition Government and Establishment of the Offices of Prime Minister, Deputy Prime Ministers and Ministers of the Government of Kenya, their functions and various matters connected with and incidental to the foregoing.

1. This Act may be cited as the National Accord and Reconciliation Act 2008.

2. This Act shall come into force upon its publication in the Kenya Gazette which shall not be later than 14 days from the date of Assent.

3. (1) There shall be a Prime Minister of the Government of Kenya and two Deputy Prime Ministers by the President in accordance with this section.

   (2) The person to be appointed as Prime Minister shall be an elected member of the National Assembly who is the parliamentary leader of -

   (a) the political party that has the largest number of members in the National Assembly; or

   (b) a coalition of political parties in the event that the leader of the political party that has the largest number of members of the National Assembly does not command the majority in the National Assembly.

   (3) Each member of the coalition shall nominate one person from the elected members of the National Assembly to be appointed a Deputy Prime Minister.

4. (1) The Prime Minister:

    a) shall have authority to coordinate and supervise the execution of the functions and affairs of the Government of Kenya including those of Ministries;

    b) may assign any of the coordination responsibilities of his office to the Deputy Prime Ministers, as well as one of them to deputise for him;

    c) shall perform such other duties as may be assigned to him by the President or under any written law.

(2) In the formation of the coalition government, the persons to be appointed as Ministers and Assistant Ministers from the political parties that are partners in the coalition other than the President's party, shall be nominated by the parliamentary leader of the party in the coalition. Thereafter there shall be full consultation with the President on the appointment of all Ministers.

(3) The composition of the coalition government shall at all times reflect the relative parliamentary strengths of the respective parties and shall at all times take into account the principle of portfolio balance.

(4) The office of the Prime Minister and Deputy Prime Minister shall become vacant only if -

    (a) the holder of the office dies, resigns or ceases to be a member of the National Assembly otherwise than by reason of the dissolution of Parliament; or

    (b) the National Assembly passes a resolution which is supported by a majority of all the members of the National Assembly excluding the ex-officio members and of which not less than seven days notice has been given declaring that the National Assembly has no confidence in the Prime Minister or Deputy Prime Minister, as the case may be; or

    (c) the coalition is dissolved.

(5) The removal of any Minister nominated by a parliamentary party of the coalition shall be made only after prior consultation and concurrence in writing with the leader of that party.

5. The Cabinet shall consist of the President, the Vice-President, the Prime Minister, the two Deputy Prime Ministers and the other Ministers.

6. The coalition shall stand dissolved if:

(a) the Tenth Parliament is dissolved; or

(b) the coalition parties agree in writing; or

(c) one coalition partner withdraws from the coalition by a resolution of the highest decision-making organ of that party in writing.

7. The prime minister and deputy prime ministers shall be entitled to such salaries, allowances, benefits, privileges and emoluments as may be approved by Parliament from time to time.

8. This Act shall cease to apply upon dissolution of the tenth Parliament, if the coalition is dissolved, or a new constitution is enacted, whichever is earlier.

Notes

[1] Campaigns had actually started in 2005 during the referendum on a new Constitution. The political rhetoric at the time was divisive and balkanizing along ethnic lines. Opinion polls conducted by a number of research institutions predicted a close election whose results would be determined mainly by the voter turn-out.

[2] Whereas it may be possible that some returning officers had made themselves inaccessible to ECK headquarters, others may have had genuine technical challenges with their mobile phones including lack of connectivity and failure to recharge the battery. The insinuation by the ECK Chairman that returning officers may have been 'cooking' the results was insensitive to the tension in the country and was quite unprofessional, a fact that Judge Johannes Kriegler was to note at the Independent Review Commission of the 2007 Elections (IREC).

[3] The Kriegler Commission investigated the 2007 elections and did not find any evidence of vote rigging at KICC. In the Commission's view rigging was undertaken by PNU and ODM in the polling stations. Furthermore, the Commission noted that the alterations of the results may have been undertaken because returning officers were requested to transmit provisional results to headquarters. Cancellations of the partial results were done on transmission of final results.

Although results from Molo, Juja, Limuru, Lari and Kieni were widely cited as evidence of rigging, the Kriegler Commission found no evidence of such. The report says "IREC has not been able to discover information demonstrating that the official results from these constituencies are not correct." *See* Review Commission Report 2008 p. 122-123. There have been claims that IREC was not thorough enough.

[4] See Review Commission Report 2008 p. 127. Apparently, some forms 16A never made it to the constituency tallying centres and were therefore not included in forms 17A. Two, all parliamentary and presidential election results for the constituencies sampled were erroneous. This meant that very few of the officially published figures were accurate. In one constituency (090 Kirinyaga Central) parliamentary candidate with most votes –if properly transferred and aggregated- was not declared the winner by the returning officer. IREC concluded that the results transfer from polling stations to constituencies, the tallying centres to constituencies, the transfer of constituency level presidential election results and the tallying at national level was of incredibly low quality and unacceptable.

[5] The purposive sampling adopted by IREC was contested by Kenyans for Peace, Truth and Justice in their piece titled "Evaluation of IREC's Statistical Analysis and Claims dated 1 October 2008." KPTJ argued that IREC should not infer population parameters from results based on a non-random sample. In a rebutall, Jorgen Elklit argued that the IREC analysis was 'so strong and so unequivocal' that there is no reason to doubt the validity of IREC conclusions. More particularly, IREC claimed that because the differences between ECK tallies and IREC re-tallies did not systematically favour any one candidate, we can conclude that discrepancies did not favour any one Presidential candidate. In their response to Jorgen Elkit, KPTJ stood its ground that the discrepancies favoured one candidate. Aware of this contestation, we make reference to the IREC Report because it was the official document released to Kenyans under Agenda 4 of the KNDR process.

[6] *Fears Mount over Kenya Violence,* January 1 2008. UK Prime Minister Gordon Brown urged both sides to work for a solution after what his government called "horrific killings". Mr Brown telephoned Mr. Kibaki and Mr. Odinga amid diplomatic efforts to broker a compromise, urging both to work for "unity and reconciliation". *See* BBC News on *http://news.bbc.co.uk/2/hi/africa/7166515.*

[7] Mediation is an intermediary activity which is undertaken by an acceptable and impartial third party and the primary intention is to voluntarily achieve a compromise settlement of issues that created the crisis in the first place. The stature and experience of the Panel members must have contributed building consensus especially on the sticky political question of power-sharing. Furthermore, the Negotiators knew each other well politically and socially.

[8] See Martin Griffiths interview with Kofi Annan titled: *The Prisoner of Peace,* Geneva, 9 May 2008.

References

Juma, Monica Kathina. 2009. Africa Mediation of the Kenya Post -2007 Election Crisis. *Journal of Contemporary African Studies*, 408 Routledge.

Khadiaga, Gilbert M. 2009. Regionalism and conflict resolution: Lessons from the Kenyan crisis. *Journal of Contemporary Africa Studies*, 437 Routledge.

Ki Moon, Ban. 2008. Address to the Opening of the 10th ordinary session of the AU heads of stae and government assembly. United Nations Economic Commission for Africa (UNECA), Addis Ababa.

Konare, A. 2008. Opening Address of the African Union Summit, 26th January in Addis Ababa.

Lafargue, Jérôme. (ed.) 2009. Special Issue: The General Elections in Kenya, 2007. *IFRA's Journal Les Cahiers d' Afrique de l'Est, No. 37*. Dar es Salaam: Mkuki na Nyota Publishers.

Ludeki, Chweya. (ed.) 2002. *Electoral Politics in Kenya*. Nairobi: Claripress.

Madior, F. Ismaila. 2008. Elections and Conflict Resolution: The West African Experience. *African Security Review*, 17(4):30-42.

Maupeu, Hervé. *et al.* (eds.) 2005. *The Moi Succession: Elections 2002*. Nairobi: Transafrica Press.

Mwagiru, Makumi. 2008. *The Water's Edge: Mediation of Violent Electoral Conflict in Kenya*. Nairobi: Institute for Diplomacy and International Studies.

Paul, Collier. 2009. *Wars, Guns, and Votes: Democracy in Dangerous Places*. New York: Harper Collins Publishers.

Walter O. Oyugi., *et al.* (eds.) 2003. *The Politics of Transition in Kenya: From KANU to NARC*. Nairobi: Heinrich Böll Foundation.

Acts and Charters

Article 4 (L) of the Constitutive Act of the African Union.

The United Nations Charter.

The Truth, Justice and Reconciliation Commission Act, 2008.

Reports

Commission of Inquiry into the Post Election Violence (CIPEV) Report, 2008.

A Report on the General Elections held in Kenya on 27th December, 2007 by Independent Review Commission (IREC), September 2008.

Roots Causes and Implications of The Post Election Violence of 2007. A Report of the research undertaken by Thabiti Taskforce 2008 Commissioned by Inter Religious Forum 2009.

Kenya National Dialogue and Reconciliation: Basic Documents. The African Union Panel of Eminent African Personalities and the Kofi Annan Foundation.

Transcripts

Rannerberger, Michael. 2008. *Kenya: Assessing the Political and Humanitarian Crisis*. Centre for Strategic and International Studies (CSIS) teleconference transcript (pg. 5)

Websites

http://news.bbc.co.uk/2/hi/africa/7166515 BBC January 1st 2008.

http://uk.reuters.com/article/2008/01/02/uk-kenya-idUKKRA12484320080102

Annan, K., and Griffith, M. 2009, The Prisoner of Peace -An Interview with Kofi A. Annan, Centre for Humanitarian Dialogue, Geneva, Switzerland *http://reliefweb.int/sites/reliefweb.int/files/resources/6F9DC0AD3921DFA7C12575890033E862-Full_Report.pdf.*

Newspapers

Daily Nation.

The Standard.

Chapter 7

Electoral Justice: The Antidote for Post Election Violence in Kenya

PLO Lumumba

Introduction

The most prominent political trend in the last half of the 20th century was the wave of democratization that swept through Africa, Eastern Europe and Latin America. Reasons for the wave, described by Samuel P. Huntington as *the Third Wave*,[1] are varied, ranging from the granting of political independence to previous colonies, to the international politics occasioned by the Cold War. In Kenya, for example, the politics of democratization started in earnest immediately after independence and dragged on to the 1990s. Subsequently, the study of democratization and comparative politics dominated the fields of law and political science. These studies attempted to understand and explain democratization. Interestingly, a common perspective on the nature of democracies remains elusive. Academic and non-academic definitions of the term "democracy" remain as numerous as the number of scholars in the field of social science.

Less studied has been the role, if any, of the electoral process in securing a peaceful and democratic State. Little attention has been given to the nature and consequences of different electoral systems. In fact, there has been a general assumption that the prevalent plurality and majoritarian electoral systems in most African countries, including Kenya, are the simplest, natural and most democratic systems of converting votes into representation.[2] In this paper, we analyze the significance of electoral processes in securing a peaceful and democratic society. Against this backdrop, we examine the Kenyan electoral design and evaluate whether, thus far, it has promoted or undermined peace and democracy. Consequently, we make recommendations on implementing electoral reforms. A congenial starting point in this discussion would be a brief attempt at a definition of democracy.

What is democracy?

Various scholars have developed varying perspectives to the study of democracy. Joseph Schumpeter talks of the 'classical theory', and the 'democratic method'[3]. Samuel P. Huntington developed three approaches: democracy in terms of sources of authority for government; democracy as a form of government; and lastly, democracy as procedures for constituting government.[4] Abdulla Bujra mentions three types of democracies; liberal democracy, social democracy, and socialist democracy.[5] In this study, we adopt Larry Diamond's approach in *Developing Democracy Toward Consolidation*, as a working formula.[6] Diamond mentions three approaches to the study of democracy: the electoral democracy, liberal democracy, and 'developmental perspective' democracy.

The electoral perspective is a somewhat reduced notion of democracy. It posits that democracy is nothing more than an electoral system that allows the people to choose their leaders in free and fair elections, and that elections should produce a legislature that is representative of the division of political opinion amongst the electorate. This perspective has been criticized by Huntington in his observation that governments produced by elections may be inefficient, corrupt, shortsighted, irresponsible, dominated by special interests, incapable of adopting policies demanded by the public good...but still democratic.[7] Terry Karl faults the minimalist theory as the "fallacy of electoralism," adding that this "flawed conception of democracy privileges elections over other dimensions of democracy and ignores the degree to which multiparty elections may exclude significant proportions of the population from contesting for power or advancing and defending their interests, or may leave significant arenas of decision-making beyond the control of elected officials."[8]

The second approach is the liberal perspective of democracy. This approach extends beyond the formal and intermediate conceptions of electoral democracies. It is characterized by exercise of power only by elected officials, the checks and separation of power, increased freedoms, pluralism, egalitarianism, a competent judiciary and respect for the rule of law. Richard Sandbrook argues that despite its well-known limitations, liberal democracy "confers benefits upon currently excluded citizens; it can also constitute an important stage in the socialist quest to extend democratic control to the social and economic, as well as political spheres"[9]

The third approach, the developmental perspective, recognizes that even the most liberal democracies may have shortcomings that may breed poverty, corruption, inequity and inequality. This necessitated the introduction of the development dimension in the conceptualization of democracy. This perspective holds that human development is an important aspect in the attainment of democracy. Ingelhart Ronald and Christian Welzel (2005) argue that "human development is meant to proceed as people attain greater autonomous choice in shaping their lives. Democratization promotes this process in so far as it institutionalizes freedom of choice based on civil and political liberties."[10] To this extent, a proper democracy should introduce a State that guarantees and works towards the social, political and economic development of the people. A democracy in this sense suffers the least levels of poverty, corruption, exclusion, inequity and inequality. With its focus on human development, it guarantees fundamental rights to its adherents, and gives similar weight to socio-economic rights as well as civil and political rights.

In discussing the role of electoral processes in attaining democracy, we adopt developmental perspective as the appropriate definition of democracy in the Kenyan context.

Significance of electoral designs in democratization and peace-building

One of the most important decisions for any new democracy is usually the choice of an electoral system. The advent of Huntington's Third Wave (the post 1960 shift of several states from authoritarian—predominantly military—to democratic rule) was accompanied by the search for an ideal electoral system for the new political dispensations. Indeed, the 1990s witnessed an explosion of innovation and reform in the electoral systems, especially as the new democracies in Africa, Asia, Eastern Europe, Latin America and the former Soviet Union began actively reforming their political and electoral systems, and looking for options and experiences from elsewhere.

Electoral systems are, at the most basic level, mechanisms for translating individual political preferences in an election into seats won by parties and candidates. These seats constitute the governance structure of a State. The integrity of the electoral process ultimately has weighty implications on governance of the State. Beyond the basic procedural essence of an electoral system, there are other implications on peace and [developmental] democracy in a State. This is evidenced from the following criteria for choosing an electoral system design, as proposed by the International Institute for Democracy and Electoral Assistance (IIDEA).[11] This criteria sums up the goals of a particular political system, the pitfalls it aims to avoid, and, in a broad sense, what the governance structure should look like.

Criteria for an electoral design

Representation: The foremost goal of an electoral process is to realize electoral democracy: the authority to exercise power derived from the will of the people. This popular will takes various shades: geographical, ideological, party-political, and descriptive representation. Geographical representation implies that every region should have a member of the legislature whom it seconds into the governance structure, and who is ultimately accountable to them. Ideological representation ensures that different opinions on governance are represented in the State structure. Party-political representation implies that the party with the most electoral votes has more say in the governance structure, for example, by having majority seats in the legislature, thereby representing the majority view. Finally, the concept of descriptive representation considers that the legislature should reflect the constitution of a particular society by including both men and women, the young and the old, the wealthy and the poor, and all the ethnic, racial, religious and other social groupings in the society. An electoral democracy must provide these four types of representation.

Making elections accessible and meaningful: Electoral democracies should give the electorate a chance to take part in governance, either directly or indirectly, through electoral choice. This is a fundamental right as provided by Article 21 of the Universal Declaration on Human Rights (UDHR) and Article 25 of the International Covenant on Civil and Political Rights (ICCPR). The electoral design should therefore ensure three things. First, there must be *ease of voting* so that everyone has an opportunity to exercise their political rights. Second, the electoral design should ensure that *every vote cast is significant* to the outcome of the elections, and alters the future direction of government. Third, the elections should ensure that the *body being elected has power to effect changes in governance*, and hence reflect policy preference in governance. Hollow elections in authoritarian systems of government where the legislature is subordinate to the executive make little impact on governance.

Providing incentives for conflict management and conciliation: Electoral systems can also become causes of civil strife or tools of building peaceful and stable societies. Electoral systems that allow for exclusive governance and the manipulation of ethnic, racial, religious, geographic or other divisions ultimately result in war when some of the excluded groups feel short-changed by the electoral process. The excluded groups then resort to other unlawful means to include themselves in governance.

On the other hand, electoral systems can also be modeled to provide incentives for conflict management and conciliation, especially in conflict-prone societies, and also societies emerging from civil strife. Some systems will encourage political parties to make inclusive appeals outside their core voter base. Ultimately, this is reflected in mainstream, inclusive and unifying party manifestos, and the phasing out of exclusive and divisive parties and policies modeled along ethnic, racial, religious or extremist and fanatical lines. Such an electoral system creates peaceful and stable societies.

Facilitating stable and efficient government: Sound electoral designs can facilitate stable and efficient governments in three ways. First, the fact that the electorate sees an electoral system as fair will grant legitimacy to the government. Popular legitimacy of a government extends to acceptance of the government's programmes and policies, e.g. tax collection. This stabilizes society. Second, the electoral process should put into power a government that can comfortably govern and enact legislation. An electoral process that puts into power a lame-duck President who lacks legislative support is defective. Third, the electoral system should avoid discrimination against particular political parties or interest groups.

Political accountability, legislative opposition and oversight: Electoral democracy is a crucial agency for representative democracy. To that extent, one very important tenet of representative democracy that should be secured by an electoral system is accountability. Indeed, representative democracy posits that governments or individual representatives produced by electoral processes should be accountable to the electorate to the very highest degree. This means that the electoral process should give the voters a mechanism to control governance by electing parties and leaders prepared to implement the will of the people, and remove those that betray that will.[12] This is the only way that democracy can remain true to the needs of the people. Aside from accountability, the electoral system should ensure that alternative voices are represented in governance through legislative opposition and oversight. This is indeed crucial in that it gives effect to the maxim "Give the majority their way, and the minority their say".

Democratic consolidation: One of the ironies of electoral democracies in Africa is that they have been used to undermine the very essence of democracy – the will of the people. This is where electoral processes are conducted under one—party autocratic regimes. An ideal electoral design should promote democratic consolidation by encouraging multi-partyism, thereby giving effect to fundamental liberties such as freedom of expression, conscience and speech. John M. Carey argues that a broader range of winning parties leads to greater representation of diverse values. Thus, it should follow that a country with more political parties will be more democratic by representing more of the public's views.[13]

Conforming to international and regional standards: Any country designing an electoral system should conform to international and regional standards on electoral democracies, contained in international and regional covenants and treaties in force at that time. International treaties include the 1948 UDHR and the 1966 ICCPR that includes principles such as free, fair and periodic elections that guarantee universal adult suffrage, secrecy of the ballot, freedom from coercion, and the principle of one person, one vote. These principles are indeed critical to the realization of democracy in the human development perspective.

From the foregoing discussion, we can see that electoral democracy is a critical aspect of democracy and peaceful and stable States. It is also agreeable that particular electoral designs either promote or undermine peace-building and democracy in a State. The choice of an electoral system should ensure that the political cleavages of a society are properly addressed by the electoral legal framework in such a way that the main conflicts and differences between and among social groups can be accommodated through the system of political representation. This is to guarantee political inclusiveness and representation.[14]

Below are the four main types of electoral systems and their essential characteristics:[15]

Single Member Plurality (SMP)

Commonly known as "First-Past-The-Post" (FPTP), this system is considered the simplest. The country is divided into electoral constituencies, each of which chooses only one candidate as its representative in Parliament. The winner in each constituency is the candidate who receives a minimum of one more vote than each of the other candidates, and does not have to obtain more votes than all the others combined. Although this system may mean that a party with a minority of votes countrywide becomes the ruling party and although it unduly disadvantages small parties, the SMP system is reputed to entrench the accountability of the MP to the constituency.

Single Member Majority (SMM)

In a Single Member Majority (SMM) system the country is also divided into constituencies but the advantage of the SMM over the SMP system is that the winner must obtain an absolute majority of votes in the constituency. Some states, e.g. Zimbabwe, use this system for Presidential elections. Where a Presidential candidate fails to secure an outright majority, a run-off election is often required.

Proportional Representation System (PR)

Although there are various types of Proportional Representation systems, the commonly used variant is the closed party list system. In most PR systems the whole country is taken to constitute a single constituency so no constituency delimitation process is required, as would be the case with the FPTP and SMM. The PR system generally ensures that all parties contesting an election have some representation in Parliament in proportion to the total number of valid votes cast. Although this system is reputed to ensure better representation of minority groups and a better reflection of public opinion, it tends to link Members of Parliament to parties rather than to the electorate.

Mixed Member Proportional System (MMP)

The Mixed Member Proportional system combines the key elements of the FPTP and the PR systems. The system allows for some Members of Parliament to be elected through the FPTP system while others occupy legislative seats through the closed party list system. Although many ordinary voters find the MMP confusing it tends to maximize the positive aspects of both the PR and the FPTP, namely broad representation and accountability. On the other hand, the MMP also embodies the negative aspects of both PR and FPTP.

Electoral democracy in Kenya

Today, Kenya prides itself as a 48–year-old democracy. The country has a brief history of electioneering. The December 2007 General Elections were Kenya's tenth General Elections since Independence. The elections which produced the first independence government were held in May 1963, under the supervision of the then colonial government. Subsequent General Elections were held 1969, 1974, 1979, 1983, 1988, 1992, 1997, 2002 and 2007. Out of these, only the 1963 and the 2002 elections have been credited as democratic.[16]

Despite the frequency of elections in Kenya, the country was ranked as number 103 out of 167 countries on the democratic scale by the Economist Intelligence Unit in 2008, and classified as a hybrid regime. The scale ranged from full democracies, flawed democracies, hybrid regimes and authoritarian regimes.[17]

It is remarkable that the Kenyan electoral process has time and again left the country in civil unrest. Indeed, varying degrees of ethnic clashes have been experienced before, during, or after every multi-party General Elections since 1992. In Kenya's last election, the 2007 General Elections, the country reached the brink of a fully-fledged civil war, resulting in the deaths of more than one thousand people, internal displacement of hundreds of thousands of citizens, and the destruction of property worth hundreds of millions of shillings. The cycle of violence associated with the electoral process can be traced not only to the flawed electoral process, but also the system and nature of governance put in place by the electoral system. The electoral process has attracted the same criticism levied on Schumpeter's procedural democracy theory: it ensures the selection of elites into political office, but does not guarantee *democratic governance*.

This problem can be traced to how the designers of, and ultimately, the contestants in the electoral process in Kenya view the state: an economic largesse to be appropriated by the winner in a high-stakes, zero-sum political game. Their objective becomes primitive accumulation by an ethnic conspiracy constructed as a means of winning or retaining power. Because the electoral system essentially encourages this view, the end product of the "democratic" electoral process becomes a conflict-prone State characterized by poverty, corruption, gross inequalities, political oppression, ethnicity, nepotism and social exclusion. Below, we briefly review Kenya's electoral design before the promulgation of the new Constitution on 27th August 2010.

The electoral framework in Kenya

Kenya's electoral design was essentially a Single Member Plurality (SMP) electoral system, also known as the "First-Past-The-Post" (FPTP) system. This system was used in the Presidential, Parliamentary and Local Government elections, with additional requirements for Presidential candidates to garner 25% of the vote in at least 5 provinces to become President.[18] The electoral framework was found in international and regional instruments, and also Kenya's constitutional and legislative provisions.

International and regional instruments affecting the electoral process in Kenya

The international standards relating to elections and electoral processes were derived from a number of international instruments that describe the various components of civil and political rights and freedoms. They include the 1948 Universal Declaration of Human Rights (UDHR),[19] the 1966 International Covenant on Civil and Political Rights (ICCPR),[20] the International Convention on the Elimination of All Forms of Racial Discrimination (ICERD), the Convention on the Elimination of All Forms of Discrimination Against Women (CEDAW) and the Convention on the Rights of Persons with Disabilities (CRPWD).

Regional instruments to which Kenya is a party include the African Charter on Human and People's Rights (ACHPR), the African Union Declaration on the Principles Governing Democratic Elections in Africa (2002) and most recently the African Charter on Democracy, Elections and Governance (2007).

The former constitutional and legislative framework for elections in Kenya

Elections in Kenya were governed by the following laws:

(a) The Constitution, Act No. 5 of 1969 (as amended)

(b) The National Assembly and Presidential Elections Act, Cap. 7.

(c) The Local Government Act, Cap. 265.

(d) The Election Offences Act, Cap 66.

(e) The Kenya Broadcasting Corporation Act, Cap. 221.

(f) The Public Order Act, Cap. 56.

(g) The Preservation of Public Security Act, Cap. 57.

(h) The Registration of Persons Act, Cap. 10.

(i) The Police Act, Cap. 84.

(j) The Societies Act, Cap. 108.

(k) The Penal Code, Cap. 63.

The Constitution

Section 1A provided that the Republic of Kenya shall be a multi-party democratic state. The Constitution further stipulated that to be elected President, one needed to have the highest numbers of votes cast; 25% or more in at least five of the eight provinces; be elected to Parliament in one's constituency. It stated that the term for the President would be five years with a maximum of two terms (s.9). The Constitution divided Kenya into constituencies and stated that each constituency shall elect one Member of Parliament nominated by a political party, and that 12 members of Parliament would be appointed by the President in proportion to the representation of each party in the National Assembly (s.33).

Section 41 created the Interim Independent Electoral Commission of Kenya (IIECK) and provided for their nomination by the Parliamentary Select Committee on Administration of Justice, and appointment by the President in consultation with the Prime Minister. Section 41B created the Interim Independent Boundaries Review Commission and provided for their nomination by the Parliamentary Select Committee on Administration of Justice, and appointment by the President in consultation with the Prime Minister.[21]

Section 41C provided for electoral boundaries review and constituency and local authority units demarcation conducted by the Interim Independent Electoral Commission of Kenya (IIECK).[22] It also provided that the delimitation of election boundaries take into account the following: density of population, and adequate representation of urban and sparsely populated rural areas; population trends; means of communication; geographical features; and community interest.

Delimitation of constituencies became more significant because of the creation of the Constituency Development Fund (CDF) by the Constituency Development Fund Act[23] as a form of devolved fund. The Fund previously comprised an annual budgetary allocation equivalent to 7.5% of the

Government's ordinary yearly revenue and any other money that accrued to the Fund. However, in the Government 2009/2010 yearly budget, read by the Finance Minister in Parliament on June 11, 2009, the constituency replaced the district as the unit for channeling devolved funds through the CDF Act. To this extent, efficient and scientific delimitation of constituencies sought to improve the quality of governance through devolution of funds to the grassroots.

The promulgation of the new Constitution and the entrenchment of devolution demands a review of Acts related to elections. This process, to be led by the Commission for the Implementation of the Constitution will lay the foundation for the 2012 elections. Some of the Acts to be reviewed include the following:

(a) The National Assembly and Presidential Elections (NAPE) Act
NAPE is both the procedural and substantive law for registration of electors and holding of elections to the office of President and to the National Assembly. It also regulated the conduct of the Electoral Commission and of political parties participating in elections in Kenya and various matters connected with and incidental to the foregoing.

(b) The Local Government Act
The Act provides for the establishment for local authorities, defines their functions and provides for the election of councillors. Section 58(1) of the Act provides that whenever there are elections being held under the National Assembly and Presidential Elections Act (NAPE), there shall simultaneously be held elections of local authority councillors.

(c) The Election Offences Act, Cap. 66
The Act provides for acts that constitute electoral offences, and stipulates procedures for prosecution and the possible sanctions.

(d) The Societies Act, Cap. 108
The Act provides for the registration of political parties, which are considered societies under the Act. Before the elections, the Registrar-General provides the IIECK with a list of all political parties registered under the Societies Act. Under this Act, the Registrar-General's office has the authority to audit the accounts of political parties.[24]

(e) The Police Act, the Preservation of Public Security Act and the Public Order Act

These Acts provide for the duties of police officers in maintaining public order and preservation of security. To that extent, the Acts provide for the issuance of a notice of 3-14 days of campaign meetings held by political parties, and the hours within which such meetings can be held (between 6 a.m. and 6 p.m.).

(f) The Kenya Broadcasting Corporation Act, Cap. 221

This Act regulates the establishment of KBC, the national broadcaster. It stipulates that KBC must give fair coverage to all political parties and their viewpoints and that it must provide free air time to all political parties contesting for the elections during the campaign period. This is defined as "the period between the initiation of an election under the provisions of the relevant law pertaining to the election and the eve of the polling day."

(g) The Political Parties Act of 2007

The Act provides a regulatory framework for the registration and operation of political parties. Among its requirements is that political parties must have at least 200 registered voters as members in every constituency. This is to ensure that every political party should seek to appeal across geographical and ethnic boundaries as a means of conciliation and peace-building.

Elements of Kenya's electoral design that undermined democracy and peace-building

Since the end of the mediation process brokered by the Panel of Eminent African personalities, and chaired by Dr. Kofi Annan, and the enactment of a new Constitution in 2010, the country has witnessed fundamental electoral reforms. The Constitution of Kenya Amendment Act No, 10 of 2008 dissolved the Electoral Commission of Kenya that oversaw the highly discredited 2007 General Elections, and replaced it with a lean and independent Interim Independent Electoral Commission. Its members were nominated by the Parliamentary Select Committee on Administration of Justice, approved by Parliament, and then appointed by the President in consultation with the Prime Minister. The Interim Independent Boundaries Review Commission was also created to take over the defunct ECK's function in delimitation of boundaries, and to review electoral boundaries through a scientific criteria.

There are certain electoral features with direct links to governance, which were reviewed in the new Constitution:

i. Single Member Plurality (SMP) or the "First-Past-The-Post" (FPTP) system

As discussed further above, this system envisages a winner-take-it-all Presidential contest whereby a presidential candidate with less that 50% of the vote appropriates the entire largesse of government, coupled with the imperial Presidential powers.[25] The FPTP system creates a high-stakes zero-sum game electoral scenario. Ndegwa observes thus:

> "Indeed, for countries that adopted plurality systems, the nature of democratic governance tended towards majority rule and minority exclusion rather than legitimate government. Such post-independence governments collapsed in part from the discontent of groups shut out of the political process, first by the electoral system and, thereafter, by the more openly exclusionary military or single-party regimes."[26]

Because Kenya's political culture is extremely ethnic-based, electoral contests become ethnic contests whereby the winners engage in primitive accumulation at the expense of the losing communities, which are then excluded from governance.[27] Indeed, the winner-take-all electoral and governance design was blamed for the outbreak of violence after President Mwai Kibaki was announced winner of the Presidential poll.[28] Kenya's unsavory political history has created a society split along ethnic lines. Therefore in considering electoral reform, a critical element of the new system was an electoral model that encourages political alliances not only in electoral contests, but also in governance. The FPTP system had failed to provide such incentives.

The FPTP also failed to provide equitable representation on terms of descriptive representation. For example, gender parity in the number of legislative seats was one of the widest in the world. Equally crucial aspects such as equity in minority representation were not provided for by the FPTP system. This impacted negatively on the development levels of regions occupied predominantly by excluded groups, and also along gender demographics.

ii. Imperial Presidential Governance Structure

The significance and efficiency of an electoral system is heavily determined by the governance structure of the State. In terms of significance, the Kenyan parliamentary and civic elections did not make sufficient impact on governance, because of the overbearing shadow of an imperial executive Presidency on the legislative processes. To this extent, members of Parliament seconded by their constituents made very limited impacts on policy changes in Government. This undermined the right of a voter to determine how to be governed, as enshrined under the UDHR.

For the electoral process to be more democratic, all the institutions subject to the electoral process (including parliamentary and civic bodies) were empowered by the new Constitution to provide adequate and legitimate representation of the will of the people.

Secondly, the electoral management body, the IIEC, had inherited the same operational framework of the defunct ECK, which allowed manipulation of the electoral process and hence tainting the integrity of electoral results. The new Constitution entrenches an independent electoral body that cannot be manipulated by the executive.

The imperial Presidential structure also allowed the incumbent to use State power and resources to restrict political activity of opposition political parties. Those powers have been trimmed significantly by the new Constitution.

iii. Absence of Transitional Mechanisms for Democratic Changeover of Power from one party to Another

One less appreciated aspect of the electoral process that has direct consequences on peace and stability is the transitional arrangements of political power. Because of the nature of Kenya's problem with impunity and the collapse of the rule of law, and undemocratic governance characterized by corruption and primitive accumulation, democratic transition had become an unattractive prospect for an incumbent. This was because of two reasons: first, the fear of prosecution of the outgoing regime's leaders by the incoming government; and second, the loss of access to state resources for personal gain. Mpumlwana observes:

> "The other factor that discourages voluntary handover of political power is the use or abuse of state power or resources to persecute ex-political leaders or to settle political scores against opponents. This creates a situation similar to prisoner's dilemma or zero-sum-game in which retiring from politics or accepting defeat by political opponents is associated with risks and persecution. Political authority in many developing or underdeveloped countries is often associated with accessing resources and influence for personal well-being or

personal wealth. Clearly those benefiting would wish that these privileges and resources would last for ever."[29]

One of the reasons cited by the Independent Review Commission (IREC) for the electoral crisis in Kenya after the 2007 General Elections was the lack of a transitional mechanism for the handover of power from an incumbent to a new President elected through democratic elections. A sound and systematic transitional arrangement gives ample time for electoral disputes to be resolved before a president is sworn into office. This has the effect of removing anxieties associated with misgivings over flawed elections, and the lack of mechanisms for redress, as was seen in the 2007 General Elections.

Another crucial aspect of governance that ensures democratic and peaceful transitions after an electoral process is sanctity of the rule of law. Democratic change-over of power becomes less tense where the incoming and outgoing governments are assured of fair treatment under the justice system. Kenya's flirtation with impunity for the last 48 years has created resistance to change by those who have benefitted from the collapse of the rule of law. It is therefore important that impunity is removed from Kenya's governance and political culture.

Conclusion

Kenya is currently in a post-conflict reform mood after the successful mediation talks that ended the blood-letting in early 2008 and the enactment of a new Constitution in 2010. Chapter seven of the current Constitution of Kenya lays down the principles of the electoral system in Article 81. The system is expected to comply with the following principles:

a) freedom of citizens to exercise their political rights under Article 38;

b) not more than two-thirds of the members of elective public bodies shall be of the same gender;

c) fair representation of persons with disabilities;

d) universal suffrage based on the aspiration for fair representation and equality of vote; and

e) free and fair elections, which are:

- by secret ballot;
- free from violence, intimidation, improper influence or corruption;

- conducted by an independent body;
- transparent; and
- administered in an impartial, neutral, efficient, accurate and accountable manner.

In Article 82(1) parliament is expected to enact legislation related to the delimitation of the Independent Electoral and Boundaries Commission of electoral units for election of members of the National Assembly and County Assemblies. To ensure that electoral disputes are resolved peacefully, parliament is called upon by Article 87 to enact appropriate legislation.

There are ongoing deliberations on implementing the Constitution, including the overhaul of the institutional operations of crucial government agencies like the Judiciary, the Legislature, and the Police Force. In order to ensure that future electoral processes in Kenya consolidate democratic gains and promote peace-building, the following have been captured constitutionally:

i. An electoral system that encourages and guarantees inclusion, peace-building and accountability by the political players. The FPTP was discredited as creating a zero-sum game scenario, hence creating conflict. On the other hand, the Proportional Representation (PR) system was criticized for creating unstable inefficient governments with legislative paralysis. In this scenario, Kenya considered a compromise between the FPTP and PR systems, which is both inclusive and fosters accountability and stability by government

ii. Transitional mechanisms for handing over power from one party to another were incorporated in the electoral design to lessen the anxieties associated with political transition. This includes electoral dispute resolution mechanisms to determine electoral outcome disputes, and forestall violent uprising as witnessed in Kenya in January 2008.

iii. Adoption of political party legislative regimes that consolidate the democratic culture through a vibrant multi-party structure, while at the same time ensuring peace-building and cohesion across various ethnic, racial, religious and geographical constituencies so as to foster peace-building.

iv. Governance structures such as the executive, legislature, judiciary and other government agencies e.g. the Police Force, are being reformed to reflect the democratic culture in the electoral process. This shall be achieved by upholding the doctrine of separation of powers by empowering all the three arms of Government, and ensuring that the vote is indeed significant to the governance process.

As the democratic discourse gradually shifts from the normative to the human developmental perspective, the electoral process loses its glitter in the eye of an electorate that has failed to enjoy the socio-economic benefits of democratization. To preserve its value, the electoral process should therefore play its role in consolidation and sustainability of democracy and peace. It is hoped that the implementation of the new Constitution of Kenya will ensure that this is done.

Notes

[1] *See* Samuel P. Huntington (1991), "The Third Wave: Democratization in the Late Twentieth Century," University of Oklahoma, Norman, Oklahoma.

[2] *See* Ndegwa, Stephen, The Relevance of the Electoral System: A simulation of the 1992 Kenyan Election, African Journal of Political Science, 1997, Vol. 2 No. 1, 12-40.

[3] *See* Joseph A. Schumpeter (1942) "Capitalism, Socialism and Democracy," Routledge, London.

[4] *See* Samuel P. Huntington, Supra note 1.

[5] *See* Abdalla Bujra, "Liberal Democracy and the Emergence of a Constitutionally Failed State in Kenya," in Abdalla Bujra, Ed, 2005, "Democratic transition in Kenya: The Struggle from Liberal to Social Democracy," Nairobi, DPMF/ACEG.

[6] *See* Larry Diamond (1999), "Developing Democracy Toward Consolidation," John Hopkins University Press. An analysis of all these approaches uncovers substantive similarities in the different procedural definitions.

[7] *See* Samuel Huntington, Supra note 1.

[8] Terry Lynn Karl, Imposing Consent? Electoralism versus Democratization in El Salvador," in "Elections and Democratization in Latin America, 1980-1985," by Paul Drake and Eduardo Silva (eds) Hispanic American Historical Review, vol. 67 no. 2 (May 1987).

[9] *See* Sandbrook Richard (1988), Liberal Democracy in Africa: A Socialist- Revisionist Perspective, Canadian Journal of African Studies, XXII, 2 (**1988**), pp. 240-268.

[10] *See* Ingelhart Ronald and Christian Welzel (2005), "Democracy as the Growth of Freedom: The Human Development Perspective", in The Japanese Journal of Political Science, 6, (3): 313-343. 2005. They argue that modernization provides human resources that increase people's emphasis on autonomous choices. Linked through their common focus on autonomous human choice, human resources and liberty aspirations provide overlapping sources for pressure for

growth of freedom. Within the limits set by the extent to which freedom is not yet present, human resources and liberty aspirations are conducive to the growth of political freedom in interchangeable ways.

[11] *See* IIDEA (2005), "Electoral System Design: The New International IDEA Handbook."

[12] The right to periodic elections is provided under the UDHR and the ICCPR.

[13] J.M. Carey (1997), Institutional design and party systems in Larry Diamond et al. (eds), "Consolidating the Third Wave democracies," Baltimore, MD: Johns Hopkins University Press.

[14] *See* International Institute for Democracy and Electoral Assistance (IDEA) (2002), International Electoral Standards: Guidelines for reviewing the legal framework of elections, Bulls Tryckeri, Halmstad, Sweden.

[15] *Ibid.*

[16] *See* the Report of the Independent Review Commission on the general Elections held in Kenya on the 27th December 2007. See also the *Report on the 1997 General Elections in Kenya 29-30 December* by Institute for Education in Democracy (IED), Catholic Justice and Peace Commission, and the National Council of Churches in Kenya (NCCK).

[17] *See* Laza Kekik, The Economist Intelligence Unit Index of Democracy (2008), available at *graphics.eiu.com/PDF/Democracy%20Index%202008.pdf* (last accessed on 16/06/09). The Economist Intelligence Unit's democracy index is based on five categories: electoral process and pluralism; civil liberties; the functioning of government; political participation; and political culture. The five categories are interrelated and form a coherent conceptual whole.

[18] *See* the previous Constitution of Kenya, the National Assembly and Presidential Elections Act, Cap. 7, and the Local Government Act, Cap. 265. These are discussed further below.

[19] Article 21 of the UDHR states that: (1) everyone has the right to take part in the government of his country, directly or through freely chosen representatives... (3) The will of the people shall be the basis of the authority of government; this will shall be expressed in periodic and genuine elections which shall be by universal and equal suffrage and shall be held by secret vote or by equivalent free voting procedures.

[20] The ICCPR states as follows at Article 25: "Every citizen shall have the right and the opportunity, without any of the distinctions mentioned in Article 2 and without unreasonable restrictions: (a) To take part in the conduct of public affairs, directly or through freely chosen representatives; (b) To vote and to be elected at genuine periodic elections which shall be by universal and equal suffrage and shall be held by secret ballot, guaranteeing the free expression of the will of the electors; (c) To have access, on general terms of equality, to public service in his country."

[21] These provisions were introduced by Constitutional Amendment Act No. 10 of 2008, as part of the implementation of the Mediation Agreements reached by the Orange Democratic Movement (ODM) and Party of National Unity (PNU) during the mediation talks chaired by Dr Kofi Annan, as a response to the post-election crisis. Previously, the electoral management body, the Electoral Commission of Kenya (ECK) conducted both the electoral process and the delimitations of electoral units.

[22] There has been, and currently is, a fierce political debate regarding the delimitation of electoral units. When the Electoral Commission of Kenya was still charged with constituency delimitation, the Kenya African National Union (KANU) government manipulated the process to create more constituencies in regions perceived as KANU strongholds, and in similar measure, stifled the creation of more constituencies in Opposition strongholds. This resulted in a skewed system of electoral units, whereby some regions produced fewer members of Parliament, but more electoral votes than other regions with comparatively more members of Parliament. This clearly violated the principle of equality of the vote. Indeed, this also violates the principle of proportional representation. It has resulted in Constitutional litigation by marginalized groups e.g. the Il Chamus, who moved to the Constitutional Court in 2004 to enforce their right to representation by seeking orders for the ECK to create a constituency for them. See Rangal Lemeiguran & Others v. the Attorney General & Others Miscellaneous Civil Application No. 305 of 2004.

[23] Act No. 11 of 2003.

[24] The political parties are regulated under the Political Parties Act 2007. It came on force on July 1, 2008.

[25] In 1997, the incumbent President Moi won a final term as president with 35% of the popular vote and a minority share of seats in Parliament. This was despite the fact that 65% of the voters essentially voted against the incumbent. In electoral systems whereby a run-off was expected, it is doubtful whether President Moi would have won another term.

[26] See Ndegwa, Supra note 1.

[27] See Peter Wanyande (2006), Electoral Politics and Election Outcomes in Kenya, Africa Development, Vol. XXXI, No. 3, 2006, pp. 62–80.

[28] See Report of the Independent Review Commission on the General Elections held in Kenya on the 27th December 2007, supra note 9.

[29] See Thoko Mpumlwana (2009), The Electoral process and the Democratic Changeover of Political Power between Parties, paper delivered at the International Conference on Challenges of Democratic Succession in Africa, under the Institute of Human Rights and Promotion of Democracy: Cotonou, Benin, 23-25 February 2009.

References

Abdalla Bujra, (ed). 2005. *Democratic Transition in Kenya: The Struggle from Liberal to Social Democracy*. Nairobi, DPMF/ACEG.

Carey John M. 1997. *Institutional Design and Party Systems.* In Larry Diamond et al. (eds), "Consolidating the Third Wave democracies." Baltimore, MD: Johns Hopkins University Press.

Diamond, Larry. 1999. "Developing Democracy Toward Consolidation," John Hopkins University Press.

Huntington, Samuel P. 1991. "The Third Wave: Democratization in the Late Twentieth Century." Norman, Oklahoma: University of Oklahoma.

Ingelhart Ronald and Christian Welzel. (2005), "Democracy as the Growth of Freedom: The Human Development Perspective." In *The Japanese Journal of Political Science*, 6, 2005.

IDEA. 2005. "Electoral System Design: The New International IDEA Handbook."

International Institute for Democracy and Electoral Assistance (IDEA). 2002. *International Electoral Standards: Guidelines for Reviewing the Legal Framework of Elections*. Halmstad, Sweden: Bulls Tryckeri.

Kekik, Laza. 2008. *The Economist Intelligence Unit Index of Democracy* available at *graphics.eiu.com/PDF/Democracy%20Index%202008.pdf* (last accessed on 16/06/09).

Lynn, Terry Karl. 1987. *Imposing Consent? Electoralism versus Democratization in El Salvador."* In "Elections and Democratization in Latin America, 1980-1985," by Paul Drake and Eduardo Silva (eds) Hispanic American Historical Review, Vol. 67 No. 2 (May 1987).

Mpumlwana, Thoko. 2009. *The Electoral Process and the Democratic Changeover of Political Power between Parties*. Paper delivered at the International Conference on Challenges of Democratic Succession in Africa, under the Institute of Human Rights and Promotion of Democracy: Cotonou, Benin, 23-25 February 2009.

Report of the Independent Review Commission on the General Elections held in Kenya on the 27th December 2007.

Ndegwa, Stephen. 1997. *The Relevance of the Electoral System: A simulation of the 1992 Kenyan Election,* African Journal of Political Science, 1997, Vol. 2 No. 1.

Report on the 1997 General Elections in Kenya 29-30 December by Institute for Education in Democracy (IED), Catholic Justice and Peace Commission, and the National Council of Churches in Kenya (NCCK).

Sandbrook, Richard. 1988. *Liberal Democracy in Africa: A Socialist- Revisionist Perspective,* Canadian Journal of African Studies, XXII, 2 (**1988**).

Schumpeter, Joseph A. 1948. "Capitalism, Socialism and Democracy." London: Routledge.

Wanyande, Peter. 2006. *Electoral Politics and Election Outcomes in Kenya*. In Africa Development, Vol. XXXI, No. 3, 2006.

Chapter 8

Post Election Violence and Crimes Against Humanity in 2007

Mbuthi Gathenji

Introduction

Election violence in Kenya has since 1992 been cyclic and predictable. Every five years violence dictates who wins or loses in the presidential, parliamentary and civic election in specific ethnically charged areas of the Rift Valley, Coast, Western and North Eastern Provinces. The forecast is that on or before the election of 2012, there will be election violence similar to the one in 2007 or worse unless the issue of impunity is conclusively addressed[1]. The actors and victims have earned notoriety and the crimes have now been classified as so serious as to justify international identity. -*"They have attained their jus cogens status i.e. they threaten the security peace or essential values of society as a whole and thus stands to be redressed by the international community as a matter of urgency"*[2]. In 1992, state sponsored violence left over 779 dead, 654 injured and 54,000 displaced persons. This necessitated the setting up of a Parliamentary Select Committee (Kiliku Committee[3]). Again in 1997 and 1998, the violence recurred and caused a great number of deaths, destruction and displacement. Another Commission of Inquiry- Akiwumi Commission- was appointed despite the fact that the recommendations made by the Kiliku Committee had not been implemented. The acts of omissions by successive governments of not implementing recommendations made by both commissions have led to impunity and consequently recurrence of violence in 2002, 2005, 2007 and 2008. Another Commission of Inquiry on Post Election Violence (CIPEV) otherwise known as Waki Commission[4] was again set up to inquire into what is described as "post election violence".

This paper examines the events that led to the violence and the nature of offences committed in the 2007- 2008 election period. It is a reflection on what has been a common phenomenon on Kenya and the reasons why it has been impossible to effectively address the impunity that has now brought the country to the "brink of the precipice". The paper observes the apathy of the politicians, the judicial system and the Attorney General in the investigation and prosecution of those involved in violence. It further examines consistent failure of the office of the Attorney General to effectively order investigation and prosecution of organizers and planners of the violence. It examines the resolve by the international community to deal with impunity in Kenya through recommendations made by The Panel of Eminent African Personalities led by Dr. Kofi Annan, former Secretary General of the United Nations. It reflects the recommended reforms i.e. constitutional, legislative and social reforms as panacea for election violence and impunity. If this initiative fails, what is the future of Kenya as it relates to dealing with crimes that seem to be part of the calendar of election violence?

The Commission of Inquiry into the Post Election Violence (CIPEV) *aka* Waki Commission

One of the recommendations of The Panel of Eminent African Personalities was setting up of a Commission to investigate the causes and identify perpetrators of the post election violence. The commission was mandated "*to investigate the facts and surrounding circumstances related to acts of violence, and make recommendation on measures to prevent, control, eradicate similar deeds in future*". More importantly, "*recommend measures to bring to justice those persons responsible for criminal acts*"[5].

The Commission in its report suggests that it reviewed a significant amount of reports, literature and documentation on past and contemporary causes of violence in Kenya. Part II of the report, headed "Facts and Surrounding Circumstances Relating to the Post Election Violence", traces the roots of violence in Kenya and gives a glossary of memorandum and inquiries done by scholars, civil societies, international and national human rights groups.

The main causes of violence as identified by the Commission are:-

(i) Use of violence by the State as a tool to ensure control;
(ii) The personalization of presidential power and deliberate weakening of public institutions;
(iii) Land and inequality;
(iv) Unemployed youth.

It reaches the conclusion that the above factors "have been dovetailed to make violence the method of choice to resolve a range of political differences and obtain political power". This generalized cause of the violence may, therefore, explain the wide range of perpetrators of crimes against humanity in Kenya.

On the individual criminal responsibility, the Commission found as a fact that specific persons and institutions in the political arena committed crimes to achieve "their own political change". The Waki Commission received oral and written evidence recounting the events as they unfolded from political meetings, church sermons, hate speeches from prominent politicians and opinion leaders, Members of Parliament, councillors and their agents. Threats on communities were issued from the period of the 2005 referendum on the Constitution through the campaign period for presidential and parliamentary candidates and climaxing with the violence at the announcement of the election results in December 2007 and the post election violence in January and February, 2008. The real stories told by the victims changed the mandate given to the Waki Commission to which, as per *Gazette Notice*, was only limited to inquire into the events that occurred after the announcement of results of the election on 30th December 2007. The Commission was in full agreement with the previous findings and recommendations of the Akiwumi Commission that election violence was always pre-planned. It confirmed that the causes of the crimes committed went beyond the announcement of election results, and that the violence was organized and directed against members of specific ethnicities, communities and political parties. This underlines the importance of identifying the period of the Commission of the crimes for purposes of investigation and prosecution.

In the Rift Valley region, the violence was directed against the Gikuyu, Kisii, Kamba and to some extent members of the Abaluhya ethnic groups who were perceived to support the Party of National Unity (PNU). The perpetrators, mainly supporters of the Orange Democratic Movement (ODM) party, included the Kalenjin or (Kamatusa), the Luo and other affiliated communities. In all, the victims were identified as anti-change (or anti-majimbo) and had to be removed from areas where they were considered as "outsiders", "madoadoa"[6] and "makwekwe[7]". In contrast, violence in the form of retribution occurred in areas where the residents were identified as members of the communities targeted in the areas above and their sympathizers . This included inhabitants of Naivasha, Nakuru and areas of Central Province and Nairobi. In Coast

Province, the same pattern was identified; the persons considered as "Wabara" (up-country people) became victims of violence. In Western and Nyanza Provinces the outsiders were Kisii, Gikuyu, Kamba and other communities associated with PNU.

The deployment of criminal gangs as aggressors or in defence cannot be justified under international and national laws and is being equally investigated and prosecuted. Groups such as Kalenjin warriors and Mungiki and their financiers are amenable to investigation and prosecution. The age of the perpetrators would be a key factor in determining their culpability. In some areas, school going children were directly involved in the violence.

In urban areas the same patterns and stereotypes were identified depending on the population of respective tribes and political affiliations. In slum areas where there were mixtures of all ethnic groups, there was a clear attempt to segregate the population through violence. This led to balkanization of populations into zones for ODM or PNU parties or Gikuyu and Luo communities. There was mass destruction of infrastructure which was attributed to organized gangs. The security agents throughout the country both in rural and urban areas also reflected a pattern based on the allegiance to one ethnic group or party. In drawing the charges for crimes committed in Kenya it is important to identify the broad categories of perpetrators and victims bearing in mind the rural and urban populations.

Nature of offences committed

In its findings, the Waki Commission while admitting its lack of time to hear a substantial number of victims and inadequate statistics, gave the number of dead as a consequence of post election violence as 1,333 (the highest number being in the Rift Valley): over 3,561 suffered injuries from assaults, 117,216 private properties were allegedly destroyed. It confirms that certain communities were targeted. They were either killed or forcefully evicted[8]. The Commission also enumerates pointers to the organization of the violence.

- *In certain instances, warnings were issued to the victims before the attacks;*
- *The violence involved large numbers of attackers, often mobilized from areas outside the location of the violence;*
- *Petrol and weapons were used in various places to carry out the attacks and destruction, which required arrangements as regards to acquisition, concealment and transport; and*

- *Sometimes the attacks specifically targeted only members of given ethnic groups to the exclusion of others (page 348).*

The Commission made findings that the pattern of crime was widespread, systematic and continuous upto the signing of the National and Reconciliation Accord. Hence, the crimes met the threshold of crimes against humanity. The International Criminal Court (ICC) definition of a crime against humanity includes:-

(a) "Murder;

(b) Extermination;

(c) Enslavement;

(d) Deportation or forcible transfer of population;

(e) Imprisonment or other severe deprivation of physical liberty in violation of fundamental rules of international law;

(f) Torture;

(g) Rape, sexual slavery, enforced prostitution, forced pregnancy, enforced sterilization, or any other form of sexual violence of comparable gravity;

(h) Persecution against any identifiable group or collectively on political, racial, national, ethnic, cultural, religious, gender as defined in paragraph 3, or other grounds that are universally recognized as impermissible under international law, in connection with any act referred to in this paragraph or any crime within the jurisdiction of the court;

(i) Enforced disappearance of persons;

(j) The crime of apartheid;

(k) Other inhumane acts of a similar character intentionally causing great suffering, or serious injury to body or to mental or physical health ".

Section 7 of the Rome Statute underlines that such acts must be committed "as a part of a widespread or systematic attack directed against civilian populations with knowledge of attack". As is clearly stated in the Akiwumi Commission Report, these offences are not new in the Kenyan jurisdiction. The former Chairman of the Law Society of Kenya, Nzamba Kitonga, while addressing the Akiwumi Commission pointed out that the offences committed between 1992 – 1998 were crimes against humanity[9]. Indeed one of the findings of the Kiliku Committee in respect of land grievances was "the misconception that some ethnic communities could chase away other ethnic communities in order to acquire their land". The intention to forcefully evict those civilians from their lawfully acquired habitation constituted an element of crimes against humanity i.e. the forceful eviction of 54,000 people from their own lawfully acquired habitation. Again the Kiliku Committee identified specific individuals and prominent members of cabinet and parliament[10] and recommended their investigation for organizing and financing the warriors. The role of politicians in the clashes was identified as the making of inflammatory and inciting statements which caused animosity. During the Akiwumi Commission, evidence was given by one of the raiders on why murder was committed during clashes. He stated ...

> "The raiders' explanation for violence was because the Kikuyus had shown they will not vote for Mzee (Moi) in the General Election which was due later that year. They had decided to kill them along with any other person who like them would be unwilling to vote for him. He further explained that they were paid 500 shillings for every adult non Kalenjin and 200 for every non Kalenjin male child killed and they had received their training in Bomet District."[11]

As early as January 2008, the Attorney General, Hon. Amos Wako, warned that the offences then being committed were of a serious nature to classify them as crimes against humanity. He, however, seems to have done nothing to stop their escalation. Nor did he address the offences committed during the referendum and election campaign, such as incitement, assault, arson and eviction that culminated in the post election violence[12]. There is evidence that a number of incidents could fall within the offence of genocide as defined by S.6 of Rome Statute especially in Kiambaa and Burnt Forest in the Rift Valley during the 2008 post election violence. The record of the three major commissions of inquiry in Kenya conclusively found a deep-seated hatred for some communities in the Rift Valley which has been wrongly attributed to historical injustices. The communities bearing the brunt of the violence were wrongly blamed for land issues and marginalization of others. They have often been subject to attack every election period. However, no serious land issues have been identified as a core reason for violence save for demographic alignment of voters.

The Rome Statute recognizes that an intention to kill a community for whatever reason is a serious crime, hence genocide does not concern itself with the number of people killed but the intention to eliminate more than one person by a group of persons so organized for that purpose. The intention to kill members of non-Kalenjin groups in the Rift Valley was explicit in public meeting and social gatherings. Such pronouncements were made by known individuals and later carried out. There is credible evidence that in some areas, roads were closed by the marauding groups who demanded that passengers identify their ethnicity. On so doing they were killed or grievously injured. A case study in point is the killing of a catholic clergy Fr Michael Kamau Ithondeka and the Kiambaa church case.

The Kiambaa case has important legal significance. The incident of burning of KAG Kiambaa church constitutes genocide, whereas the events which occurred in its vicinity constitute crimes against humanity.

Persons who were evicted forcefully from their farms in Kimuri, Rehema, etc, moved into the church for shelter. They were all from one ethnic group, the Kikuyu or non-Kalenjin. Others forcefully evicted were Kamba, Kisii and Luhya. Those who evicted them were from the Kalenjin community and their sympathizers. They were well organized with traditional weapons, arrows, bows, spears, axes, machetes, stones and clubs. They systematically moved from one farm to another meeting little or no resistance from the victims. They were smeared on their faces and bodies with white ochre, sang war songs and had a central command that directed their movements to farms occupied mainly by non-Kalenjin, especially Gikuyu.

On reaching the church the hostile gang of warriors decided that they would *eliminate* the entire group of victims in the church. They had a common intention and made it clear from their speeches outside the church that they would kill the Gikuyu in the church. They proceeded to carry out their intention by hacking their first victims to death with machetes; even those who surrendered to them carrying green twigs and pleading for their lives. The warriors killed eleven (11) people outside the compound of the church. They then proceeded to set the church on fire using foam mattresses and petrol.

According to the police officers in charge of the scene of crime, twelve (12) bodies were burnt beyond recognition inside the church. The number of people is more than sufficient to constitute an act of genocide. The essential element of the offence is the "*intention to carry out the act of the elimination of an ethnic group.*" Other areas where offences for genocide were likely to have been committed include Burnt Forest where a couple and their children were hacked to death even after surrendering all their possessions, including their farm to the raiders. They were informed by the raiders their fate had been decided and there was no mitigation. Their community must die.

It was obvious that groups had organized themselves for a long time to evict and kill members of non-Kalenjin communities e.g. in Molo, Sotik, Kericho, and so on. Investigation will reveal that such pockets and groups of people were organized and indoctrinated by traditional leaders to kill members of specific ethnic group using reasons such as "historical injustices", land issues, et cetera.

In some areas of the Rift Valley, threats to evict the Gikuyu started as early as 26th December 2007. Burning of houses in Kimuri area which neighbours Kiambaa started on 29th December 2007 before results of the election were announced. Tension in Kiambaa was already high on 31st December 2007. They had been warned by the Nandi, a sub-ethnic group of the Kalenjin, that whatever the outcome of the election, the Gikuyu had to be evicted from the area. The victims were able to identify some of their attackers as they were neighbours, former school mates, and so on. The Kiambaa crimes were committed in broad daylight at eleven o'clock in the morning and hence conditions favourable to proper identification existed.

The attackers were well co-ordinated and used military-like formations. They alerted others by using coded call signs, singing Kalenjin songs and using whistles, and other facilities. They were in large numbers of over 1,000 raiders. When burning the church, they sprinkled petrol on blankets and mattresses and threw them over the church. They were meticulous on how to get maximum ignition of the materials in the church. They blocked the road leading to the church with logs and stones to prevent escape of any of the victims or any assistance reaching the scene.

Elaborate meetings to plan the mayhem took place in homes of well known personalities nights before the attacks on 30/12/07. They surrounded the church and prevented people from escaping from the burning inferno. There is evidence that they pushed back children and women who attempted to get out of the burning church. The police arrived at Kiambaa Church only to find Red Cross Society staff removing the debris of the burnt church.

The people inside the church were composed mainly of women, children, elderly and persons with disabilities. According to the pastor in charge of the church, it could accommodate about 250 people. The crowd inside the church was over 300 people.

Seeds of impunity

The question that comes to mind for any scholar of criminology is why these offences recur at least every five years.

The real seed of impunity is the misconception by politicians, some Western governments and human rights activists that quick restoration of peace is the priority. As one scholar in international crimes would argue, *"The states that have emerged from conflicts give priority to attainment of peace rather than justice for the victims. Opportunities to fully investigate, punish and hence put permanent deterrent measures are lost for short term gains[13]"*.

The 1992 atrocities committed by the Moi regime were supposed to be addressed by the government that took power after the multi-party elections in the same year. The perpetrators of these crimes won the elections and became members of the cabinet. They decided the national policy priorities. These decisions did not include the investigations and prosecution of the perpetrators of violence or the resettlement of internally displaced persons.

In 1998 again after the atrocities were repeated, the perpetrators became the members of the cabinet. They proceeded to appoint the Akiwumi Commission to inquire into ethnic offences. After the Commission of Inquiry revealed the persons involved in the atrocities and recommended their investigation and prosecution, the Attorney General published a rejoinder and exonerated them, stating the report was biased against certain tribes"[14]. He declined to make the report public until he was ordered by a court to release it to one of the victims in July 2002[15]. The same Attorney General and implicated individuals continued to serve the Moi Government beyond 2002 when a majority of the Moi Members of Parliament were voted out. The miracle is that some managed to jump ship midstream and formed the incoming National Rainbow Coalition (NARC) government. Again they became members of the cabinet in 2003.

The hybrid and fragile government of NARC had no confidence or audacity to prosecute the perpetrators although part of the reason for change was the previous bad record of ethnic violence meted out on those perceived to support political change. Again the card of reconciliation and peace was used to perpetuate impunity. The reason given not to prosecute them was "this may result in retribution". Daniel Arap Moi was forgiven, so was his oppressive regime. The planners, organizers of genocide and crimes against humanity for the period 1992 – 2002 were also forgiven. However, they only became dormant like the virus awaiting resurrection in 2007/8.

The deep division in the NARC government became obvious during the 2005 referendum on the new constitution. A series of meetings held by the factions precipitated ethnic balkanization.

It is noted by the Kenya Human Rights Commission Report that the 2005 referendum had all the characteristics of a mini election[16]. The same phenomenon of election fever and violence characterized by deep division based on ethnicity emerged. The two camps "Banana" and "Orange" exchanged bitter hate speeches that culminated in the rejection of the New Proposed Constitution. As the Waki Commission observed, the tension which accompanied referendum campaigns matured into the 2007/8 violence.

It is obvious that the signing of an Accord[17] to establish a coalition government on 28th February 2008 by the two Principals (Mwai Kibaki and Raila Odinga) who were accused of precipitating the violence compromised justice for the victims. This is borne out by the fact that despite a clear road map by the Waki Commission on steps to be taken by the Government to establish a tribunal to try the perpetrators, parliament rejected the draft statute. The pattern of voting again reflected the party division and loyalties. The Accord took no consideration of the victims of injustices committed in 2007/ 2008 violence. In any event, victims were not parties to the Accord.

The inability of the Government to make a decision whether it will settle for the ICC at The Hague or a local tribunal is basically grounded on its complicity in the violence. The state security agencies failed to put an effective machinery to stop crimes. The coalition government has in its cabinet some of the named organizers of violence. This makes it difficult to try any of the most "responsible perpetrators" through the local courts or even the much hyped local tribunal, unless the real stakeholders in peace and justice are included in the initiative.

The Rome Statute of ICC

The coming into force of the Rome Statute of ICC in July 2002 has given the victims of violence an avenue to seek for justice. Kenya became a signatory to the Statute and ratified it on 15th March 2005. This means ICC is not a foreign court. Kenya became a member state and hence can under article 13(a) of the Statute refer a situation within its jurisdiction for investigation and prosecution.

It can do so if it is unable or, for reasons explained in the Article, or is unwilling to undertake prosecution for the offences committed in 2007 – 2008.

Under the ICC Rome Statute Article 15, the victims can bring to the attention of the ICC Prosecutor sufficient evidence to justify an investigation of the Kenya "situation". The Prosecutor can initiate investigations and prosecute with permission of the pre-trial chamber. The debate in Kenya on whether ICC is the appropriate court for trial of perpetrators has exposed ignorance on part of the political leaders and public alike. The suggestion that Kenya will surrender its sovereignty is devoid of any merit.

The complementarity principle only gives the Kenyan courts a priority to try the offences committed within its jurisdiction. When Kenyan signed and ratified the Rome Statute, it engaged the organs of the court to try Kenyan citizens for offences within ICC jurisdiction. Kenya has now domesticated the ICC Statute by the enactment of the International Crimes Act 2008 (Act 16 of 2008). The Act commenced on 1st January 2009.[18]

The misnomer about the ICC being a foreign court needs rectification. The perception spread by the politicians and media in Kenya is that the ICC is a foreign court based at The Hague, Netherlands, and shall try Kenyans as foreigners. The politicians, especially some Members of Parliament, have even stated that Kenya will lose its sovereignty by making referral to ICC.

A close examination of the establishment, structure and operation of the ICC will dispel this misconception. The ICC was established by the Assembly of State Parties. These are defined in Article 112. Kenya became a State Party on signing of the Rome Statute of ICC. State parties have one vote each. The role of the Assembly of State Parties includes an oversight role on the Presidency, the Prosecutor, etc. Kenya, therefore, is part of the ICC. The effect of making reference to the court is not a derogation of its sovereignty. It is not a foreign jurisdiction as stated. It can deal with such offences as defined in Articles 6 and 7 of the Statute by way of investigation and trial. The court is not restricted to sitting in The Hague. It can sit in other places, including Kenya , as may be designated by Article 3 of the Statute and now provided in Section 8(2) of the International Crime Act 2008.

What would victims in Kenya be looking for in the ICC? Once the court determines that the six individuals namely, Uhuru Kenyatta, Amb. Francis Muthaura, Hussein Ali, William Ruto, Henry Kosgey and Joshua Sang referred to it by the Chief Prosecutor Luis Moreno Ocampo have a case to answer, it may transmit a request and surrender of a person or persons, together with material supporting the request outlined in article 91 to any state on the territory of which that person may be found and shall request the co-operation of the state in the arrest and surrender of such person. State parties shall in accordance with provisions of this part and the procedure under their national law comply with requests for arrest and surrender. The Kenyan sought by ICC and visiting any of the State Parties may be liable to arrest and surrender. The Kenya government will be obliged to co-operate with the International Criminal Court in the investigation and prosecution of perpetrators in Kenya. It must facilitate the voluntary appearance of persons as witnesses and experts before the court. It must comply with the requirement for transfer of persons to the ICC at The Hague or any other place chosen as the sitting of the court.

Special Tribunal for Kenya

The Special Tribunal for Kenya proposed by the Waki Commission was an enhancement of the court's jurisdiction in Kenya to try the offences committed in the post election period. The offences triable under the proposed special tribunal for Kenya included the International Crimes and Penal Code. The passing of the International Crimes Act which domesticates the ICC Statute has further given the High Court jurisdiction to deal with these offences in the future. The Special Tribunal for Kenya must be specifically empowered to apply retrospectively. The Bill tabled in parliament, although imperfect in some areas, was meant to take care of any of the constitutional and local issues which could affect the operation of the Tribunal. These included, *inter alia*, retroactivity, immunities and current powers of the Attorney General with regard to prosecution.

The Commission Investigating Post Election Violence (CIPEV) recommended the setting up of the Special Tribunal as a court to sit within the territorial boundaries of the Republic of Kenya. This recommendation was so crucial that the Commission put its implementation under the auspices of the Panel of Eminent African Personalities. They were to consult with the President and the Prime Minister of Kenya with full co-operation of the Parliament, the judiciary and the office of the Attorney General. The recommendation gave a specific time table for the establishment and operationalization of the Tribunal.

Although Parliament adopted CIPEV recommendations, it failed to give the necessary co-operation for the setting up of a local tribunal. The two principals - the President and the Prime Minister- signed the Agreement in December 2008 to give the impetus for implementation of the Report and hence the setting up of the Court.

The Report recommended that the Bill establishing the Special Tribunal provide for jurisdiction to adjudicate over the crimes brought against persons bearing greatest responsibility, particularly crimes against humanity related to the 2007 post-election violence. The Bill presented in Parliament[19] by and large conformed to the CIPEV recommendations, save for details that had to be modelled on the International Standard concerning issues of amnesty, retroactivity and presidential immunity. The rejection of the Bill by Parliament was, however, predictable as the environment in which the debate was conducted indicated that a wider consultation of stakeholders and building of consensus had not been done by the Government. The failure of Parliament to pass the Bill left the option of handing over the envelope prepared by the Waki Commission and containing the list of alleged perpetrators and the accompanying evidence to the prosecutor of the International Criminal Court by Dr. Kofi Annan. This was done in June 2009.

It is important to note that the role of the African Union (AU) personalities was completed as determined by both the CIPEV recommendations and the agreement of the principals on the implementation of the Report. After the failure by Parliament to set up a local tribunal, the ICC prosecutor proceeded to open the envelope and together with all the other evidence in his possession determined that he could initiate investigations on crimes committed against humanity in Kenya. This action removed the matter from parliament and the government.

Although a section of the government has lobbied the African Union and the United Nations through the Vice President, Kalonzo Musyoka, these efforts are essentially political rather than judicial. The conditions for the initiation of investigation in Kenya do not require any further consultation with AU or the Kenya Government. The decision whether or not the prosecutor has sufficient evidence to commence investigations and prosecution within Kenya now rests with the pre-trial Chamber of the ICC Court. The Special Tribunal for Kenya has been overtaken by events and the majority of Kenyans seem to have decided that the local solutions will not deliver justice, provide protection to witnesses and create necessary confidence among the victims of post election violence.

Truth Justice and Reconciliation Commission

One of the mandates of the CIPEV was to make such recommendations to the Truth Justice and Reconciliation Commission as it would deem appropriate. This was probably based on an assumption that Truth, Justice and Reconciliation Commission would be established by Parliament and would be operating at the same time as the CIPEV. However, the Truth Justice and Reconciliation Act was not passed until November 2008. It is clear from the Act that the objectives and purposes of the Truth Justice and Reconciliation Commission are neither investigation nor prosecution of crimes. The period covered by the Act dates back to 1963 and will not include trials of perpetrators of genocide or crimes against humanity. The aim of the Truth Justice and Reconciliation is to provide a forum for healing the psychological wounds of the victims of injustice. The Truth, Justice and Reconciliation Commission is obliged to make recommendations for prosecution of perpetrators who have committed serious crimes. The Act provides for the application of amnesty for certain categories of people to enable them make confessions. Such serious crimes include trespass, assaults, thefts, arsons against neighbours and other third parties. The Commission is obliged to consider such application within the framework given by the Act. The Truth, Justice and Reconciliation Commission is not a substitute for the Special Tribunal or the International Criminal Court. It has not been so used in any other jurisdictions, including South Africa and South American countries.

The Truth, Justice and Reconciliation Act 2008 was assented to on 28th November 2008 and Gazetted on 2nd December 2008. (Kenya Supplement No. 84 Acts No. 6). It was commenced on 9th March 2009 and appointment of Commissioners, Chairman and Deputy Chairman was done in July 2009. The preamble to the said Act just like the Gazette Notice establishing CIPEV gives a false impression that violence followed the announcement of the 2007. However, the period subject to the inquiry is between 12th December 1963 and end of February 2008. It excludes from amnesty crimes against humanity but is not explicit on the crime of genocide. In the marginal note in S.34 the Act does not specifically make any reference to genocide though both have been defined in section 2 of the Act. The original S.34 in the Bill presented in Parliament in May 2008 included both offences. The presumption is that the subsection (3) of S.34 which stipulates that no amnesty may be recommended in respect of gross violation of human rights including genocide if facts presented before the Commission indicate that such an offence was committed. The

TJRC is again mandated to make recommendations to the President for prosecution of individuals who may be implicated in its findings[20]. It has powers to also investigate gross violations and abuses of human rights, identify the victims, make appropriate recommendations for redress and reparation for the victims. The responsibility of implementing the Report of the Commission is vested in the Minister responsible for matters relating to Justice and Constitutional Affairs. He is obliged to operationalise the implementation mechanism in accordance with the recommendations of the Commission. This involves the formation of the implementation committee which publishes the Report. However, two steps are necessary before the Minister acts on the Report. It must be submitted to the President and Parliament. It is not clear from the Act what is the role of the President or Parliament on receiving the Report. It is apparent the two organs have not been given any power to modify or vet the Report. Equally, the office of the Attorney General seems to have no role except receiving a recommendation for amnesty under Section 39 of the Act.

From the agenda drawn by the two Principals, the Waki Commission Report should have been the first document to be received by the Truth, Justice and Reconciliation Commission covering the period within its jurisdiction. As stated earlier, the Waki Commission was obliged to make recommendations to the TJRC. Its term expired before the establishment of the TJRC.

On receiving the TJRC Report, the Attorney General is apparently bound to institute or continue with prosecution of such a case subject to the amnesty application.

The actors, role of police administration, politicians and media

The specific mandate of the Waki Commission included investigating the acts of commission or omission of State security agencies during the course of the violence[21]. In its findings on acts of commission, the Waki Report confirmed it received evidence of several cases involving police shooting civilians[22]. Persons killed and injured through gunshots included women and children.

Most serious was the encouragement to civilians to commit crimes by taking no preventive action through a deliberate act of indifference. The ICC Statute specifically makes provision for persons with command responsibility. Article 28 provides that the military commanders and other superiors are criminally responsible for acts of their forces. With specific reference to the police officers, the junior officers are individually responsible for acts outside the established legal procedures. If such actions are done with approval or connivance of their seniors, the latter also become liable to prosecution.

As in respect of Akiwumi Commission, the Waki Commission was mandated to identify the persons responsible for the violence. Though the wording was generally to investigate facts and surrounding circumstances, the Commission was expected to recommend "measures with regard to bringing to justice those people responsible for criminal acts". Some of the individuals' names were listed in an envelope which was subsequently handed over to Mr. Kofi Annan with an intention of forwarding them to the Prosecutor of ICC if a credible local tribunal was not set up. The names were not disclosed to the public. The Kenya National Commission on Human Rights issued a report which categorized the perpetrators of offences under three groups. The triangle of responsibility identified the following classes:-

(a) Remote perpetrators which composed of "overseers, planners, financiers, instigators and organizers.

(b) Mid-level perpetrators comprising of those who gave and received instructions or orders and led local implementation of plans.

(c) The lower lever perpetrators who were directly committing acts of violence.

This document was part of the evidence tabled before the Waki Commission[23]. Besides this there were other evidence from human rights organizations and individuals. The list includes Chiefs, Administration Police officers, Police Officers and other members of the security agencies. Their role ranges from actual participation to aiding and abetting commission of murders, arsons, rape, forceful evictions and assaults. The evidence in the public domain includes preparation of acts of murder by concealment of information on individuals engaged in training of warriors and making of weapons used in the violence. The procurement of petrol, arrows, bows, guns and other weapons was - in some places -done with full knowledge of administrators. Others provided information about the residents' movements and state of their habitation to raiders to facilitate the attacks. In some cases, motor vehicles belonging to administrators and other officials of government were used to ferry the warriors.

Earlier, politicians, had started arming their supporters with propaganda and weapons to attack their opponents. During the campaign period they negatively referred to some communities and urged their supporters to evict, destroy and kill their neighbours. The Members of Parliament, cabinet ministers and councillors are implicated in financing youth and supplying them with means of travel to various areas where attacks took place. The Permanent Secretary of the Ministry of Information, Bitange Ndemo, in his testimony before the Commission[24] confirmed that in the 2005 Referendum and the 2007 General Election, most media houses took partisan positions and engaged in unbalanced reporting. The crimes relevant to media include incitement which resulted in violence. In his submission to the Waki Commission, Bitange Ndemo identified a number of FM Radio Stations as having engaged in incitement to violence. A number of these stations were listed by the PNU in their Memorandum before the Commission and other witnesses who understood the language of the inciters.

The incitement to violence is not new in both the Ad hoc Tribunals of International Criminal Tribunal for Rwanda (ICTR) and International Criminal Tribunal for Yugoslavia (ICTY). The reports of the Kenya National Commission on Human Rights and other human rights organizations have categorized the media as part of the perpetrators of crimes against humanity in the Kenya jurisdiction. The indictment of Joshua Arap Sang by the ICC on account of his activities at KASS FM is instructive.

Evictions and threats to remove the "madoadoa" were received as early as April 2007. In the Rift Valley, incidents of preparation for war were evident in August 2007 during school holidays during which young men would allegedly attend traditional rituals and indoctrination sessions. Traditional weapons like bows and arrows were being manufactured in large quantities. Specific individuals perceived to support PNU had already received warnings that they would be evicted forcefully from their lawful habitation. The media captured these events as they occurred, including the movement of civilians to internally displaced persons (IDP) Camps. Such places as Kuresoi in Rift Valley had recorded violence since early 2006.

Investigation of post election violence

It is not possible to have a detailed overview of the whole country. However, a case study of Kiambaa in Eldoret may give a sample of major violence experience in Rift Valley (*see also Warigi, this Volume*).

The investigation of criminal offences by Kenyan Police is guided by, among others, Criminal Procedure Code Cap 75, Evidence Act 80 and Force Standing

Orders. Investigation into serious offences such as murder requires the intervention of the office of the Attorney General. The prosecution is undertaken by the State Counsel after a file is compiled by the police within the jurisdiction. It is mandatory that the cause of death be confirmed through a post-mortem by the Government pathologists. Identification of the deceased by relatives or persons well-known to him/her is also a necessary step in the investigation of murder or unlawful killing. The challenge faced by the police was the lack of capacity in terms of professionals, for example, the doctors to conduct autopsy and prepare the post-mortem reports. The incidents of arson where individuals were burned beyond recognition presented extreme difficulties. Victims could not identify their relatives and there were no adequate facilities to carry out DNA profiles, for instance, with respect to Kiambaa arson.

The insecurity and displacement of victims further made it difficult to access the hospital for purposes of identification. Some identification was done more than seven (7) days after the event. Even by April 2009, two bodies had not been identified by a private pathologist to prepare them for burial. Some of the victims' bodies were eaten by dogs. There was lack of prompt action to preserve the bodies. Some bodies were still in the field on 2/1/08. Other bodies had been left in remote places where they were decomposing due to exposure. The magnitude of the problem due to the large number of deceased and many suspects seems to have overwhelmed the police.

Investigations require taking of statements from witnesses and compiling inquiry files. Crucial to the investigation was examination of exhibits, e.g. weapons used. The ballistics expert report was necessary where firearms were used and so was the analysis of other forensic evidence by Government chemists and analysts. It was quite obvious that the police department was not adequately equipped to meet the magnitude of offences created by the post-election violence even where they were willing to take action.

Besides issues of capacity, a substantial number of the police officers were complicit in the commission of offences and turned a blind eye to obvious cases. There was open flouting of the Force Standing Orders with respect to receiving and recording of complaints. As found by a majority of victims and confirmed by many human rights organizations, sexual offences were the least attended to. Issues of ethnicity of victims and political affiliation determined priority of cases to be investigated.

Police investigation was further hampered by the biased and partisan stand taken by the administration officers. The lack of co-operation from the chiefs and assistant chiefs compromised the identification and arrest of suspects. In many cases, the chiefs themselves were parties to the crime, especially in planning and instigating evictions of persons identified as PNU activists or sympathizers in Rift Valley, Nyanza and Western. The politicians maintained protective attitudes to those who acted at their behest. They issued threats of more violence and even where arrests were made, visited police stations to procure the release of suspects from their ethnic group or political party.

The special tribunal operating within the international regime must conform to certain standards. These include rules that ensure fair trial of suspects and access to justice by the victims.

The crimes committed in Kenya in the last two decades are so serious as to justify the intervention of the international community. The excuse that Kenya is a sovereign state loses sight of the fact that in 2007/8 violence, the country faced a threat of self-destruction. It is incumbent for any nation that subscribes to the Universal Declaration of Human Rights and is governed by a Constitution to give value to life at all costs. The struggle for power has dominated politics in Kenya and has led to the current state of affairs. Parliament and the cabinet have shown serious inability to lead and resolve issues of impunity. There is need to urgently investigate and prosecute the perpetrators of the election violence to deter the imminent recurrence as the country prepares for the next election in 2012.

Victims of violence require redress for their grievances, including reparation and compensation for their loss. The spirit of reconciliation can only be provided through punishment of the perpetrators and ensuring a sound judicial reform is undertaken. The time taken in the debate for the Special Tribunal clearly demonstrated there is no intention of providing a local solution. Justice is being delayed and denied. Trials at ICC provide a phenomenal opportunity to end impunity in Kenya.

The new Constitution offers a sustainable solution by addressing- amongst others- judicial reform, and providing permanent institutions strong enough to withstand individual political ambitions and check abuse of power. It entrenches sufficient checks and balances to reduce ethnic tension and inequalities.

Notes

[1] Kreigler Independent Review Commission (IREC) Report 2008.

[2] International Criminal Law and Human Rights by Claire de Than/Edwin Short.

[3] The National Assembly Report on the Parliamentary Select Committee (Kiliku Committee) to Ethnic Clashes in Western and other parts of Kenya in 1992.

[4] The Report of the Commission of Inquiry into Post Election Violence. October 2008. Government Printer Nairobi

[5] Kenya Gazette Notice No. 4473 of 22nd May 2009.

[6] "Madoadoa" means exemplified by spots as on the skin of a hyena. The animal is depicted in most of African traditions and folklores as greedy and dirty, feeding on decomposed carcasses and its own cubs. It connotes those who spoilt the pattern of voting.

[7] "Makwekwe" means weed; unwanted in that it interferes or destroys the crop. It connotes persons who were not in conformity with the community in terms of political direction in voting. Both of these terms were frequently used during 1992 – 1998 violence. Other derogatory words included "sangari", "cowdung", "urine" and "bunik".

[8] See Waki Commission Report pages 346 – 347.

[9] Appendix E statement by Nzamba Gitonga, Chairman Law Society of Kenya.

[10] Page 83 Kiliku Report. *The list included the names of party leaders, prominent politicians and members of the cabinet in the KANU government.*

[11] Extract from Akiwumi Commission report page 120 paragraph 219 with respect to clashes in Sondu area.

[12] See the reports of Kenya National Commission on Human Rights (KNCHR).

[13] Paper presented to LSK Seminar on Continuing Legal Education "Relevance of International Law. A comparative study. The Proposed Special tribunal for Kenya and International Criminal tribunals" on 6th February 2009 at Sarova Hotels, Nairobi by Boniface Njiru Advocate, High Court of Kenya.

[14] Comments by Attorney General 1999.

[15] Pradhan –vs- Attorney General & Another (2002)(1) K.L.R.1 High Court held, inter alia that "the failure of the Attorney General to supply the applicant with the Report of the Judicial Commission of Inquiry into the tribal clashes in Kenya (the Akiwumi Commission) was a breach of the applicants constitution rights. Applicant, Rashanali Karmali Khimji Pradhan was a commercial farmer at Ziwani Farm in Kwale District in the coast Province of Kenya. He had reported to the police and provincial administration certain information he had received that some people were taking oaths and training with a view to causing violence in his farm. He later wrote to Attorney General stating that authorities had failed to act on his information with the

result that his farm had been invaded, one of his workers killed and his property looted and destroyed. He thereafter instituted a suit for damages against the Attorney General accusing him of among others breach of duty in failing to take any action to prevent the raid on his farm. He requested Attorney General for the Akiwumi Report for the purposes of using it in the suit but the Attorney General failed to advise the Government to supply such copies in contravention of S.26 of the Constitution. Among the points noted by the court was failure by the Government or Attorney General to investigate the vandalizing of the applicants property and to protect it.

[16] Kenya Human Rights Referendum Report.

[17] Agreement on the Principles of partnership of the coalition Government.

[18] Legal Notice No. 66 of 29th May 2009 Kenya Gazette Supplement No. 35 of 29/5/09.

[19] Chapter thirteen of CIPEV Report Pg 472 – 475. The Special Tribunal for Kenya Bill 2009 Kenya Gazette Supplement No. 7 (Bills No. 2).

[20] S.6(f) and (S.48(2)(b).

[21] Gazette notice 4474 see the Executive Summary of the Report at page xiii – xv.

[22] *See* Waki Commission Report pages 387 – 423.

[23] "Kenya National Commission on Human Rights. On the Brink of the Precipice: A Human Rights Account of Kenya's post 2007 Election violence: Final Report". (Edited version of the Final Report presented to the commission investigating post Election Violence Waki Commission) prepared for and on the directions of the Commission issued on the 19th August 2008. It is important to note there exists unedited confidential report exhibited before Waki which contain names and particulars. It is also important to see other reports including drafts leaked to press which contain raw data. In contrast other versions such as COMPREHENSIVE MEMORANDUM TO THE POST ELECTION TO WAKI COMMISSION ON THE 2007 POST ELECTION VIOLENCE BY PNU (edited by Beatrice Elachi and Daisy Amdany 8/12/08 are equally relevant). Report from OHCHR fact finding mission to Kenya 6–28 February 2008. United Nation High Commission for Human Rights (Geneva). Patterns of Violence (page 8 – 10), Human Rights Watch and so on.

[24] Report by Bitange Ndemo, Permanent Secretary, Ministry of Information and Communication to the Commission of Inquiry into the Post Election violence. Exhibit 127 entitled Media Conduct Prior to, During and After the December 2007 General Election.

About the Contributors

Koki Muli is a lawyer and Advocate of the High Court of Kenya. She is an electoral and constitutional expert.

Simiyu Barasa is a film maker and writer.

Gakiha Weru is a journalist with the Nation Media Group.

William Oloo is the Chairman of the Kenya Correspondents Association.

Gitau Warigi is a columnist with the Nation Media Group.

Kimani Njogu is a cultural analyst and Director of Twaweza Communications.

PLO Lumumba is a lawyer and Advocate of the High Court of Kenya.

Mbuthi Gathenji is a lawyer and Advocate of the High Court of Kenya.

www.ingramcontent.com/pod-product-compliance
Lightning Source LLC
Chambersburg PA
CBHW022313280326
41932CB00010B/1091